Microsoft®
Windows Vista™
VISUAL™
ENCYCLOPEDIA

by Kate Shoup Welsh and Kate J. Chase

Microsoft® Windows Vista™ Visual Encyclopedia™

Published by
Wiley Publishing, Inc.
111 River Street
Hoboken, NJ 07030-5774
Published simultaneously in Canada

Library of Congress Control Number: 2006939469

ISBN: 978-0-470-04635-7

Manufactured in the United States of America

10 9 8 7 6 5 4 3 2 1

Trademark Acknowledgments

Contact Us

For general information on our other products and services please contact our Customer Care Department within the U.S. at (800) 762-2974, outside the U.S. at (317) 572-3993, or fax (317) 572-4002.

For technical support please visit www.wiley.com/techsupport.

Wiley Publishing, Inc.

Sales

Contact Wiley at (800) 762-2974 or fax (317) 572-4002.

CREDITS

Project Editor
Sarah Hellert

Acquisitions Editor
Kim Spilker

Product Development Supervisor
Courtney Allen

Copy Editor
Nancy Rappaport

Technical Editors
James Floyd Kelly
Don Passenger

Editorial Manager
Robyn Siesky

Business Manager
Amy Knies

Special Help
Barbara Moore

Wiley Bicentennial Logo
Richard J. Pacifico

Manufacturing
Allan Conley
Linda Cook
Paul Gilchrist
Jennifer Guynn

Book Design
Kathie Rickard

Production Coordinator
Adrienne Martinez

Layout
Elizabeth Brooks
Sean Decker
LeAndra Hosier

Screen Artist
Jill A. Proll

Illustrators
Ronda David-Burroughs
Cheryl Grubbs

Proofreader
Linda Quigley

Quality Control
Christine Pingleton
Charles Spencer

Indexer
Steve Rath

**Vice President and Executive
Group Publisher**
Richard Swadley

Vice President and Publisher
Barry Pruett

Director of Composition Services
Debbie Stailey

ABOUT THE AUTHORS

During the course of her career as a freelance writer, **Kate Shoup Welsh** has written or co-written several books on various topics, including *Look & Learn FrontPage 2002*, *What Can You Do with a Major in Business*, *Not Your Mama's Beading*, *Not Your Mama's Stitching*, *Microsoft Windows Vista Visual Encyclopedia*, and *Webster's New World English Grammar Handbook*. She has also co-written a screenplay and worked as the Sports Editor for *NUVO Newsweekly*. Prior to striking out on her own, Kate worked as an editor at a computer-book publishing company, where she engaged in such diverse professional activities as consulting on the development of new series, consulting on ways to improve the publishing workflow, and editing numerous standout titles. When not writing, Kate loves to ski (she was once nationally ranked), make jewelry, and play video poker — and she plays a mean game of 9-ball. Kate lives in Indianapolis, Indiana, with her husband, their daughter, and their cat.

Kate J. Chase of Woodbury, Vermont, has written books on the Windows operating system, Microsoft applications including the Microsoft Office Suite, Web design and publishing, and the Internet. She has previously written *Norton All-in-One Desk Reference For Dummies* and *Build It Yourself Visually: The Ultimate Media Center PC.* A general freelance writer as well as a columnist and journalist, Kate also works on science, medical, political, and other topics. She is perhaps best known as PC Kate (www.pckate.com) from America Online and the Microsoft Network where she led thriving technical communities for more than a decade and is a Microsoft MVP (Most Valuable Professional).

PREFACE

Do you look at the pictures in a book or newspaper before anything else on a page? Would you rather see an image instead of read about how to do something? Search no further. This book is for you. Opening *Microsoft Windows Vista Visual Encyclopedia* allows you to read less and learn more about Windows Vista.

Who Needs This Book

This book is for a reader who has never used Windows Vista operating system. It is also for more computer-literate individuals who want to expand their knowledge of the different features that Windows Vista has to offer.

Book Organization

This book consists of sections, all listed in the book's table of contents. A *section* is a set of steps that show you how to complete a specific computer task.

Each section, usually contained on two facing pages, has an introduction to the task at hand, a set of full-color screen shots and steps that walk you through the task, and a set of tips. This format allows you to quickly look at a topic of interest and learn it instantly.

What You Need to Use This Book

To perform the tasks in this book, you need a computer with these specific requirements:

- Windows Vista Ultimate Edition. However, most of the tasks work as written using the Windows Vista Home Basic, Home Premium, and Business Editions.
- 512MB RAM
- PC with 800 MHz 32-bit (x86) or 64-bit (x64) CPU
- 15GB of available hard disk space
- CD or DVD drive
- Keyboard and pointing device, such as a mouse
- SuperVGA display capable of a resolution of 800x600 or greater
- Internet connectivity strongly recommended

The Conventions in This Book

Typographic and layout styles have been used throughout *Microsoft Windows Vista Visual Encyclopedia* to distinguish different types of information.

Bold

Bold type indicates text and numbers that you must type into a dialog box or window.

Italics

Italicized words introduce new terms and are followed by a definition.

Numbered Steps

You must perform the instructions in numbered steps in order to successfully complete a section and achieve the final results.

Indented Step Text

You do not have to perform these steps; they simply give additional information about a feature. Indented step text tells you what the application does in response to a numbered step. For example, if you click a certain menu command, a dialog box may appear, or a window may open. Indented step text may also present another way to perform a step.

Notes

Notes give additional information. They may describe special conditions that may occur during an operation. They may warn you of a situation that you want to avoid, for example, the loss of data.

 You can easily identify the tips in any section by looking for the TIP icon. Tips offer additional information, including tips, hints, and tricks. You can use the TIP information to go beyond what you learn in the steps.

In order to get this information to you in a timely manner, this book was based on a pre-release version of Microsoft Windows Vista. There may be some minor changes between the screenshots in this book and what you see on your desktop. As always, Microsoft has the final word on how programs look and function; if you have any questions or see any discrepancies, consult the online help for further information about the software.

Table of Contents

W

A

B

C

D

X

INTRODUCTION

As long-time users, technicians, and experts in Windows operating systems as well as other Microsoft programs, we feel that Windows Vista Ultimate is the most stable and secure Windows version available. It is our hope that this is your experience as well, especially after you use this book to take advantage of all that this operating system offers to you.

Because Windows Vista Ultimate is so comprehensive and encompasses so many different tools and features, it lends itself extraordinarily well to an encyclopedia. Instead of reading countless pages of text on a particular topic, you can use this book to easily look up a feature by alphabetic entry and find all the steps you must perform in order to complete the task at hand.

The moment you can master many of the basics of file management, Internet, and other network connectivity, as well as hardware and software installations, you can enjoy significantly more control over your desktop workspace. This book, with its steps and visual presentations, helps you to do just that quickly and efficiently. Once mastered, you can move on to your real work of enjoying the Internet and all the digital world and its ever-changing revolution can provide to you. This includes your ability to run applications, transfer files to and from your system, play today's top PC games — even watch TV.

Windows Vista Visual Encyclopedia is divided into two parts.

Part I is a comprehensive A to Z reference of tools. Tools can be icons found in palettes, panes, or toolbars. Tools can also be specific commands accessed from the menu bar. A named dialog box, window, or panel that is used to accomplish a specific task can also be a tool, as might a wizard designed to step you through a complex operation such as setting up a wireless home network.

Within Part I, you learn about key components such as the Windows Firewall, engineered to protect your network and Internet connections; the Backup and Restore Center, where you manage your computer's backup processes; Windows Vista programs such as Windows Calendar, Windows Contacts, and Windows Mail; and more. You can also read about the Ease of Access Center to help you work in Windows if you have special physical or cognitive challenges. In addition, you can explore tools such as Remote Desktop Connection that will enable you to work remotely from home to the office, or between different computers on your home or small office network.

Part II is an alphabetical reference of techniques, including basic tasks as well as advanced, solutions-based operations. Techniques represent results from an operation that may involve the use of one or more tools.

Inside Part II, you will find useful techniques, such as how to secure your files or share them with others. You will also see how to adjust security options such as Windows Update and Windows Defender. Screenshots and callouts assist you throughout your efforts to get the right results the first time you try, which is the beauty of a visual encyclopedia.

By using the tools and techniques covered in this book, you will quickly and easily master the necessary skills to use Windows Vista Ultimate Edition to its fullest.

Kate Shoup Welsh
Indianapolis, IN

Kate J. Chase
Woodbury, VT

Windows Vista
Visual Encyclopedia

Part I: Tools

Most people use Windows Vista for both work and personal enjoyment. Regardless of how you use it, Windows Vista offers many tools that can help you do your work more quickly, easily, and accurately, and that can enhance your personal computer experience.

The first part of this book describes tools that empower you to do just about anything that you want with your Windows Vista computer. These tools help you to communicate with your office network or set up a home network, add a printer, connect to the Internet, back up and restore your files, import video to your Vista PC, and more.

Whether you are an administrator or a rookie, a computer enthusiast or an occasional user, the tools in Windows Vista offer a range of options and features to help you master your system.

ADD PRINTER WIZARD

Although many of today's newer printers are *plug and play*, meaning you can simply plug them in to your computer in order to install them, others may require you to use the Add Printer Wizard. This wizard is an all-inclusive tool to locate, add, and configure a printer for use with your Windows desktop, an associated network, or even a printer connected via Bluetooth or infrared. (Note that you might need the disk that accompanied your printer to complete the wizard.)

The Add Printer Wizard can detect many printers and install the appropriate printer driver. Keep in mind that you must turn on the printer before you run the wizard. You must also know the name of the printer you want to add. If you are not the person who named the printer, see if it is posted on the printer itself, contact the owner of the printer, or ask your network administrator.

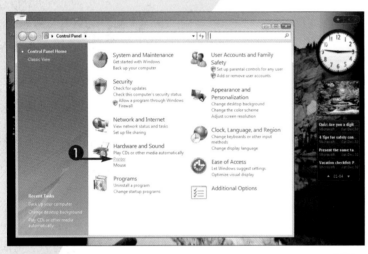

① In the Control Panel window, click the Printer link under Hardware and Sound.

Note: Click Start and click Control Panel to open the Control Panel window.

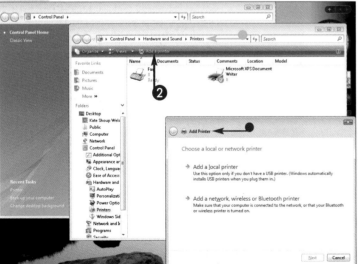

● The Printers window opens.

② Click the Add a Printer button.

● The Add Printer Wizard window opens.

AUTOPLAY

AutoPlay enables you to select what program to use for various types of media or hardware. For example, you can specify that both CDs containing music and DVDs containing movies open automatically in Windows Media Player, that media card readers containing image files open in Photo Gallery, and so on.

If you do not want AutoPlay to launch a particular program when you insert media with certain types of files, you can configure it to prompt you to select the program you want to use on a case-by-case basis. Alternatively, you can disable AutoPlay entirely.

To change your PC's AutoPlay settings, you use the AutoPlay window, accessible via Control Panel.

See also>> **Start Menu: Open**

1 In the Control Panel window, click Play CDs or Other Media Automatically under Hardware and Sound.

● The AutoPlay window opens.

● To enable AutoPlay globally, select the Use AutoPlay for All Media and Devices checkbox. (Alternatively, disable the feature by clearing the checkbox.)

● To specify that a certain program run when you insert a specific type of media, click the media type's drop-down list and choose the action you want to occur.

   Note: If you want Windows to always launch the AutoPlay dialog box when you insert that type of media, choose Ask Me Every Time. If you want AutoPlay to do nothing when the media is inserted, choose Take No Action.

● Click Reset All Defaults to return each setting to its default.

2 Click Save.

BACKUP AND RESTORE CENTER

You should back up your files to protect them from the many kinds of disasters that can befall a computer — theft, loss, breakage, and the like. Using Windows Vista's Backup and Restore Center, you can make copies of files, programs, and even settings for the entire system, and save these copies in another location, such as an external hard drive, a CD, or a DVD. The Backup and Restore Center is the launching point for several backup operations, including the File and Folder Backup Wizard, CompletePC Backup, and System Restore.

See also>> **File and Folder Backup**

See also>> **CompletePC Backup**

System Restore: Create

System Restore: Roll Back

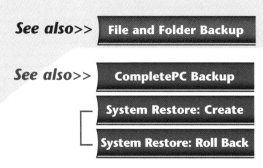

① Click Start.

② Click Control Panel.

● The Control Panel window opens.

③ Click Back Up Your Computer under System and Maintenance.

The Backup and Restore Center opens.

● Back up files here.

● Restore files here.

● Click here to access Windows Vista's System Restore feature.

● Click here to set a restore point. (*Restore points* save information about your computer in order to allow you to undo problematic or unwanted system changes.)

CALCULATOR

You can use Windows Vista's Calculator program to perform both basic and advanced math tasks. Calculator works very much like a handheld calculator. To enter numbers for calculations, either use the numeric pad on your keyboard or use your mouse to click the corresponding numeric key within Calculator. Specific Calculator keys perform math functions: Click the asterisk key (*) to multiply, the plus key (+) to add, the minus key (-) to subtract, and the slash key (/) to divide.

Windows Vista's Calculator allows two modes of operation: Standard and Scientific. Use Standard mode, the default, for all basic calculations, and Scientific mode to handle complex mathematical formulas and statistics. You can also convert your values to other number systems, such as hex or binary, and use digit grouping to view numbers as logically grouped. Calculator's extended precision feature enables you to ensure accuracy to 32 digits.

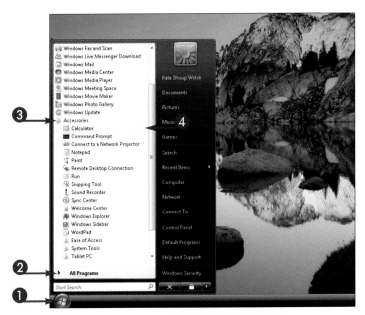

1 Click Start.

2 Click All Programs.

3 Click Accessories.

4 Click Calculator.

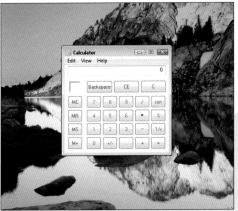

Calculator opens on the desktop.

CALENDAR

Windows Vista's Calendar function can be employed both as your personal calendar and as a calendar you *publish*, or share with others as you see fit. If you like, you can maintain multiple calendars — for example, one for work and one for home. You can also download iCalendars directly into Windows Calendar. (iCalendars are special online calendars to which you can subscribe.) You can view and print your calendars by day, work week, week, or month.

With Windows Calendar, you can schedule appointments, be they one-time events (such as a meeting) or recurring (such as a standing lunch

date). You can also keep a running list of tasks you need to complete.

You can configure Windows Calendar to send you a reminder about any appointments you enter minutes, hours, or days in advance. Reminders can also be sent for tasks in your task list on the day a task is due.

See also>>

Calendar: Manage

Calendar: Publish

Calendar: Set

❶ Click Start.

❷ Click All Programs.

❸ Click Windows Calendar.

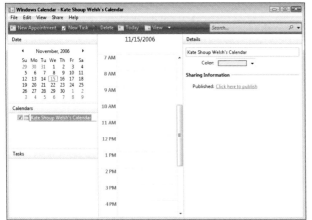

Windows Calendar opens.

CARDSPACE

CardSpace enables you to create Information Cards, which contain information about your identity. You can send an information card to any Web site that supports their use. This frees you from having to keep track of the user names, passwords, and other information required to use Web sites. (Note that the precise steps for submitting an information card vary by site.)

CardSpace offers two types of Information Cards: personal cards and managed cards. Personal cards include information such as your name, address, phone number, and so on. Managed cards are issued by trusted businesses and organizations such as banks, employers, or government agencies. Examples of managed cards include credit cards, membership cards, and so on.

CardSpace also enables you to obtain information about sites you visit, such as the name of the organization associated with the site, its geographic location, even a privacy statement that indicates how your information will be used.

See also>> CardSpace

① Click Start.

② Type **cardspace** in the Start menu's Search box.

③ Click Windows CardSpace.

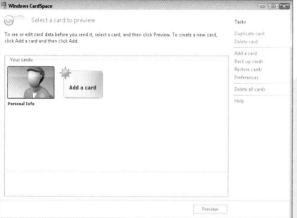

The Windows CardSpace window opens.

COMMAND PROMPT

If you are comfortable with an old-style command-line interface, where you type DOS and other computer commands rather than clicking to run programs or open files, then you can use Windows Vista's Command Prompt. The Command Prompt is a separate window that opens on the desktop; in it, you can issue commands through your keyboard. When you use the Command Prompt, your mouse does not function, and there is nothing to click.

You may sometimes need the Command Prompt to run certain troubleshooting programs as well as very old utilities and software. The majority of command-line tools available in Windows XP are also supported by Windows Vista; in addition, Windows Vista includes a few new command-line tools. In general, however, unless you attempt to complete a task whose instructions specifically require the use of the Command Prompt, you probably will not use it much.

❶ Click Start.

❷ Click All Programs.

❸ Click Accessories.

❹ Click Command Prompt.

The Command Prompt window opens.

COMPUTER FOLDER

C

Like previous versions of Windows, Windows Vista uses *folders* to store and organize your documents and programs. Unlike previous versions of Windows, however, Vista features a Computer folder, which you use to access files and programs on your hard drive, CD or DVD drive, removable media such as an external hard disk, or network location.

From within the Computer folder, you can view your system properties, uninstall or change a

program, or map your network drive. You can also change how the icons in the Computer folder are displayed by clicking the Views button and choosing a different view option. To find a specific file or program stored in the Computer folder, type its name in the Search box; Windows Vista searches the folder for your file, and displays files whose names match what you type.

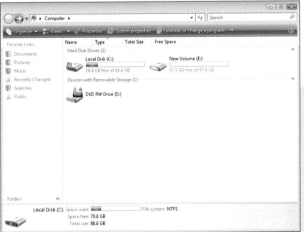

1 Click Start.

2 Click Computer.

The Computer folder opens.

CONNECT TO A NETWORK PROJECTOR WIZARD

Windows Vista supports the use of *network projectors* — that is, video projectors connected to a local area network. If your computer can connect to a network projector, you might use it to, say, deliver a presentation from your office PC to an audience in a conference room in a different building. You can connect to a network projector using the Connect to a Network Projector Wizard.

Audience members must be in the same room as the projector in order to view your presentation. That said, you can deliver your presentation to multiple audiences simultaneously by connecting to multiple projectors; simply follow the steps outlined here as

many times as necessary to connect to the various projectors.

Although network projectors *can* transmit high-bandwidth presentations that include video streams, they are not expressly designed to do so. For this reason, video transmitted via network projector may appear choppy. For best results, limit your presentations to still images, such as PowerPoint slides and digital photographs.

Information you send to the network projector can be encrypted, ensuring that any confidential information in your presentation *remains* confidential.

① Click Start.

② Click All Programs.

③ Click Accessories.

④ Click Connect to a Network Projector.

⑤ If asked whether you want the network projector to communicate with your computer through the Windows Firewall, click Yes.

Note: *If prompted, type the administrator password or click Continue.*

The Connect to a Network Projector Wizard starts.

CONNECT TO A NETWORK WIZARD

To set up a home network in Windows Vista, install the network hardware, connect the computers, and if the network is wireless, run the Set Up a Wireless Router or Access Point Wizard to finish the job.

After the network is established, you may later decide to add more computers to it. If a computer is wired (as opposed to wireless) and running Windows Vista, adding it is a simple matter of plugging it in to your network's hub, switch, or router and turning the computer on. If the computer is wireless (and running Vista), however, you add it using the Connect to Network Wizard.

(You add a wired hardware device, such as a printer, to a network by plugging it into the network's hub, switch, or router. To add a wireless hardware device, turn it on and follow the instructions that came with the device. To confirm that the device has been added, check the Network folder.)

See also>> **Network Folder**

Set Up Wireless

1 Click Start.

2 Click Connect To.

The Connect to a Network Wizard starts.

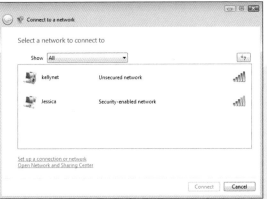

CONNECT TO THE INTERNET WIZARD

A critical aspect of any computer system is Internet connectivity. Fortunately, Windows Vista's Connect to the Internet Wizard makes connecting your machine to the Web a snap by guiding you through the process.

Before you start the wizard, you need to have established an account with an Internet service provider (ISP for short). You also need the appropriate hardware for connectivity: a dial-up modem if you plan to use your phone line to access the Internet or a cable modem or DSL modem if you plan to use a broadband connection. Chances are,

your computer came pre-installed with a dial-up modem; cable and DSL modems are typically provided by the cable or DSL ISP when you sign up for an account.

If your computer already has an Internet connection, you can use the Connect to the Internet Wizard to configure a second connection. For example, if your broadband connection is unreliable, you might decide to configure a dial-up connection as a backup.

See also>> **Internet Options**

① Click Start.

② Click Control Panel.

● The Control Panel window opens.

③ Click the Network and Internet link.

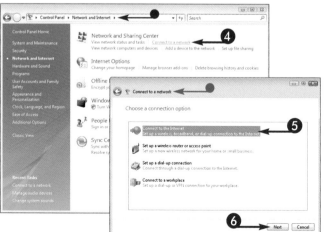

● The Network and Internet window opens.

④ Click the Connect to a Network link under Network and Sharing Center.

● The Connect to a Network window opens.

⑤ Click Connect to the Internet.

⑥ Click Next.

Windows launches the Connect to the Internet Wizard.

CONTACTS

Windows Vista's Contacts function stores information you enter about people and organizations — phone numbers, fax numbers, e-mail addresses, postal addresses, Web site addresses, and so on. Contacts also allows you to store notes about a contact as well as enter personal information about the contact — for example, the name of the contact's spouse or boss. You can even store a photograph of the contact.

In addition to serving as a repository for contact information, Contacts also functions as the address book for Windows Mail and other compatible e-mail programs. When you create an e-mail message using one of these programs, you can select the recipient from Contacts. (If you frequently send e-mails to the same group of people, you can group those contacts; that way, you do not have to enter each name individually.) You can also share contact information with others by sending contacts via e-mail.

See also>> Mail

See also>> Contacts: Import Export

Contacts: Manage

❶ Click Start.

❷ Click All Programs.

❸ Click Windows Contacts.

The Contacts window opens.

CONTENT ADVISOR

Although the Internet can be both educational and entertaining, it can also expose users to unwanted subject matter, such as sexually explicit or violent content. To restrict what types of Internet sites and other Web resources are available on your PC, enable Internet Explorer 7's Content Advisor tool.

Content Advisor uses ratings provided voluntarily by Web sites to block or allow certain content, depending on the settings you choose. (Web sites that are unrated are blocked by default.) You can also specify that specific Web sites be blocked or allowed.

With Content Advisor enabled, anyone who tries to access the types of material you have filtered cannot do so — nor can anyone modify the settings or disable Content Advisor without the supervisor password that you set when you activate the tool. (You learn how to create your password in the task "Content Advisor: Set Internet Explorer 7 Parental Controls" in the Techniques section of this book.)

See also>> **Internet Options**

See also>> **Content Advisor**

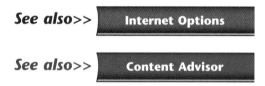

1 Within Internet Explorer 7, click Tools.

2 Click Internet Options.

● The Internet Options dialog box opens.

3 Click the Content tab.

4 Under Content Advisor, click Enable.

> ***Note:*** *If prompted, type the administrator password or click Continue.*

● The Content Advisor dialog box opens.

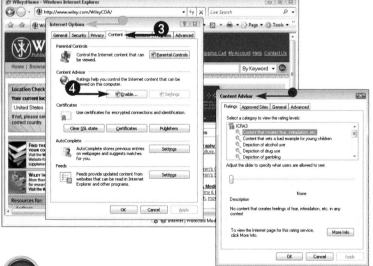

CONTROL PANEL

C

Control Panel acts like a master computer console, providing you direct access to the hardware, settings, and services that are installed on your computer. You can click a link in Control Panel to display information about a device or service or, in some cases, to launch a tool or wizard. As but a few examples, you can use Control Panel as a launching point for performing system-maintenance tasks, checking for security updates, setting up file sharing, changing mouse settings, uninstalling a

program, establishing parental controls, changing the appearance of your desktop, setting the system time and date, and setting up a microphone.

You may notice that Control Panel does not always appear identical in different Windows Vista systems. This is because various options that are installed on your computer may place new icons in the pane, changing or rearranging the icons that are listed.

① Click Start.

② Click Control Panel.

The Control Panel window opens.

15

DETAILS PANE

Folders in Windows Vista include certain panes, including the Navigation pane, the Preview pane, and so on. One such pane is the Details pane. Using the Details pane, you can quickly access information about a selected file, such as its name, type, and rating. You can also see any tags that have been applied to the file.

In addition to simply viewing details about a file in the Details pane, you can also use the Details pane to change certain properties, including tags.

If the Details pane is not visible in a folder window, you can display it by clicking the Organize button, clicking Layout, and clicking Details Pane.

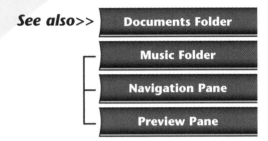

See also>>

Documents Folder

Music Folder

Navigation Pane

Preview Pane

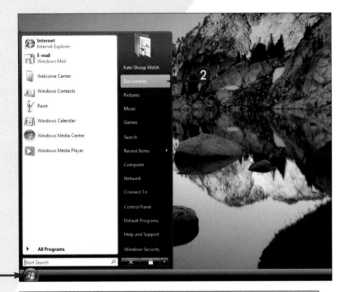

1 Click Start.

2 Click a folder you want to open (here, Documents).

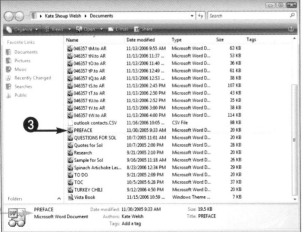

The folder opens.

3 Click a file in the folder.

● Information about the file is displayed in the Details pane.

DEVICE MANAGER

You can consult Device Manager about the hardware and *drivers* — that is, the software associated with a device to help it communicate with Windows — available on your computer. Device Manager serves as an inventory of different, mostly hardware, components, and allows you to check device status, run troubleshooting wizards, and install driver updates.

It may be that not all hardware attached to your PC appears within Device Manager, but most devices do — either for the device name itself or for the method the device uses to connect to the system. For example, even if you cannot see your printer listed, you can see the port to which it connects, such as the Universal Serial Bus (USB) port.

See also>>

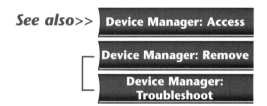

Device Manager: Access

Device Manager: Remove

Device Manager: Troubleshoot

① In Control Panel, click System and Maintenance.

② Click Device Manager.

Note: *If prompted, type the administrator password or click Continue.*

● The Device Manager window opens.

DISK CLEANUP

In addition to files you actively create or save as you work on your computer, many more files are created, changed, and saved automatically by Windows. Some of these files, called temporary files, are the result of Web browsing; others are created by applications to store the contents of open files before they are saved to disk.

These files may be stored with various filename extensions, such as .bak and .tmp. They can also be found in a number of different folders that are scattered throughout your hard disk. Over time, you can end up with a gigabyte or more of unneeded files that take up valuable space on your hard drive. You can use the Disk Cleanup tool to find and remove them, as well as to empty the Recycle Bin. In fact, it is a good idea to run the Disk Cleanup tool regularly as part of standard disk management.

See also>>   **Computer Folder**

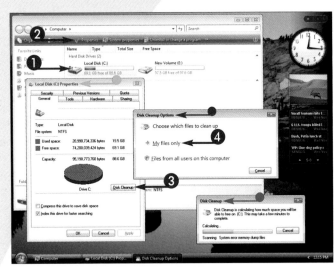

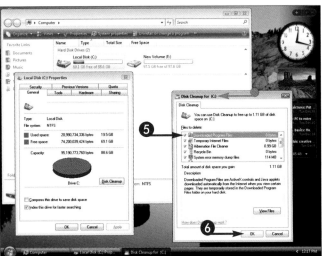

1 In the Computer folder, click the drive you want to clean up to select it.

2 Click the Properties button.

● The selected disk's Properties dialog box opens.

3 Click the Disk Cleanup button.

● The Disk Cleanup Options dialog box opens.

   Note: If prompted, type your administrator password or click Continue.

4 Specify whether you want to clean up only your files or all the files on the computer.

● Windows calculates how much space you can free up by running Disk Cleanup.

● The Disk Cleanup dialog box opens.

5 Click the checkbox next to each type of file you want to delete.

6 Click OK.

DOCUMENTS FOLDER

The Documents folder on your computer is the default folder where many of the files that you save as you work or browse the Web are stored. These can include word-processor files, spreadsheets, and Web pages. (Note that pictures and music are not stored in the Documents folder; instead, they are stored in their own folders: Pictures and Music, respectively.)

Like all folders in Windows Vista, the Documents folder contains tools for searching, navigating, and organizing your files and folders, including the Search box, the Address bar, and the Navigation, Details, and Preview panes. If any of these panes

is not visible, click the Organize button, click Layout, and choose the desired pane. Also included is a Folders list, which you access by clicking the Folders link in the bottom-left corner of the folder window.

See also>> Music Folder

Pictures Folder

See also>> File and Folder Management: View

Folders: Create

① Click Start.

② Click Documents.

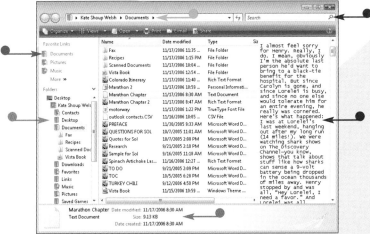

The Documents folder opens.

● The Address bar displays your current location.

● The Search box enables you to filter the contents of the Documents to find the file you need.

● The Navigation pane allows you to access any folder on your computer.

● The Folders list displays all the files and folders within the Documents folder.

● The Preview pane displays a snapshot view of the selected file.

● The Details pane displays information about the selected file.

EASE OF ACCESS CENTER

Windows Vista includes several accessibility features that can help people with physical challenges to use their computer more easily and more effectively. These features include Magnifier, which expands an area of the desktop to make it easier to read; Narrator, which reads onscreen items, such as dialog box options, aloud; and On-Screen Keyboard, which allows a user to type text on the screen rather than with a keyboard.

You can use any or all of these features, accessible from Windows Vista's Ease of Access Center, to improve your Windows experience. Some may assist you even if you do not have a physical limitation but want to do something in a different way. The Ease of Access Center also serves as a launching point for Windows Vista's Speech Recognition program, which lets you dictate text and verbally issue commands to your PC.

If you are not sure whether Windows Vista's accessibility features would be useful to you, complete the Ease of Access Center's questionnaire; it is designed to help you determine which, if any, of the accessibility features might be of help.

See also>> **Ease of Access Center**

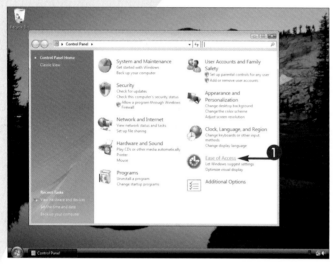

① In the Control Panel window, click the Ease of Access link.

② Click Ease of Access Center.

● The Ease of Access Center opens.

EASY TRANSFER

If you have recently purchased a new computer with Windows Vista installed, you can use Easy Transfer to copy files and settings from your old computer onto the new one — provided the old computer runs Windows 2000, XP, or Vista. Transferable files and settings include all files and folders within your Documents, Pictures, Music, and Shared Documents folders; e-mail settings, contacts, and messages; user accounts; desktop settings; Internet settings; and program settings. (Note that Windows Easy Transfer transfers program settings only, not the programs

themselves. You will need to install any programs manually.)

You can transfer your files and settings from your old computer to the new one via a network, a USB Easy Transfer cable, a DVD or CD, or a USB Flash drive or external hard drive. If you plan to port all your files and settings from your old computer to the new one, opt for the network or Easy Transfer cable route if possible. To transfer just a few files, a CD, DVD, or Flash drive will suffice.

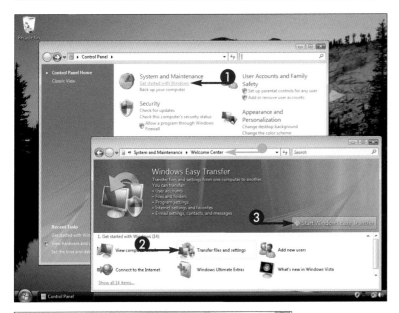

1 In Control Panel, under System Maintenance, click Get Started with Windows.

● The Windows Welcome Center opens.

2 Click Transfer Files and Settings.

3 Click Start Windows Easy Transfer.

Note: If prompted, type the administrator password or click Continue.

Easy Transfer starts.

EVENT VIEWER

One of the best ways to monitor your system and troubleshoot problems that arise is to check details about what happens on your computer. When the Windows operating system or a Windows application detects an action or occurrence, it treats this occurrence as an *event*. For example, if a service fails to launch when Windows starts, then this situation generates an event that your system records. You can use the Event Viewer to view these events.

You can also consult Event Viewer to determine which programs and services run regularly. Scheduled tasks such as backups also appear as events.

You can access Event Viewer from the Control Panel's System and Maintenance window; to open that window, click Start, click Control Panel, and click System and Maintenance.

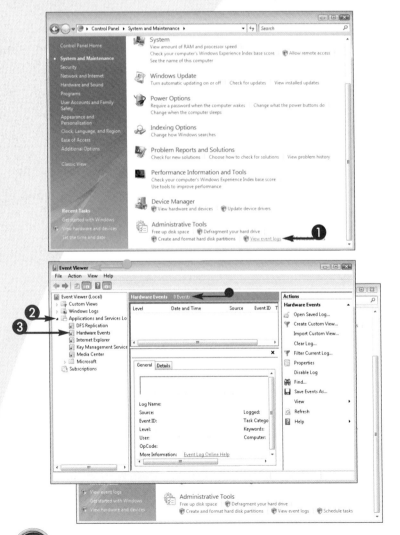

① In the System and Maintenance window, click View Event Logs under Administrative Tools.

Note: If prompted, type the administrator password or click Continue.

● Event Viewer opens.

② Double-click a folder whose events you want to view.

③ Double-click an event to view details about it.

● Details about the event appear here.

FAX AND SCAN

Typically, in order to fax a hard-copy document from a PC, you must first scan the document you want to fax. For this reason, Microsoft has combined its faxing and scanning functions into a single application: Fax and Scan. You can use Fax and Scan to scan documents, and to send, receive, organize, and view faxes. In addition to using Fax and Scan to fax hard-copy documents, you can also fax a document, picture, or other type of file that resides in electronic form on your PC.

To use Fax and Scan, you must have installed on your computer a scanner (or multifunction device with scanning capabilities) and a fax modem connected to an analog phone line. (If you are connected to a network with a fax server, a fax modem is not necessary.) You must also create a fax account in Windows Fax and Scan to enable your computer to send and receive faxes.

See also>>

Fax and Scan: Scan

Fax and Scan: Set Up

1 Click Start.

2 Click All Programs.

Note: If Fax and Scan does not appear on your Start menu, you may need to enable it. To do so, click Programs in Control Panel, click Turn Windows Features On or Off under Programs and Features, click the Windows Fax and Scan checkbox to select it, and click OK.

3 Click Windows Fax and Scan.

The Windows Fax and Scan window opens.

● Your Inbox, where faxes you have received appear, is here.

● The contents of the fax selected in the Inbox appear here.

● Click these buttons to switch between Fax and Scan view.

● You can store and organize your faxes here.

● Click here to start a new fax.

● Click here to start a new scan.

FILE AND FOLDER BACKUP WIZARD

If a disaster — such as theft, loss, breakage, or virus attack — were to befall your computer, certain files, such as digital pictures, would be impossible to replace. Others, such as files used for work, would be incredibly time-consuming and laborious to reconstruct. For this reason, you should *back up* your files — that is, copy your files to a storage medium such as an external hard drive, a CD, or a DVD, and store the backup in a safe, separate location from your computer (preferably somewhere fireproof).

Although you can run backups manually (for example, if you have just uploaded photographs to your computer or if you are about to make system changes such as adding new hardware), you should set up your system to do so automatically by using the File and Folder Backup Wizard.

See also>> **Backup and Restore**

See also>> **CompletePC Backup**

① In Control Panel, click the Back Up Your Computer link under System and Maintenance.

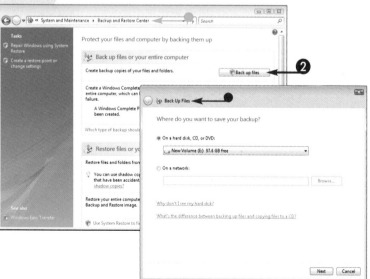

● The Backup and Restore Center opens.

② Click the Back Up Files button.

Note: *If prompted, type the administrator password or click Continue.*

● The File and Folder Backup Wizard starts.

FLIP 3D

As you work on your Vista PC, you will likely have several windows open at once. To switch among these open windows, you can use Flip 3D. This feature arranges your open windows in a stack that appears three-dimensional, enabling you to quickly see which one is which and select the one you need.

In order to use Flip 3D, your system must have an adequately powerful video card, and must be running Windows Vista's Aero interface. (Note that if the Windows Aero option is not available, it means your computer's video card is not up to the task of displaying it. Note, too, that this feature is not available for Windows Vista Starter or Windows Vista Home Basic software packages.)

See also>> **Aero**

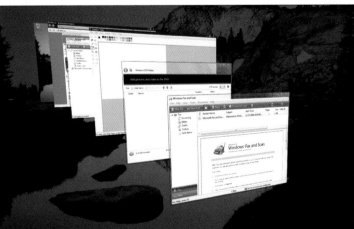

① Open several windows in Vista.

② Hold down the Windows logo key on your keyboard.

③ Press the Tab key.

Vista switches to Flip 3D mode.

④ Still holding down the Windows logo key, press the Tab key repeatedly to cycle through the open windows.

⑤ When the window you want to work with is at the top of the stack, release the Windows logo key.

GADGETS

Windows Sidebar, the vertical bar that can be displayed on the right side of your screen, houses *gadgets*. Some are mini programs that offer information such as news headlines, weather conditions, exchange rates, and stock movement. Others offer access to frequently used tools such as Calendar, Contacts, and a clock. If you seek entertainment, you can enjoy Windows' slide show or picture-puzzle gadget.

By default, the Sidebar displays a clock, a photo slideshow, and news headlines. You can, however, add and remove gadgets from your Sidebar as desired.

The great thing about gadgets is they provide instant access to the tools and information you need. For example, suppose you are creating a WordPad document that will serve as an invoice and you need to calculate the amount due. If the calculator gadget is already displayed on the Sidebar, you can simply click it to use it rather than clicking the Start button, choosing All Programs, clicking Accessories, and selecting Calculator.

See also>>

See also>> Gadgets

① To display Windows Sidebar, click Start.

② Click All Programs.

③ Click Accessories.

④ Click Windows Sidebar.

● Windows Sidebar opens, with gadgets displayed.

GAMES

Even the most dedicated professional needs to take a break now and then. Windows Vista's games offer the perfect diversion.

Game options range from traditional card games, such as Hearts and Solitaire, to simulated games such as chess and mahjong. Vista also includes a game just for kids, Purble Place, designed to teach memory, pattern-recognition, and reasoning skills.

Note that, by default, Windows games are not installed in Windows Vista Business and Windows Vista Enterprise editions. To install them, open Control Panel, click Programs, click Advanced Options, and double-click Windows Features. In the dialog box that opens, click the Games checkbox to select it and click OK.

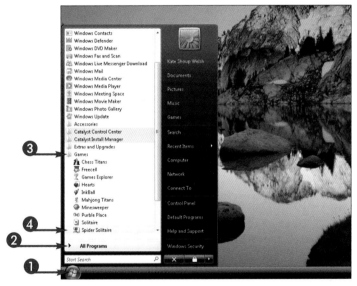

1 Click Start.

2 Click All Programs.

3 Click Games.

4 Click the name of the game you want to open (here, Spider Solitaire).

The game starts.

IMPORT VIDEO WIZARD

If you have a digital video camera, you can import video you have shot using the camera to your Windows Vista system. You might do so in order to burn the footage onto a DVD using DVD Maker or to edit the footage into a movie with Windows Movie Maker. The following digital video formats are supported: ASF, AVI, M1V, MP2, MP2V, MPE, MPEG, MPG, MPV2, WM, and WMV.

To import footage from a digital video camera, use the Import Video Wizard. First, connect the camera to your computer using an IEEE 1394 or USB 2.0

connection and set your camera mode to play recorded video. In most cases, Windows Vista automatically launches the Import Video Wizard. If the wizard does not start, you can start it from Windows Movie Maker, as described here.

See also>> Movie Maker

See also>> DVD Maker

Movie Maker: Create

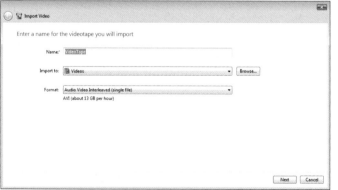

❶ Connect your digital video camera to your computer using an IEEE 1394 or USB 2.0 connection.

❷ Set the camera to its playback mode.

❸ From within Movie Maker, click File.

❹ Click Import from Digital Video Camera.

Windows launches the Import Video Wizard.

INTERNET EXPLORER 7

Internet Explorer 7 operates in much the same way as earlier versions of the Web browser. You type the URL of the site you want to visit in the Address bar, you click the Back and Forward buttons to return to previous pages and then back again, you click the Favorites button to add the sites you really like to your Favorites, and so on.

That said, Internet Explorer 7 also offers several new features. For example, *tabbed browsing* enables users to open multiple sites in a single browser window — the upshot being that there are fewer taskbar buttons to contend with.

Internet Explorer 7 also enables users to subscribe to *feeds* — that is, syndicated Web content, such as news feeds, blogs, and so on. Perhaps more important, Internet Explorer 7 includes greatly enhanced security.

To start Internet Explorer 7, click Start and click Internet.

See also>> Internet Explorer 7

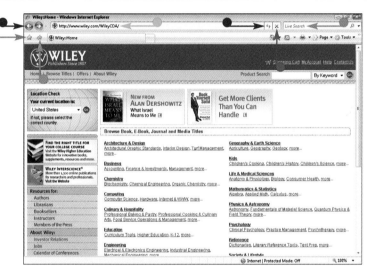

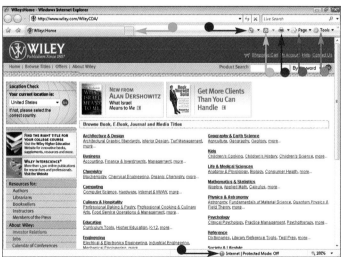

- Type a URL in the Address bar.
- Click Refresh to refresh the currently displayed site.
- Click Stop to stop the page-loading process.
- To search the Web, type a keyword or phrase in the Live Search field and press Enter.
- Click Back and Forward to return to previous pages and back again.
- Click Favorites to view your Favorites.
- Click Add to Favorites to add the currently displayed page to your Favorites.
- View and switch between tabs here.
- Click Home to return to the site displayed when Internet Explorer 7 is launched.
- Click Feeds to view subscribed feeds.
- Click Print to print the currently displayed page.
- Click Page to access page options, such as Zoom.
- Click Tools to access tools, such as the Phishing Filter.
- View security settings here, and double-click to change them.

INTERNET EXPLORER PROTECTED MODE

Microsoft strongly recommends that you run Internet Explorer 7 in Protected mode, and enables that mode by default. Protected mode warns you when a site attempts to install software on your computer, making it much more difficult for unsavory sites to install malicious software such as viruses, worms, Trojan horses, and the like on your computer. (Malicious software is also known as *malware*.)

Operating in Protected mode also allows you to install programs you *do* want as a standard user rather than as an administrator. That way, if the program you try

to install turns out to be malware, it can access only those settings on your computer that a standard user can change, *not* the settings that require an administrator password.

See also>> Internet Options

See also>> Phishing Filter

Security Zones

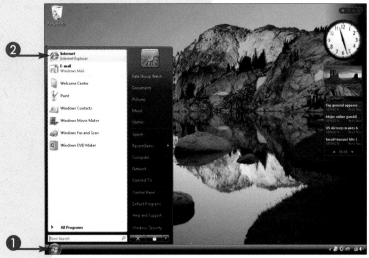

① Click Start.

② Click Internet.

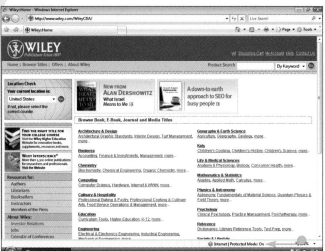

Windows launches Internet Explorer 7.

● Internet Explorer indicates whether Protected mode is turned on or off here.

INTERNET OPTIONS

You can configure various aspects of the Microsoft Internet Explorer 7 Web browser. For example, you can activate or deactivate the parental controls that restrict access to adult content. You can also custom-configure security zones that the browser uses to determine whether to accept cookies. (*Cookies* are small files that are placed on your computer by many Web sites to help to identify you while you are there.)

You can access these features through the Internet Options dialog box. There, you can

configure specific settings that are related to privacy and communications, as well as advanced options that control how the browser functions.

See also>> Internet Explorer 7

See also>> Content Advisor

Security Zones

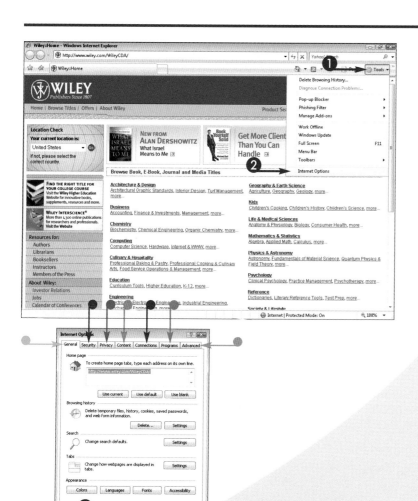

① In Internet Explorer, click Tools.

② Click Internet Options to open the Internet Options dialog box.

● Click General to access general settings such as the browser's home page, search defaults, and so on.

● Click Security to access security settings pertaining to security zones, Protected mode, and so on.

● Click Privacy to access settings that relate to privacy and pop-ups.

● Click Content to set up Parental Controls, Content Advisors, Feeds, and more.

● Click Connections to set up an Internet account, adjust settings for a LAN, and so on.

● Click Programs to choose a default Web browser, HTML editing program, and e-mail program.

● Click Advanced to access advanced settings pertaining to accessibility, browsing, multimedia, and more.

③ Click OK.

MAIL

Windows Mail is the e-mail program included with Windows Vista. In order to use Windows Mail, you must have signed up with an Internet service provider (ISP), and have set up an e-mail address with that provider. You must also set up your account within Windows Mail; to do so, you will need the e-mail address (and password) you created and set up with your ISP, as well as the names of the incoming and outgoing e-mail servers the ISP will use with your account. (Obtain this information from your ISP.)

In addition to functioning as an e-mail program, Windows Mail also acts as a newsreader. A

newsreader is a program that enables you to download, read, and post newsgroup messages. A *newsgroup* is an online discussion forum for users from all over the world with common interests.

See also>>

Mail: Create Mailing List

Mail: Filter

Mail: Send

Mail: Set Up Account

Mail: Set Up Newsreader

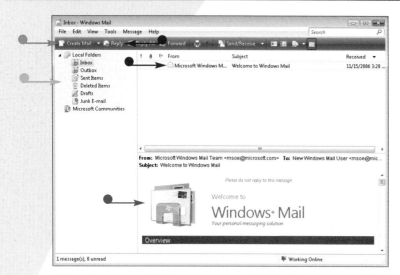

① Click Start and click E-mail. The Windows Mail window opens on the desktop.

● The folders list displays all the folders within your e-mail account.

● Messages you have received appear here.

● Preview the selected message here.

● Click the Create Mail button to create a new e-mail message.

● Click Reply to reply to the sender of the selected message.

● Click Reply All to reply to the sender of the selected message, as well as to all other recipients of the message.

● Click Forward to forward the selected message to a new recipient.

● Click Print to print the selected message.

● Click Delete to delete the selected message.

● Click Send/Receive to send any messages in your Outbox and receive any messages waiting for you on your ISP's incoming mail server.

MEDIA LIBRARY

Windows Media Player is Windows Vista's built-in tool for watching and listening to media files such as videos and music.

When you save a media file on your PC — for example, a music file in the Music folder or a digital photo in your Pictures folder — you can access it through Windows Media Player's Media Library. Windows Media Player also automatically saves any video or music files you play online in the library.

You can sort the items in your Media Library, based on ascending or descending order, for each

column of information such as Title, Album, or Artist. Click a column heading to sort the entries based on the column data. You can also specify which columns appear in the Library list. Right-click any column heading and then click to deselect any columns that you want to hide.

See also>>   Media Player

See also>>   Media Player: Find New

Media Player: Rip

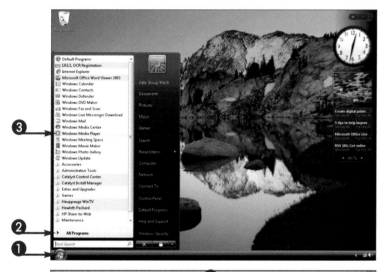

① Click Start.

② Click All Programs.

③ Click Windows Media Player.

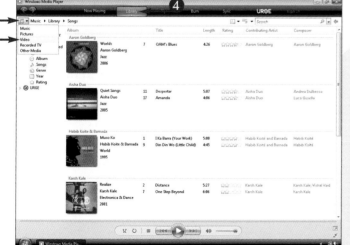

Windows Media Player opens on your desktop.

④ If the Media Library is not already displayed, click the Library tab.

⑤ To view a different category of content — say, video instead of music — click the Select a Category button.

⑥ Choose the desired category.

The library changes to display the type of content you specified.

MEDIA PLAYER

Windows Media Player allows you to listen to an audio CD or play a movie that you have downloaded. You can also turn a collection of MP3s into a custom CD that you can play in the car or send to your portable audio device, such as an MP3 player. Windows Media Player can also play streaming audio and video such as from an Internet radio broadcast site. You can even shop various online stores from within Media Player.

Media Player recognizes most of the popular media formats, including AVI movies and MP3 audio files,

and offers easy-to-use playback tools to allow you to watch DVD movies from your desktop. (Keep in mind, however, that not every graphics adapter — the part of your computer that draws what you see on the monitor screen — is capable of playing DVD movies.)

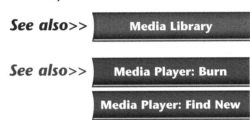

See also>>   Media Library

See also>>   Media Player: Burn

Media Player: Find New

① Click Start.

② Click All Programs.

③ Click Windows Media Player.

Windows Media Player opens on your desktop.

MICROSOFT MANAGEMENT CONSOLE

The Microsoft Management Console (MMC) houses several administrative tools called *snap-ins*, which are used to manage hardware, software, and network components.

More than two dozen MMC snap-ins are included with Windows Vista Ultimate, including Device Manager, Event Viewer, Shared Folders, Task Scheduler, and Local Users & Groups. Some of these snap-ins, such as Device Manager, are standalone tools that are accessible from within Control Panel. Others, such as Local Users & Groups, are accessible only from within the MMC.

In order to use a snap-in, you must add it to the console; you learn how in the task "Microsoft Management Console: Add Management Tools" in the Techniques part of this book.

See also>> **Microsoft Management Console**

① Click Start.

② Type **mmc** in the Search box.

The Start menu displays a list of programs that match what you typed.

③ Click the mmc link in the Start menu.

Note: If prompted, type the administrator password or click Continue.

The Microsoft Management Console opens.

MOVIE MAKER

Windows Movie Maker allows you to create movies from video or images on your hard disk, or from video footage shot using a camera. You can also use Movie Maker to add audio to your movie. You organize the movie content, or *clips*, in *collections* — special folders within Movie Maker.

When you work in Movie Maker, the program refers to your movie as a *project*. You add audio and video clips, video transitions, video effects, digital photos, and titles to the project, editing each as you see fit.

When you are happy with the arrangement of all these components, you *publish* the project; at that

point, what was formerly called a *project* is now called a *movie*.

After you publish a movie, you can share it with others by sending it as an e-mail attachment, posting it on a Web site, or using DVD Maker to burn it to a DVD.

See also>>

DVD Maker

Movie Maker: Create

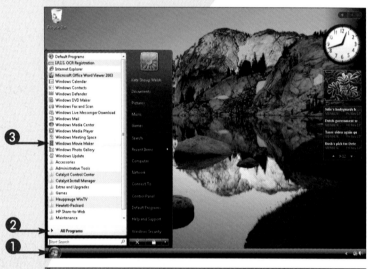

① Click Start.

② Click All Programs.

③ Click Windows Movie Maker.

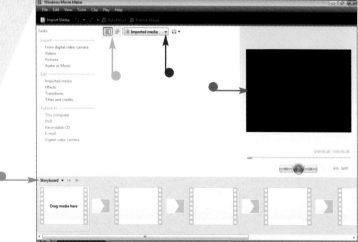

● Click these two buttons to toggle the main pane between a Tasks view, which contains links for performing common tasks, and a Collections view, which contains links to folders on your computer that house clips.

● View what clips, effects, or transitions you have added to your project in the Contents pane.

● Use the Preview monitor to preview your clips individually or to view your entire project.

● Click here to toggle this pane between a Storyboard view, which provides a visual record of the sequence of the video clips and effects in your project, and a Timeline view, which provides a more detailed view of the project.

MUSIC FOLDER

The Music folder on your computer is the default folder where audio files that you download or rip are saved. These can include MP3 files, WMA files, WAV files, and so on.

Like all folders in Windows Vista, the Music folder contains tools for searching, navigating, and organizing your files and folders, including the Search box, the Address bar, and the Navigation, Details, and Preview panes. (If any of these panes are not visible, click the Organize button, click Layout, and choose the desired pane.) Also included is a Folders list, which you access by

clicking the Folders link in the bottom-left corner of the folder window.

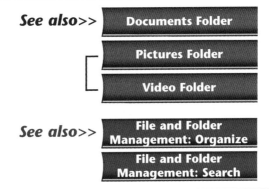

See also>> Documents Folder

Pictures Folder

Video Folder

See also>> File and Folder Management: Organize

File and Folder Management: Search

1 Click Start.

2 Click Music.

● The Music folder opens.

3 In the Folders list, click the subfolder in the Music folder that contains the music files you want to hear.

4 Click a track to select it.

● Use the Search box to locate files in the folder that is currently open.

● The Folders list, part of the Navigation pane, displays the subfolders within the selected folder.

● Play a selected track from the Preview pane.

● The Details pane contains information about the selected track.

5 Click Play All to listen to all the music files displayed in the file list. (To listen to specific songs, click them to select them and click Play.)

6 Click Share to share the selected files with other users on your PC or network.

37

NARRATOR

Narrator is an accessibility option that helps visually impaired users work on a Windows computer. Narrator is a text-to-speech tool. It reads what is written on the screen and speaks it aloud to you through your computer sound system when you cannot read it yourself. Narrator is an example of adaptive or assistive technology because it bridges the gap between those with a disability and their computers.

You can customize the voice options in Narrator. For example, you can modify the text-reading speed, the voice pitch, and the overall volume.

You access Narrator from the Ease of Access Center, which is available from Control Panel.

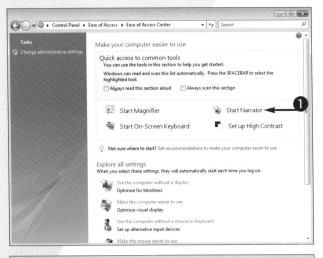

1 In the Ease of Access Center window, click Start Narrator.

● The Microsoft Narrator dialog box opens.

NAVIGATION PANE

All folders in Windows Vista include a Navigation pane, displayed by default. Using the Navigation pane, you can quickly access the more common folders such as the Documents folder, the Pictures folder, the Music folder, and so on.

The Navigation pane also includes easy access to the Searches folder, as well as to the folder containing recently changed files.

For access to even more folders, click the Folder link in the bottom-left corner of the pane. When

you click a folder in the Navigation pane, the contents of that folder are displayed.

See also>>

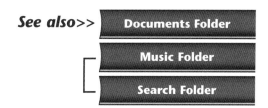

Documents Folder

Music Folder

Search Folder

① Click Start.

② Click a folder you want to open (here, Documents).

● The folder opens.

● The Navigation pane offers quick access to other main folders on your PC.

③ Click the Folders icon in the bottom of the pane.

● The folder list expands.

NETWORK AND SHARING CENTER

For real-time status information about your network, Windows Vista provides the Network and Sharing Center. In the event you experience connection problems, or if you are trying to set up a network, this information can prove invaluable.

Specifically, you can use the Network and Sharing Center to determine whether your computer is connected to your network. If so, the Network and Sharing Center also conveys the type of connection you have, and what level of access you have (if any)

to other computers and hardware devices on the network. For even more detailed information, you can access a map of your network from within the Network and Sharing Center.

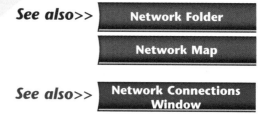

See also>> **Network Folder**

Network Map

See also>> **Network Connections Window**

① Click Start.

② Click Network.

● The Network folder opens.

③ Click Network and Sharing Center.

● The Network and Sharing Center opens.

NETWORK FOLDER

If you want to use a shared network resource such as a printer, open files on another computer on your network, or just confirm that a computer or other hardware device was successfully added to your network, use the Network folder.

If your computer is connected to a network, then all the other computers and devices currently connected to that network will be visible in the Network folder, as will all shared files and folders on the network.

You can also use the Network folder to install networked devices such as printers, and to troubleshoot network problems.

The Network folder also provides quick access to the Network and Sharing Center, where you can determine whether your computer is connected to your network, what type of connection you have, and what level of access you have (if any) to other computers and hardware devices on the network.

See also>>

Network and Sharing Center

Network Map

① Click Start.

② Click Network.

The Network folder opens.

NETWORK MAP

Both the Network folder and the Network and Sharing Center provide critical information about your network.

The Network folder lists all the computers and devices currently connected to your network, as well as all shared files and folders on the network.

The Network and Sharing Center provides real-time status information about your network, such as whether your computer is connected to your network, the type of connection you have, and what level of access you have (if any) to other computers and hardware devices on the network.

For even more detailed information about your network, however, you can access a map of your network. This is a graphical view that shows both the computers and devices on your network, as well as precisely how they are connected. (Note that although Windows Vista can detect the computers on the network that are running Windows XP, it may not be able to determine how those PCs are connected to the network.)

See also>>   **Network and Sharing Center**

Network Folder

See also>>   **Network Connections Window**

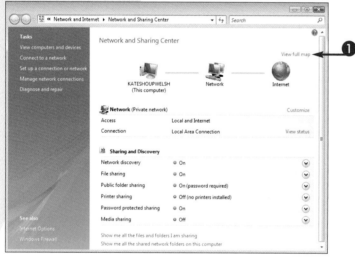

1 In the Network and Sharing Center, click View Full Map.

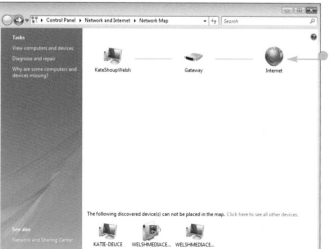

● The network map is displayed.

NOTEPAD

Notepad, one of the simplest text editors available, is ideal when you need to create, read, or edit short, text-only documents. In fact, Notepad allows you to read and create files that can be read on almost any other computer or hand-held communications device, such as a Web-enabled cell phone.

Unlike word processors that offer customized formatting to make text appear in a certain way — such as all bold or centered — Notepad works with unformatted text only. You cannot apply any fancy styles. However, plain text is an advantage for you when you need to create a document that can be opened on virtually any type of computer, regardless of what programs are installed on that computer.

All of the Notepad options are available through the menu bar near the top of the window. The size of the files that you can open or create in Notepad is limited to about 32KB, which corresponds to a few pages of text. You can open larger files through an alternate program such as WordPad, or a word processor such as Microsoft Word.

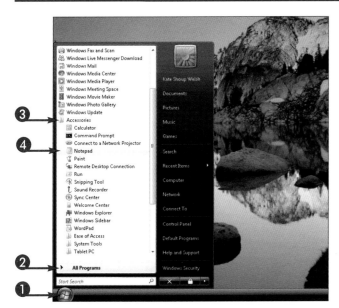

① Click Start.

② Click All Programs.

③ Click Accessories.

④ Click Notepad.

The Notepad window opens.

ON-SCREEN KEYBOARD

You can enter text through the graphical interface by using On-Screen Keyboard, a virtual keyboard that opens on your desktop. Windows includes this accessibility tool to assist those who cannot use a standard keyboard to type because of a physical challenge.

On-Screen Keyboard displays a virtual desktop keyboard through which you can type in one of three ways. The clicking mode enables you to type when you click an onscreen key with your pointing device (i.e., a mouse). The scanning mode works with some

forms of alternative input devices, such as a toggle switch, to provide extra help when you type. The hovering mode enables you to hold a pointing device over a key and have that key recognized as if you actually pressed the key.

See also>> Ease of Access Center

See also>> Ease of Access Center

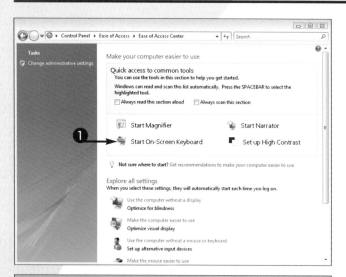

① In the Ease of Access Center, click Start On-Screen Keyboard.

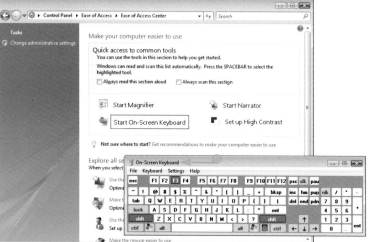

● The On-Screen Keyboard feature starts.

OPEN

Windows Vista offers a number of ways to open documents and other types of files. For example, you can double-click a filename in a folder to open that file, along with the program that is needed to read or run the file. Alternatively, you can use the Open dialog box found within many popular Windows programs to help you browse, locate, and open files.

The left section of the Open dialog box displays a list of links to several of the most commonly used folders and other file storage areas, such as the Documents folder. If the file that you want to open is not listed in the current folder in the Open dialog box, then you can click one of these alternate folders to search for the file.

Once you access the folder containing the file you want to open, simply click the file to select it and click the dialog box's Open button.

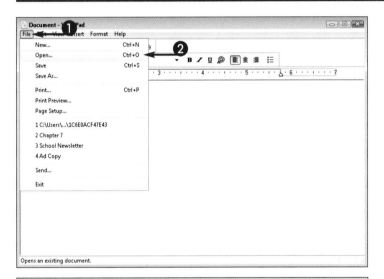

① In an open Windows program, click File.

② Click Open.

The Open dialog box appears.

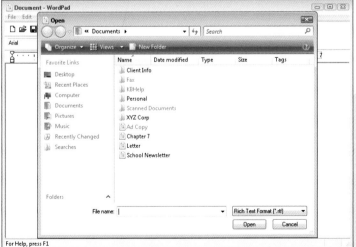

PAINT

Like many of its predecessors, Windows Vista includes a simple graphics program, called Paint. Although Paint is not as feature-rich as many graphics applications, it does offer some simple tools for creating simple drawings either on a blank canvas or on top of another image, such as a digital photograph.

On the left side of the Paint window is a toolbar, which provides easy access to various Paint tools. These include Free-Form Select, Select, Eraser, Fill with Color, Pick Color, Magnifier, Pencil, Brush, Airbrush, Text, Line, Curve, Rectangle, Polygon, Ellipse, and Rounded Rectangle. Some of these tools can be modified as needed. For example, when you select the Line tool, Paint enables you to choose the thickness of the line. In addition, Paint enables you to flip or rotate an image, to resize it or skew it, to invert colors, and so on.

Images you create in Paint can be saved as BMP, JPEG, GIF, PNG, and TIF files.

① Click Start.

② Click All Programs.

③ Click Accessories.

④ Click Paint.

Paint opens on the desktop.

● The Paint toolbox offers easy access to the program's tools.

● Choose the colors you want to use here.

PARENTAL CONTROLS

Although using a computer can be both educational and entertaining, it can also expose children to inappropriate subject matter, such as violent or sexually explicit content online or in computer games or other programs offline. Vista's parental controls enable parents to limit their kids' access to Internet Web sites and other online resources, as well as restrict the use of games and programs installed on the PC.

You can also configure Vista's parental controls to limit a child's computer use to certain hours of the day on certain days of the week, and to track how much time a user spends logged in.

To implement parental controls, each child who uses your computer must have his or her own standard user account. In addition, you must be logged in to the administrator account in order to set parental controls.

See also>> Content Advisor

Windows Media Center

See also>> User Accounts: Create

User Accounts: Manage

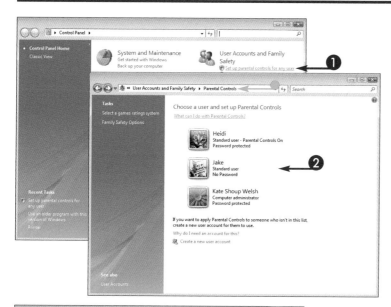

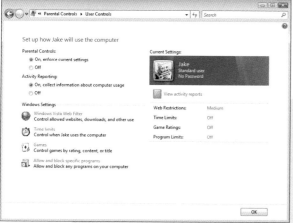

1 In Control Panel, click Set Up Parental Controls for Any User under User Accounts and Family Safety.

Note: If prompted, type the administrator password or click Continue.

● The Parental Controls window opens.

2 Click the standard user account to which you want to apply parental controls.

The User Controls window opens, enabling you to set parental controls for this account.

PERSONAL FOLDER

Windows Vista's personal folder offers easy access to folders such as Documents, Music, and Pictures folders, as well as to the Videos folder, where any videos you import or create are stored by default; the Downloads folder, where items you download from the Internet are automatically saved; and more.

The precise name and contents of the personal folder vary depending on who is logged on to Windows Vista. For example, if I am logged on, the personal folder is named Kate Shoup Welsh, and will provide access to my personal files, but not to files belonging to other users.

Like all folders in Windows Vista, the personal folder contains tools for searching, navigating, and organizing your files and folders, including the folders list, the Search box, the Address bar, the Navigation pane, the Preview pane, and the Details pane. In addition, the personal folder includes a Search pane to expedite searching. (If any of these panes are not displayed when you open your personal folder, display them by clicking Organize, clicking Layout, and choosing the pane that is missing.)

① Click Start.

② Click the personal folder.

The personal folder opens.

PHONE AND MODEM OPTIONS

You can open Phone and Modem Options in Control Panel to review information about the modem and telephony options that are installed on your system. This feature serves as the major configuration and support center for phones, fax modems, and voice over Internet protocol, or VOIP.

The Phone and Modem Options dialog box displays three different tabs. The Dialing Rules tab allows you to adjust how your computer dials out over a modem. In the Modems tab, you can check the properties of the modem. The Advanced tab displays the special services and providers that are available to your make and model of modem.

The Phone and Modem Options dialog box displays basic configuration details along with dialing rules that you can establish to save on long-distance costs or to dial around an internal phone system, such as those that are sometimes found in hotels. (Note that if you want to test and troubleshoot the working status of your modem, then you can use Device Manager.)

See also>> **Device Manager**

See also>> **Phone and Modem Options**

1 In Control Panel, click Hardware and Sound.

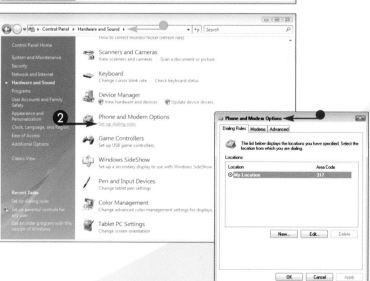

● The Hardware and Sound window opens.

2 Click Set Up Dialing Rules under Phone and Modem Options.

● The Phone and Modem Options dialog box opens.

Note: *If this is the first time you have opened the Phone and Modem Options dialog box, Windows will first display a dialog box that prompts you to enter your area code and other access codes.*

PHOTO GALLERY

Photo Gallery enables you to view and organize pictures and videos on your computer. Photos and other image files in your Pictures folder appear in Photo Gallery by default, but you can add pictures from any other folders to Photo Gallery. (Note that if Movie Maker is installed on your PC, videos will also be visible in Photo Gallery.)

You can edit your digital pictures using tools provided by Photo Gallery. For example, you can change an image's colors, improve its brightness and contrast, straighten the image, crop it, and remove red eye.

Photo Gallery enables you to rename image files in batches, bestowing meaningful names on several

image files at once. Alternatively, you can *tag* your image files, adding keywords that describe the picture to the picture's metadata. Both methods make it easier to organize and locate your files. You can also search for image files by file type and by date taken.

Finally, Photo Gallery enables you to create photo slide shows and to print your photos.

See also>>

Photo Gallery: Edit

Photo Gallery: Manage

① Click Start.

② Click All Programs.

③ Click Windows Photo Gallery.

The Photo Gallery window opens.

PICTURE LIBRARY

Windows Media Center's Picture Library provides many of the same features as Photo Gallery. For example, like Photo Gallery, Picture Library enables you to view and organize pictures on your computer. You can also edit your digital pictures using tools provided by Picture Library. For example, you can rotate and crop photos, adjust their brightness and contrast, and fix red eye. You can also use the Picture Library to print pictures and to create slide shows with them.

See also>> Windows Media Center

See also>> Windows Media Center: Set

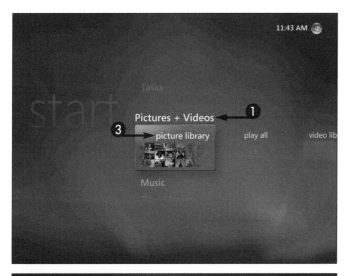

1 In Windows Media Center, scroll to Pictures + Video.

2 If necessary, scroll to Picture Library.

3 Click Picture Library.

The Picture Library opens.

PICTURES FOLDER

The Pictures folder acts as a central repository for digital image files. For example, when you scan an image or upload pictures from a digital camera, those image files are stored in the Pictures folder by default.

Like all folders in Vista, Pictures contains tools for searching, navigating, and organizing your files and folders, including the Search box, the Address bar, and the Navigation, Details, and Preview panes. (If any of these panes are not visible, click the Organize button, click Layout, and choose the desired pane.) Also included is a Folders list, which you access by

clicking the Folders link in the bottom-left corner of the folder window.

Using the Pictures folder, you can quickly and easily view your pictures. Toolbar buttons in the folder window enable you to view your pictures in a slide show, print your pictures, and share them with others via e-mail.

See also>>

Photo Gallery

Picture Library

① Click Start.

② Click Pictures.

The Pictures folder opens.

PREVIEW PANE

Although it is not displayed by default, folders in Windows Vista can be configured to include a Preview pane. Using this pane, you can see the contents of the files within the folder. For example, clicking a WordPad document displays the document's text in the Preview pane. Likewise, if you click an image file, the Preview pane displays the image.

The Preview pane is extremely useful if you are trying to find a file but you are not entirely sure

what its filename is. Instead of having to take the time to open a file — and, often, launch its associated program — to determine whether the file is the correct one, you can simply click it and view its contents in the Preview pane.

See also>>

Details Pane

Navigation Pane

❶ Within the folder in which you want to display the Preview pane, click Organize.

❷ Click Layout.

❸ Click Preview Pane.

The Preview pane is displayed.

❹ Click a file in the folder.

● The contents of the file are displayed in the Preview pane.

PROGRAMS AND FEATURES WINDOW

Windows Vista's Control Panel offers access to the Programs and Features window. From here, you can uninstall a program from your computer — something you might do to free up disk space or if you have simply stopped using a program. You can also change a program's configuration from within the Programs and Features window, or repair it in the event it becomes damaged. (Note that not all programs can be changed. Any program that does not have a Change or Repair button listed cannot be changed or repaired.)

Be aware that some programs may not be listed in the Programs and Features window. For example, programs written for other versions of Windows may not appear. If you want to uninstall a program not listed in the Programs and Features window, refer to the program's documentation for instructions.

See also>> **Default Programs Center**

① In the Control Panel window, click Programs.

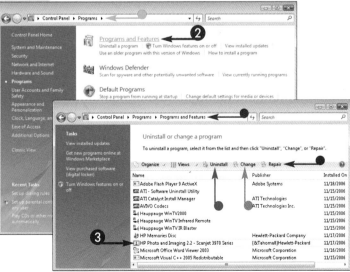

● The Programs window opens.

② Click Programs and Features.

● The Programs and Features window opens.

③ Click the program you want to uninstall, change, or repair.

● Click Uninstall to uninstall the program.

● Click Change to change the program.

● Click Repair to repair the program.

QUICK LAUNCH

Q

You can use the Quick Launch bar to launch your most frequently used programs more quickly in Windows. The Quick Launch bar is a special toolbar that contains icons for programs, utilities, and even documents so that you can open them quickly and easily.

The Quick Launch bar allows you to decide which items appear on it, although buttons for certain programs, such as Internet Explorer 7 and Windows Media Player, may appear by default. Another useful feature of the Quick Launch bar is

the Show Desktop button. When you click this icon, Windows minimizes all open application windows so that you can see the Windows desktop. You can then quickly access any of the shortcuts on the desktop to launch programs or open documents.

If the Quick Launch bar is not visible on your desktop, you can enable it.

See also>>   **Quick Launch**

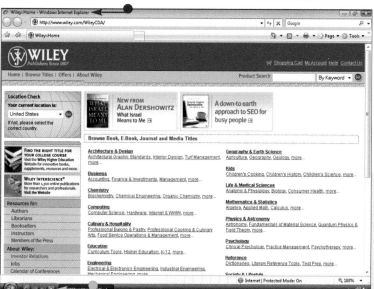

① Right-click the taskbar.

② Click Toolbars.

③ Click Quick Launch.

A checkmark appears in the menu next to the Quick Launch entry.

Note: You can also follow these steps to remove the Quick Launch toolbar from your taskbar, clicking Quick Launch to remove the checkmark.

● The Quick Launch bar is displayed.

④ To open a program from the Quick Launch bar, click the program's icon.

● The program opens.

QUICK TABS

In earlier versions of Internet Explorer, opening multiple Web pages at once involved opening a separate browser window for each page — which made it cumbersome to switch from one page to another.

To rectify this, Microsoft developed a feature called Quick Tabs view for inclusion in Internet Explorer 7. With Quick Tabs, when you open multiple Web pages at once, each one is displayed in the same browser in its own tab. To switch to a different Web page, you simply click the page's tab. You close a page by right-clicking its tab and clicking Close, or by clicking the tab's Close button.

The Quick Tabs feature also supports a special view, called Quick Tab view. In Quick Tab view, all the pages that are open in your browser are displayed at once. To open Quick Tab view, click the Quick Tab button. Alternatively, view a list containing all open Web pages by clicking the Quick Tab button's down arrow.

See also>>  Internet Explorer 7

See also>> Internet Explorer 7

① With several Web pages open in your browser window, click a page's tab to switch to that page.

● Internet Explorer switches to the page whose tab you clicked.

② Switch to Quick Tabs view by clicking the Quick Tabs button.

● Internet Explorer displays all the open pages in one window.

Note: To close Quick Tabs view, click the Quick Tabs button.

RECENT ITEMS

To locate and open the most recently accessed files on your system, use the Recent Items command on the Start menu. Doing so displays a list of the files you opened most recently, including documents, graphics, and so on. This feature helps you to save time by limiting your search for a particular file only to those that you have created, read, or modified in the recent past.

Although Windows keeps track of these files automatically to determine which files are listed under Recent Items, you can reset the display

at any time by right-clicking the Recent Items command in the Start menu and choosing Clear Recent Items List. Windows creates a fresh view, which is temporarily empty until the next time you start or open a file.

Each user with an account on your PC has his or her own separate Recent Items list. If a user resets the list on his or her account, it does not affect the lists displayed for other users.

1 Click Start.

2 Click Recent Items.

3 Click a file to open.

The file opens in its associated program on your desktop.

RECYCLE BIN

The Windows Recycle Bin is a virtual wastebasket that resides on your desktop. You can drag and drop files into it from other folders, or you can delete a file from within a folder to send it automatically to the Recycle Bin.

Regardless of the approach you use, when you delete files from your drives, these files remain on the disk, in the Recycle Bin. That way, in the event you determine you deleted a file in error, you can

restore it to its previous location and condition. When you want to make more disk space available on your computer, you can empty the Recycle Bin; when you do, the file is permanently removed from your PC and cannot be restored.

See also>> **Recycle Bin**

1 Double-click the Recycle Bin icon on your desktop.

The Recycle Bin window opens, displaying files you have deleted.

REGIONAL AND LANGUAGE OPTIONS

As more companies share information with users in different countries, documents and files need to be exchanged in an increasing number of languages.

For this reason, Windows Vista includes the Regional and Language Options dialog box. Using this dialog box, you can change the language used in menus and dialog boxes (called the *display language*) as well as the language used to input data (called the *input language*). In addition, you can set regional options that determine how time, date, currency, and other numbers should be displayed.

Adding support for some languages, including Arabic, French, German, Hebrew, Japanese, Korean, and Spanish, is a simple matter of selecting the language in the Regional and Language Options dialog box. If the language you want to enable is not listed in the dialog box, you must first install it; to do so, you will need your Windows Vista install CD handy.

See also>> **Regional and Language Options**

❶ In Control Panel, click Clock, Language, and Region.

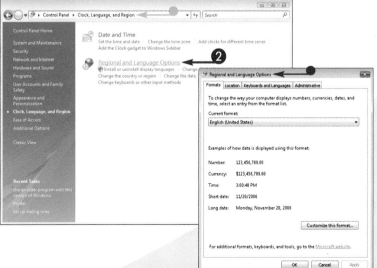

● The Clock, Language, and Region window opens.

❷ Click Regional and Language Options.

● The Regional and Language Options dialog box opens.

RESTORE FILES WIZARD

If you used Windows Vista's File and Folder Backup Wizard to back up the files and folders on your PC, you can use Vista's Restore Files Wizard to restore your files and folders in the event of system failure or some other disaster.

To restore the files, you must first make available to your computer the media on which the backed up files are stored. For example, if you stored the

backed up files on a CD or DVD, insert the disc in your drive. Alternatively, if you saved the backed up files on an external hard drive or a Flash device, connect the hardware to your PC.

See also>>   **Backup and Restore**

See also>>   **File and Folder Backup**

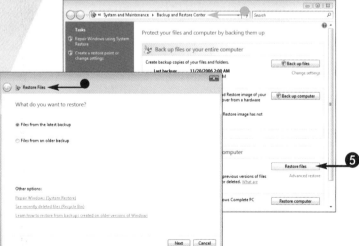

1 Click Start.

2 Click All Programs.

3 Click Maintenance.

4 Click Backup and Restore Center.

● The Backup and Restore Center opens.

5 Click Restore Files.

● The Restore Files Wizard starts.

SAVE AS

Many Windows applications launch a standard Save As dialog box when you save a file for the first time or if you attempt to close a file without saving it. To save a file, click File and click Save, press Ctrl+S on your keyboard, or click the Save toolbar button. (Note that you should save your files often so that if your computer crashes, little or no work will be lost.)

You can also open the Save As dialog box to save a copy of the file you are working on, but with a new name. To do so, click File and click Save As.

Within the Save As dialog box, you can type a name for the file, choose a file type, specify the folder in which your file should be saved, and in some cases add tags to the file.

After you have saved a file with the Save As dialog box and closed the file, you can open the file later with the Open dialog box.

See also>> **Open**

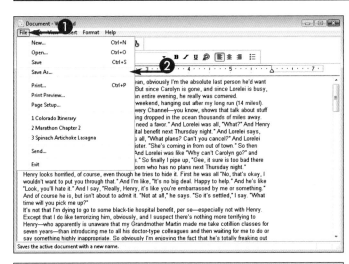

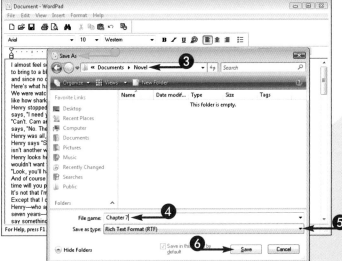

① With the file you want to save open on your screen, click File.

② Click Save or Save As.

● The Save As dialog box opens.

Note: To expand the dialog box, click the Show Folders button in the lower-left corner.

③ Open the folder in which you want to save the file.

④ Type a name for the file.

⑤ Choose a file type.

Note: *The file types available in this list differ depending on what type of file you are working with. For example, if you are working with a document file, you will see file types such as Rich Text Format (RTF), Text Document (TXT), and so on; available file types for images include JPEG, GIF, and the like.*

⑥ Click Save.

Windows saves the document.

SCANNER AND CAMERA INSTALLATION WIZARD

Typically, when you connect a camera or scanner (or just about any other piece of hardware) to a Windows PC and turn the scanner or camera on, Windows automatically locates and installs the necessary *drivers* — that is, the software that enables Windows and the camera or scanner to interact.

On occasion, however, Windows does not have access to the appropriate drivers, especially if the scanner or camera is older or, in the case of the scanner, networked. If, when you attach your scanner or camera to your PC and turn the camera or scanner

on, Windows fails to recognize the hardware, you can run the Scanner and Camera Installation Wizard to locate and install the necessary drivers. (If you have the CD that came with your scanner or camera, be sure to keep it handy; you may need it in order to successfully install the camera or scanner.)

See also>> **Fax and Scan**

See also>> **Fax and Scan: Set Up**

① In the Control Panel window, click Hardware and Sound.

● The Hardware and Sound window opens.

② Click View Scanners and Cameras.

● The Scanners and Cameras window opens.

③ Click Add Device.

● The Scanner and Camera Installation Wizard starts.

SEARCH BOX

S

If you misplace a file or folder in your Windows system, you can use Vista's search tools to find it. If you have a general idea where the item is located — for example, if you know it is somewhere in your Documents folder — you can search for it from within that folder using the folder's Search box. Simply type one of the following in the box: the name of the file (or folder), a broad description of what the file contains (such as "music"), the file type (DOC, JPG, MP3, and so on), tags (these are words or phrases you can add to your files to describe them), or author. As you type, Windows sifts through the files and folders on your system, displaying only those that match your criteria.

If you have no idea where your file or folder is, or if you want to apply more advanced search criteria, use the Search folder.

See also>> **Search Folder**

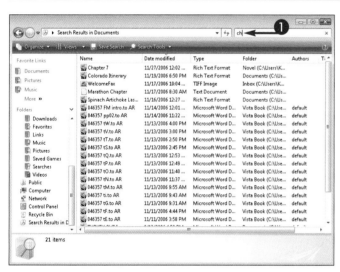

① In the folder that houses the missing file or folder, enter part or all of the file's name, type, author, or other criteria in the Search box.

● As you type, Windows displays the files and folders within the active folder that match your criteria.

② When you see the file you want, double-click it to open it.

63

SEARCH FOLDER

If you misplaced a file or folder in your Windows system, you can use Vista's search tools to find it.

Vista offers several search options, each serving different needs. If you have a general idea where the file you seek is located — for example, you know it is somewhere in your Documents folder — you can search for it from within that folder using the folder's Search box.

Another search option, the Search folder, is a good choice when you do not know where a file or folder is located, or when you want to conduct a more advanced search.

When Windows searches for a file, it combs through certain folders only, called *indexed locations*, by default. These folders include Documents, Pictures, Music, Desktop, and others; e-mail files; and offline files.

See also>> Search Box

See also>> Search Folder

① Click Start.

② Click Search.

● The Search folder opens.

③ Type a word or part of a word in the folder's Search box.

● As you type, Windows displays the files and folders in all indexed locations that match your criterion.

● To show only certain types of files, such as documents or pictures, click a filter button.

● To access additional filters, click the Advanced Search button.

● Open the Location list and click an alternative folder or drive to search it.

SECURITY CENTER

The Windows Security Center provides you with a central location where you can view the status of various security-related settings, including firewall settings, automatic update settings, anti-malware (i.e., virus protection) settings, Internet security settings, and User Account Control settings.

You can also change the settings of certain security-related features from within Vista's Security Center. For example, if you use Windows Firewall, you can access that feature's settings directly from within Security Center. Likewise, if you use the Internet Explorer 7 Web browser, you can adjust its security settings here.

One way to access the Security Center is to double-click the Security Center icon on the taskbar. This icon is displayed anytime Windows detects a problem with one of your security features. If the Security Center icon is not displayed, access the Security Center via Control Panel.

See also>>

See also>>

① In Control Panel, click Check This Computer's Security Status.

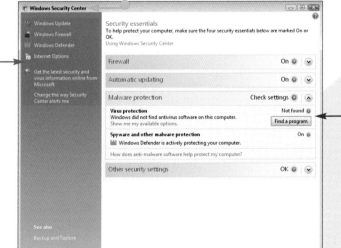

● The Security Center opens.

● View your system's security status here.

● Access security-related programs and tools here.

SECURITY REPORT

If you plan to use the Internet for any type of online transaction, such as with a bank or merchant, you want to ensure that the transaction is secure, and that your private information remains just that: private.

That is why Internet Explorer 7 includes a Security Report button. When you click it, it displays information about the online-transaction site that is open in your browser window, such as whether it has a certificate from a trust organization, such as BBB Online, TRUSTe, or WebTrust.

See also>> Internet Explorer 7

Internet Explorer Protected Mode

See also>> Internet Explorer 7

Phishing Filter

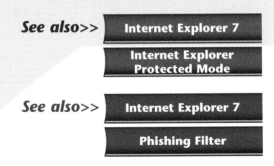

① Click the lock icon in the Security Status bar.

Information about the site appears.

② To learn more about the site, click View Certificates.

● The Certificate dialog box opens.

SET UP A WIRELESS ROUTER OR ACCESS POINT WIZARD

Before you set up a wireless network, first confirm that all computers destined for the network have a wireless network adapter. (See Vista's help files for details.) If you want the computers on the network to share an Internet connection, you also need a wireless router, a broadband modem, a cable or DSL jack, and an Internet connection.

After you set up the required hardware, run the Set Up a Wireless Router or Access Point Wizard. It steps you through the network setup process, enabling you to add more computers and hardware such as printers to the network.

When you complete the wizard, test the network by opening the Network folder. It should display icons for all the computers and hardware on the network. (You can also remove a computer or other device from the network here; click its icon and press the Delete key on your keyboard.)

See also>>

Network and Sharing Center

Network Folder

① Click Start.

② Click Network.

● The Network folder opens.

③ Click Network and Sharing Center.

● The Network and Sharing Center opens.

④ Click Set Up a Connection or Network.

● The Set Up a Connection or Network window opens.

⑤ Click Set Up a Wireless Router or Access Point.

⑥ Click Next.

Windows launches the Wireless Router or Access Point Wizard.

SOUND NOTIFICATIONS

By default, Windows produces sounds to alert you to certain problems or errors that may occur as you work with your computer. However, if you are hearing-impaired or you have the sound disabled, then these alerts cannot attract your attention. To rectify this, Windows Vista includes Sound Notifications. It converts sound alerts into visual alerts, such as a flash on the screen. Unfortunately, not every program or tool that you run on Windows Vista will support Sound Notifications, but many of the more common ones do.

In addition to displaying visual alerts, Sound Notifications can also display text captions, much like those used in closed captioning with television, to inform you when your computer engages in an operation, such as starting or finishing a print job.

See also>> **Ease of Access Center**

See also>> **Ease of Access Center**

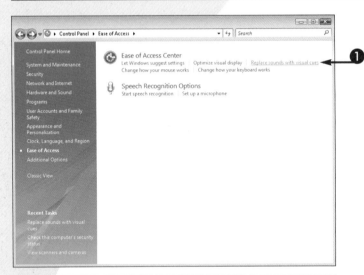

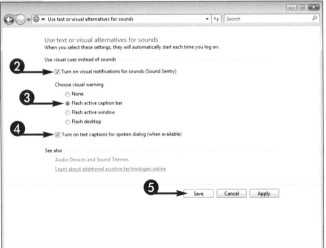

① In the Ease of Access Center, click Replace Sounds with Visual Clues.

The Use Text or Visual Alternatives for Sounds window opens.

② Select Turn On Visual Notifications for Sounds (Sound Sentry) to replace system sounds with visual clues.

③ Choose what kind of visual warning you want to see.

④ Select Turn On Text Captions for Spoken Dialog (When Available) to see text captions in place of sounds.

⑤ Click Save.

((ϙ)) SPEECH RECOGNITION

Using Windows Vista's Speech Recognition feature, you can dictate and edit text, be it to type a report in a word-processing program such as WordPad or to fill out a form online. In addition to using Speech Recognition to dictate text, you can also use it to control your computer — that is, issue commands to run programs and otherwise interact with Windows — rather than using your mouse and keyboard.

Setting up Windows Speech Recognition involves two steps: setting up a microphone and creating a voice profile. A *voice profile* includes information

about how you speak, such as whether you have an accent and how you pronounce certain words, as well as information about your environment, such as whether certain common office sounds are present.

Optionally, you can run the program's 30-minute Speech Tutorial to learn the various commands required by Speech Recognition to control your computer and to dictate and edit text.

See also>> **Speech Recognition**

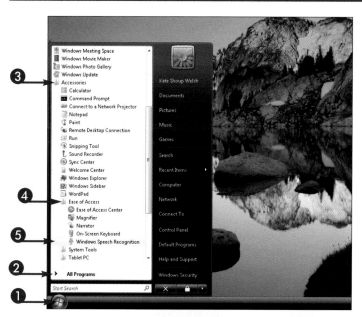

1 Click Start.

2 Click All Programs.

3 Click Accessories.

4 Click Ease of Access.

5 Click Windows Speech Recognition.

● Windows Speech Recognition opens.

START MENU

Windows' Start menu is the gateway to the programs, folders, and files on your PC.

The menu's left pane lists commonly used programs, with the entries in the lower portion of the list reflecting the programs you have used recently. To access programs not on the list, click All Programs.

The right pane provides access to Windows' main folders (Documents, Pictures, Music, and so on); Windows features, including Control Panel, Help and Support, and games; and buttons that enable you to power off, lock, log off of, shut down, or restart your computer, and to switch users.

If you cannot find a program or folder on the Start menu, or if you want to initiate a search for a program, folder, or file, type a keyword or phrase in the Start menu's Search box. Windows displays the results of the search in the left pane; click a result to open it.

See also>>

❶ Click Start.

Windows displays the Start menu.

SYNC CENTER

If you sometimes work with offline files, or use a portable device such as a personal digital assistant (PDA), you must eventually synchronize, or *sync*, the files in the offline folder or portable device with those on the network or on your PC.

To sync files, use Sync Center. It compares files on your PC with files on the network or portable device to determine whether any have changed. If so, Windows refers to the appropriate *sync partnership* (the set of rules you establish to dictate how and when files should be synced

between two specific devices) to determine which version of each file should be saved.

You can run syncs manually, or schedule automatic syncs on a daily, weekly, or monthly basis. Alternatively, you can instruct Windows to sync when a specific event occurs — such as every time you log on to your PC.

See also>>   **Offline Files: View**

Sync Center

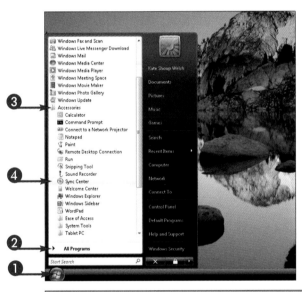

① Click Start.

② Click All Programs.

③ Click Accessories.

④ Click Sync Center.

The Sync Center window opens.

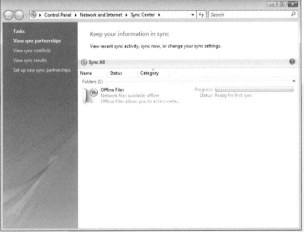

SYSTEM INFORMATION WINDOW

The System Information window displays details about your computer at a glance. Information about hardware resources, software environment, and components is listed by category. Under System Summary, you find general information about your PC such as its name, workgroup, and domain; its manufacturer; the amount of memory installed; and the PC's processor type and speed. You also find details about the operating system installed.

The System Information window's Find What box enables you to search for the information you need by typing a keyword. The left pane of the System Information window provides several links to various system settings and tools.

You can use the System Information window to troubleshoot a problem with your system, and to review the effects of changes that you make through an upgrade. Finally, technical service representatives may ask you to open this window to obtain details about your system when you call a customer support line.

See also>> **Performance Information**

① Click Start.

② Click All Programs.

③ Click Accessories.

④ Click System Tools.

⑤ Click System Information

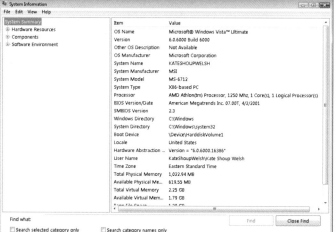

The System Information window opens.

TASK MANAGER

You can use the Task Manager dialog box to check your system, close a program that you cannot exit normally, or do a quick check of overall system performance.

Task Manager provides you with multiple options through a multi-tabbed window, each tab displaying a label for the information or services that it allows you to view or perform. These tabs generally include Applications, Processes, Services, Performance, Networking, and User, although additional tabs may appear, based on your Windows setup. More options are available from the menu bar, such as opening a new task.

Just as its name implies, Task Manager tracks all open programs, which you can see in the Applications tab. Task Manager also lists services that run invisibly in the background, which you can view from the Processes tab.

You can use the Networking tab to see what is presently occurring on your network, just as you can view real-time performance through the Performance tab.

See also>> **Performance Information**

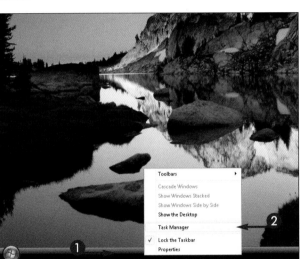

① Right-click a blank area of the taskbar.

② Click Task Manager.

● The Windows Task Manager dialog box opens.

TASK SCHEDULER

Most computer users perform certain tasks on a regular basis. For example, they might run Disk Cleanup on a weekly basis, or work with a financial program each month to balance their checkbooks.

If you are one such user, you can use the Create Basic Task Wizard to configure Windows Vista's Task Scheduler utility to launch the necessary programs according to the schedule you choose. For example, you can configure Task Scheduler to launch Disk Cleanup on the prescribed day, at which point Disk Cleanup will await your input to complete the task.

Task Scheduler offers a few different choices. You can opt to launch the program daily, weekly, or monthly, or when certain computer events occur, such as when the computer starts, when you log on, and so on.

You launch Task Scheduler from the System and Maintenance window in Control Panel.

See also>> **Disk Cleanup**

1 In the System and Maintenance window, under Administrative Tools, click Schedule Tasks.

Note: Click Start, Control Panel, and then System and Maintenance to open the System and Maintenance window.

Note: If prompted, type the administrator password or click Continue.

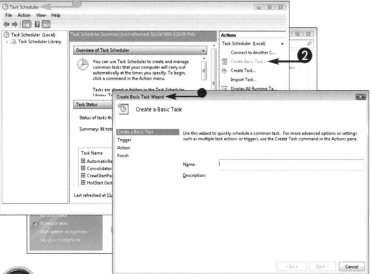

● The Task Scheduler window opens.

2 Click Create Basic Task.

● Windows launches the Create Basic Task Wizard.

TASKBAR AND START MENU PROPERTIES

The taskbar, which appears across the bottom of your desktop, is home to the system tray, sometimes called the *notification area*. In the system tray, you can check the time, view system messages, and access certain programs and tools. Also available from the taskbar are the Quick Launch bar, which provides ready access to shortcuts to your favorite programs, and buttons representing open programs. Perhaps most important, however, the taskbar houses the Start button, which you click to view the Start menu.

Microsoft has grouped the properties and settings for both the Start menu and the taskbar in a

single dialog box: the Taskbar and Start Menu Properties dialog box.

In addition to customizing the taskbar via this dialog box, you can also drag it to another position on your screen (along one of the side edges, perhaps). In addition, you can drag the edge of the taskbar that abuts the desktop to increase its size, allowing quick access to more open programs.

See also>> **Taskbar**

1 Right-click a blank area of the taskbar.

2 Click Properties.

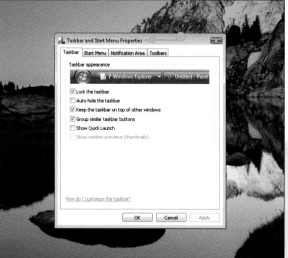

● The Taskbar and Start Menu Properties dialog box opens.

USER ACCOUNT CONTROL

User Account Control (UAC) enables users to run Vista with a Standard account rather than an Administrator account for day-to-day use. With a Standard account, the user can surf the Internet, send e-mail, use a word processor, and so on. If someone using a Standard account attempts to install a program or perform some other operation that requires administrator privileges, UAC prompts that user for the administrator password before permitting the user to proceed. (If the user is logged on as the administrator, UAC prompts the user to click a button to continue.)

UAC also displays a warning message if an unidentified program is attempting to access the computer or if a program has been blocked.

If these warning messages annoy you, you can disable UAC by clicking User Accounts and Family Safety in Control Panel, clicking User Accounts in the window that appears, clicking Turn User Account Control On or Off, and following the onscreen instructions.

See also>>

User Accounts: Create

User Accounts: Manage

① Launch an operation that requires administrator privileges.

● In this example, I clicked the Device Manager option in the Hardware and Sound window in Control Panel to open Device Manager. Notice the shield icon next to that option; it indicates that administrator privileges are required to launch the operation.

● Windows displays a warning box.

② Type the administrator password or, if you are logged on to the Administrator account, click Continue.

● Windows finishes launching the operation.

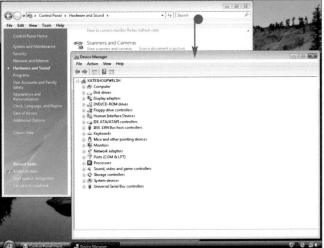

VIDEO LIBRARY

Using Windows Media Center, you can watch live or recorded television, listen to digital music, view your photographs, play games, burn CDs and DVDs, listen to FM or Internet radio, or access other online content. In addition, you can use Windows Media Center to house your videos in the Video Library.

The Video Library is not unlike the Windows Media Center Picture Library. It enables you to view and organize videos on your computer, and to apply

search criteria to locate the video you want to view. These videos can be footage you import from your digital video camera, or can be video you download from the Internet.

See also>>

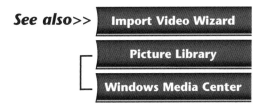

Import Video Wizard

Picture Library

Windows Media Center

① In Windows Media Center, scroll to Pictures + Video and click Video Library.

The Video Library opens.

VOLUME MIXER

Although the speakers attached to your computer often allow you to adjust audio volume, and sometimes treble and bass levels, you can control volume directly through the Volume Mixer window. This feature offers you dynamic control directly from your Windows desktop; you do not need to adjust the controls on the actual hardware.

From the Volume Mixer window, you can adjust the volume for your speakers as well as for other audio devices that you have installed on your system. You can also adjust the volume of Windows system

sounds — for example, the audible alert you hear when you receive an e-mail message. In addition, you can adjust the volume of certain programs running on your system, independently. For example, if you are running Windows Media Player and Narrator, you can adjust the volume of one without affecting the volume of the other.

In addition to fine-tuning the volume, you can also use the Volume Mixer window to mute the sound from a specific device or program.

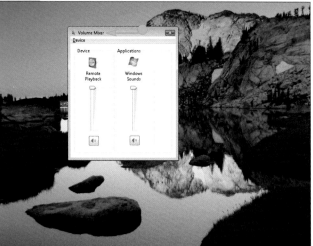

① Right-click the Volume icon in the taskbar's Notification Area.

Note: If the Volume icon is not visible, right-click the taskbar, click Properties, click the Notification Area tab, click the Volume checkbox to select it, and click OK.

② Click Open Volume Mixer.

● The Volume Mixer opens.

WELCOME CENTER

When you start Windows Vista and log on to your account, the operating system displays the Welcome Center. From this window, you can view details about your computer, transfer files and settings from a different computer to this one, add new users, personalize Windows, register your copy of the operating system, view Windows Vista demos, and more. You can also access Windows online technical support and respond to offers from Microsoft. To access one of these various tools, or features, simply click its icon in

the Welcome Center and then click Show More Details.

If you no longer wish to see the Welcome Center at system startup, simply click the Run at Startup checkbox to deselect it. If you later decide you wish to open the Welcome Center screen, you can do so by clicking Get Started with Windows under System and Maintenance in the Control Panel.

1 Launch Windows.

2 Log in to the desired account.

● Windows displays the Welcome Center window.

3 Click an item in the Welcome Center (in this example, View Computer Details).

4 Click Show More Details.

*Note: The item you click in Step **4** depends on the item you selected in Step **3**. For example, if, in Step **3**, you clicked Transfer Files and Settings, you would click Start Windows Easy Transfer in Step **4**.*

● Windows displays more details about the selected item.

5 Click the Close button to close the Welcome Center window.

WINDOWS DEFENDER

Spyware is software that is installed on your computer usually without your knowledge or consent. It can overwhelm your system with unwanted pop-up ads, and will almost certainly monitor and record your Web-surfing activities and transmit this data to one or more third parties. Although these third parties may simply be companies seeking marketing data, they can be more sinister forces: hackers who want your personal information, such as passwords, or who want to sabotage your computer. Even if the spyware on your computer is relatively benign, its

presence can dramatically affect the performance of your machine.

To combat this, use Windows Defender to scan your system for spyware and uninstall spyware if detected. You can even schedule automatic scans to occur on a regular basis. Windows Defender also offers a real-time protection feature — enabled by default — to alert you if a spyware program attempts to install itself on your machine or if any program attempts to change your Windows settings without your knowledge.

① In the Control Panel window, click Security.

● The Security window opens.

② Click Windows Defender.

The Windows Defender window opens.

WINDOWS FIREWALL

You can configure and use Windows Firewall to protect your computer from privacy intrusions or other problems when you connect to a network or the Internet. The Windows Firewall software is designed to act as a barrier between your private computer files and outside connections.

When you enable Windows Firewall, it monitors all programs that either access the Internet from your computer or try to communicate with your computer from an external source. You should enable the firewall if you do not have a third-party program such as Norton Internet Suite, which provides this protection.

Once you enable Windows Firewall, it automatically acts to block certain programs that may compromise the security of your system. When the firewall detects a potential problem, a message appears onscreen asking what you want to do. You can choose to either continue blocking the software or stop blocking it.

See also>>

Windows Firewall: Configure

Windows Firewall: Manage

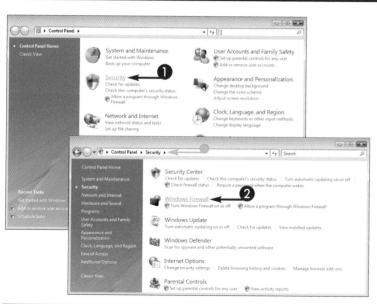

① In the Control Panel window, click Security.

● The Security window opens.

② Click Windows Firewall.

The Windows Firewall window appears.

WINDOWS LIVE MESSENGER

Instant messaging (IM) enables two or more people to communicate in real time using typed text. Although Windows Vista does not include an IM program by default, it does provide a link in the Start menu to download Windows Live Messenger, an update of Microsoft's MSN Messenger. Simply download and install the software (click the Start button, click All Programs, and click Windows Live Messenger Download) and, if necessary, create a Windows Live account.

Windows Live Messenger has retained many of the more popular features of MSN Messenger, such as contact lists and support for emoticons. In addition,

Windows Live Messenger includes several new features. For example, with Windows Live Messenger, users can share folders and files with others, conduct PC-to-phone calls throughout North America and western Europe, and send messages to (and receive messages from) virtually any mobile phone number, regardless of whether the person at that number uses Windows Live Messenger. Users can also converse with *bots*, which are automated interactive applications, to access information from such resources as Encarta.

See also>> **Windows Live Messenger: Create**

---

① Click Start.

② Click All Programs.

③ Click Windows Live Messenger.

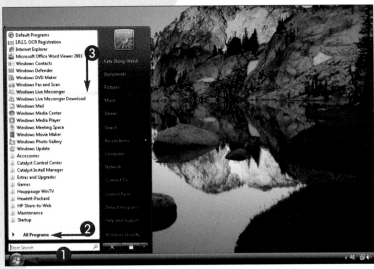

● The Windows Live Messenger sign in window opens.

④ Type the e-mail address you chose when you created your Windows Live Messenger account.

⑤ Type your password.

⑥ Click Sign In.

● The Windows Live Messenger window opens.

WINDOWS MALICIOUS SOFTWARE REMOVAL TOOL

If your computer is running slowly or exhibiting other mysterious behaviors, you may have a virus.

Even if you use Windows Firewall, Windows Defender, an industry-standard anti-virus program such as Windows Live OneCare, and Windows Update to obtain security patches and so forth from Microsoft, a virus or other form of malicious software can occasionally slip through. To remove it, you can use Microsoft's Malicious Software Removal tool.

This tool, which is updated by Microsoft on a monthly basis, scans your computer for viruses and other malicious software and attempts to

remove any "infections." Even if your computer seems asymptomatic, Microsoft recommends you run the tool on a regular basis.

The Malicious Software Removal tool is not installed in Windows Vista. Instead, you run it from a special Microsoft Web site. To locate it, visit www.microsoft.com and type **"malicious software removal tool"** (quotes included) in the site's Search box.

See also>>

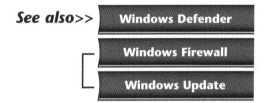

- Windows Defender
- Windows Firewall
- Windows Update

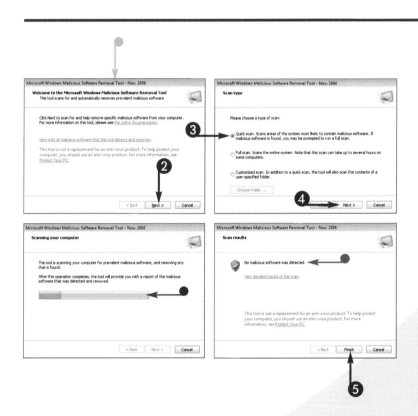

❶ Follow the steps on Microsoft's Web site to download and run the Malicious Software Removal tool.

● The first screen of the Malicious Software Removal tool appears.

❷ Click Next.

❸ Choose the type of scan you want to perform.

❹ Click Next.

● The Malicious Software Tool scans your system.

● The results of the scan are displayed.

❺ Click Finish.

WINDOWS MEDIA CENTER

With the appropriate hardware — namely, a TV tuner and an FM tuner — you can turn your Windows Vista PC into an entertainment center using Windows Media Center.

Windows Media Center, included in the Home Premium and Ultimate editions of Windows Vista, enables you to watch and record TV shows (in HDTV, no less), listen to digital music (and create your own playlists), view digital pictures and videos, play games, listen to and burn CDs (including your own music CDs), watch and burn DVDs, listen to FM and Internet radio stations, and access content from online services.

You can even set up Windows Media Center to play your digital media anywhere in your home — for example, you can wire speakers throughout your home to your Windows Vista computer so you can enjoy your digital music collection from any room in the house. In addition, with the use of special Windows Media Center Extenders and a home network, you can enjoy Windows Media Center on any television in your home.

See also>> **Windows Media Center: Set**

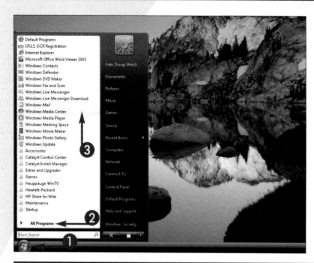

1. Click Start.
2. Click All Programs.
3. Click Windows Media Center.

Windows Media Center opens.

WINDOWS MEETING SPACE

W

Using Windows Meeting Space, you can share notes, documents (called *handouts*), programs, even your desktop with nine other computers on a network (all of which must be running Windows Vista), and vice versa. All communication is encrypted to ensure that only authorized session participants can access the shared information.

Computers in a Windows Meeting Space session connect using *peer-to-peer technology*; each computer in the session communicates with the others over the Internet or a private network, without requiring a server. If no network is present, Windows Meeting Space can set up an *ad hoc network*, in which the computers in the session

connect wirelessly, with wires, or some combination thereof to each other rather than to a network hub or router.

To use Windows Meeting Space, your firewall must be configured to allow it. If your system runs Windows Firewall, check the Windows Meeting Space checkbox in the Windows Firewall dialog box's Exceptions tab.

See also>>

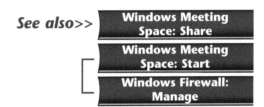

Windows Meeting Space: Share

Windows Meeting Space: Start

Windows Firewall: Manage

❶ Click Start.

❷ Click All Programs.

❸ Click Windows Meeting Space.

Note: If this is the first time you have launched the Windows Meeting Space program, you will be prompted to enable People Near Me, which is a technology that identifies people using computers near you and allows them to identify you. You may also be asked whether you want Windows Meeting Space to communicate through Windows Firewall; in order to use Windows Meeting Space, you must choose Yes.

The Windows Meeting Space window opens.

WINDOWS SIDEBAR

Windows Vista can display a long, vertical bar on the right side of your desktop called the Windows Sidebar. This bar houses special mini-programs, called *gadgets*, which offer easy access to information and frequently used tools. For example, suppose you create a WordPad document that serves as an invoice and you need to calculate the amount due. Rather than clicking the Start button, choosing All Programs, clicking Accessories, and selecting Calculator, you can simply use the Calculator gadget on the Sidebar.

By default, the Windows Sidebar includes a clock gadget, a slide-show gadget that cycles through the images in your Pictures folder, and a newsfeed gadget, which streams headlines directly onto your desktop. That is not to say, however, that those are the only gadgets available to you. You can easily add more gadgets, including the aforementioned Calculator gadget, to the Sidebar or remove any you do not want.

See also>> 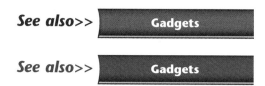 Gadgets

See also>> Gadgets

① Click Start.

② Click All Programs.

③ Click Accessories.

④ Click Windows Sidebar.

● The Windows Sidebar appears on the desktop.

WINDOWS SIDESHOW

With Windows SideShow, you can use certain devices to access the gadgets on your Windows Sidebar — even if your computer is turned off. For example, you might use a SideShow-enabled device to access the Calendar gadget to view your appointments, access the Mail gadget to read e-mail messages, and so on.

Windows SideShow supports the use of two types of devices: those that are integrated into your computer, such as the color displays that are sometimes embedded into the lid of some newer laptops, and devices that are separate from your PC, such as a mobile phone.

Whatever type of device you intend to use, it must be compatible with Windows SideShow. (Check its documentation to find out.) Once you have determined that a device is compatible, you must install the device on your PC. (Again, check the device's documentation for details.) You must also enable the use of each gadget with the device; to do so, click the checkbox next to the gadget in the Windows SideShow screen.

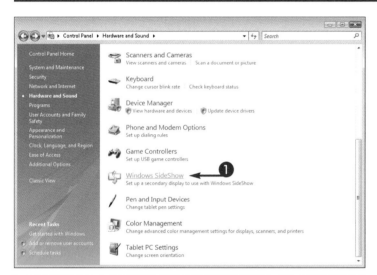

① In the Control Panel's Hardware and Sound window, click Windows SideShow.

The Windows SideShow window opens.

WINDOWS UPDATE

Windows Vista is a complex operating system that requires *updates* or *patches* — that is, additions to software that can prevent or fix problems or enhance security or performance. Microsoft constantly develops and publishes updates for Windows to make it work better, and to make it more secure and reliable.

Using Windows Update, you can manually obtain updates and patches or automate the update and patch process. For example, you can schedule Windows Update to automatically download and install updates on a regular basis, such as every day at 3:00 a.m. If you like, you can configure Windows

Update to download the updates but not install them until you direct it to do so. Whatever route you take, updates are downloaded in the background while you are online. In the event an important update cannot be installed, Windows Update will notify you.

See also>>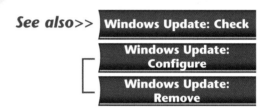

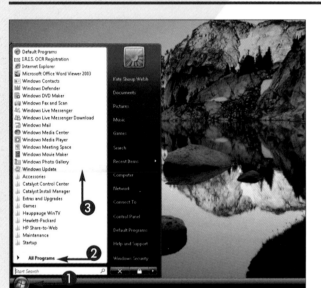

① Click Start.

② Click All Programs.

③ Click Windows Update.

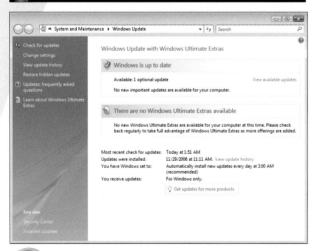

The Windows Update window opens.

WORDPAD

WordPad is a basic word-processing tool that is built into Windows Vista. You can use WordPad to write letters, keep a text list, type an address to print on an envelope, or read a document. You can also copy information from a Web page and paste it into an open WordPad document where you can save it to disk for later reference.

While Windows Notepad allows you to create and view only plain-text files, WordPad works with the

Rich Text Format, or RTF, which shows more stylized text features than a plain-text file.

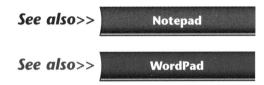

See also>> Notepad

See also>> WordPad

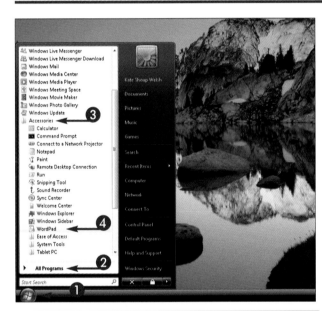

① Click Start.

② Click All Programs.

③ Click Accessories.

④ Click WordPad.

The WordPad window opens on the desktop, displaying a blank document.

Windows Vista Visual Encyclopedia

Part II: Techniques

Although Windows Vista Ultimate offers a lot of powerful tools and features, it may not be immediately clear how you can use them — at least, not until you arrive at the second part of this book.

From Ease of Access options to working with media files, the Techniques section walks you through some of the tasks that you will frequently perform with the tools and features in Windows Vista. You will also discover new options that you may not have thought possible without the use of third-party software. For example, Windows Vista allows you to copy or move files directly to a recordable CD or DVD drive; you no longer need to install special software to do this. Other programs, such as Windows Media Player, Windows Media Center, Calendar, Contacts, DVD Maker, Mail, Movie Maker, Photo Gallery, and Windows Collaboration, enable you to listen to music, watch TV, manage your calendar, organize your contacts, burn DVDs, e-mail friends and family, edit home movies, organize and edit digital photos, and collaborate with others, respectively.

In addition, if you share your computer with others, you can configure individual user accounts. If children use your system, then you can enable and configure parental controls to restrict access within Windows Vista, as well as to limit which Web sites your children can visit. All these tasks are covered in this section.

AERO:
Set Up Aero

Windows Vista includes a new, special setup called Aero, which may be displayed on your PC by default. This setup features a transparent glass design, subtle window animations, and new window colors. Aero, whose name is an acronym for Authentic, Energetic, Reflective, and Open, supports the use of Windows Flip 3D, which you use to preview your open windows in three-dimensional stacks, and live taskbar buttons, which display thumbnail-sized previews of your open windows.

If your Windows Vista machine is not currently using the Aero setup, you can easily switch to it provided your system supports its use. Specifically, your PC will need a 1 gigahertz, 32-bit or 64-bit processor; 1 gigabyte of system memory; and a Direct X 9 compatible graphics processor with a WDDM driver and at least 128 megabytes of video RAM.

See also>>   Flip 3D

① Right-click a blank area of the desktop.

② Click Personalize.

The Personalization window opens.

③ Click Window Color and Appearance.

● The Appearance Settings dialog box opens.

4 Click Windows Aero.

5 Click OK.

Windows Aero is activated.

6 To use Aero's live taskbar button feature, hover your mouse over a taskbar button.

TIP

More Options!

In addition to the Aero setup, Vista also supports a Windows Vista Basic setup (used throughout this book), and Windows Standard and Windows Classic setups, which hearken back to earlier editions of the operating system.

BACKGROUND:
Set the Desktop Background

One of the easiest ways to customize your Windows Vista workspace is to use a different image for your default desktop background, as well as specify how that image should be positioned onscreen.

You can choose one of the predesigned backgrounds available in Windows, which include black-and-white photographs, light auras, paintings, macro photographs of various textures, and landscape images (called, appropriately, "Vistas").

Alternatively, you can use a favorite digital image as your desktop background, such as a photo depicting family members, your dog, your friends, or your favorite vacation spot. Your only limitation is your imagination and the images that are available to you.

See also>> **Themes**

① Right-click a blank spot on your desktop.

② Click Personalize.

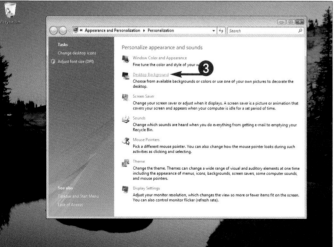

The Personalization window opens.

③ Click the Desktop Background link.

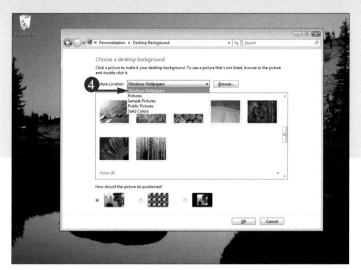

The Desktop Background window opens.

4 From the list, select the location where the picture you want to use is stored.

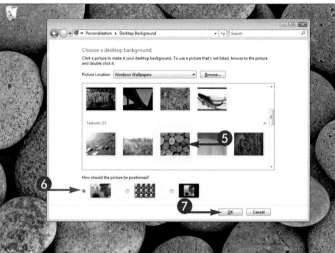

The available pictures in the selected location appear.

5 Click a background picture to select it.

Windows applies the selected picture to the desktop.

6 Specify how the picture should be positioned.

7 Click OK.

The new desktop background remains on the desktop.

Did You Know?

Files used for background images are usually Windows bitmap files that end with the .bmp file extension, but you can also use GIF, JPG or JPEG, DIB, PNG, HTM, or HTML files as the desktop background.

Did You Know?

To use a digital image of your own as a desktop background, click Pictures in the list of background categories in Step **4**. The photos stored in your Pictures folder appear; click a picture to select it. (To use a picture that is stored elsewhere on your computer, click the Browse button and locate the picture you want to use.)

CALENDAR:
Manage Tasks

Many people make lists to keep track of tasks they need to complete. To aid in this, Windows Calendar includes a personal task list. When you enter a task into your personal task list, you can specify a start time, a deadline, and a priority ranking for the task, as well as set a reminder. You can also enter notes about the task — for example, you might list other people who are involved in completing the task. When you complete a task, simply check it off your list.

See also>> | Calendar

See also>> | Calendar: Publish
Calendar: Set

① Click Start.
② Click All Programs.
③ Click Windows Calendar.

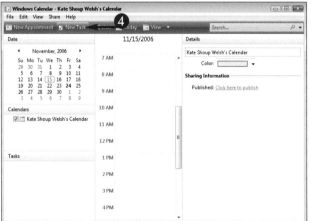

Windows Calendar opens.
④ Click the New Task button.

⑤ At the top of the Details pane, type a description for the task.

⑥ Optionally, click the down arrow next to the Priority field and choose Low, Medium, or High to prioritize the task.

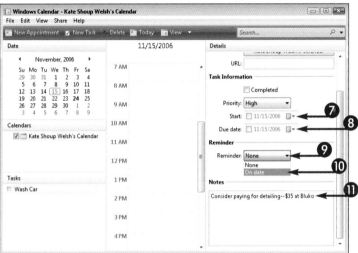

⑦ Click the down arrow next to the Start field and click the start date in the calendar that appears.

⑧ Click the down arrow next to the Due date field and click the due date in the calendar that appears

⑨ To set a reminder, click the down arrow next to the Reminder field.

⑩ Choose On Date.

⑪ Type any notes about the task.

Try This!

Search for an appointment or task by typing a few letters or words in the task's description in the Search box. As you type, results appear, narrowing as you provide more information.

Try This!

To edit an appointment or task, double-click it and type over the existing text in the Details pane as needed.

Try This!

To print your calendar, open the File menu and choose Print. In the Print dialog box, choose Day, Work Week, Week, or Month; specify the range of dates you want to print and the number of copies; and click OK.

CALENDAR:
Publish a Calendar

You can *publish* a calendar in order to share it with others. For example, you might share your calendar with your spouse and your kids.

There are two main ways to share a calendar. One is to publish it in your computer's Public Downloads folder, enabling you to share it with others who use the same computer as you do or whose computers reside on the same network as yours.

The other is to publish it online so that users who do not share your Windows Vista system or your network can access it. (Note that in order to publish your calendar online, you need access to a WebDAV

server — coverage of which is beyond the scope of this book.)

After you publish your calendar, others can subscribe to it by following the steps in the next task

See also>> Calendar

See also>> Calendar: Manage

Calendar: Set

Calendar: Subscribe

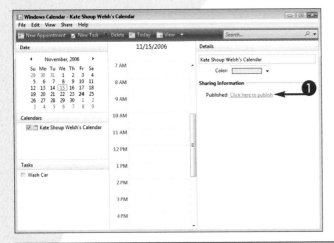

① Click the Click Here to Publish link in the Details pane of the Windows Calendar window.

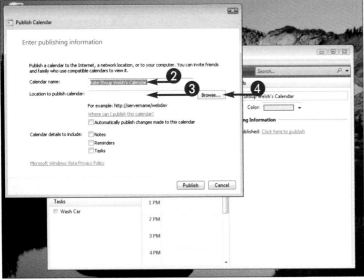

The Publish Calendar dialog box opens.

② By default, the calendar that is currently open is the one that will be shared. To share a different calendar, type its name.

③ Type the path to the folder where the shared calendar will be located.

④ If you are not sure of the path to the folder or Web site where you want to share your calendar, click Browse.

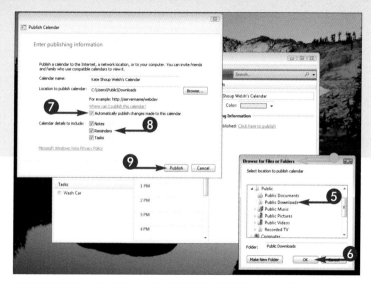

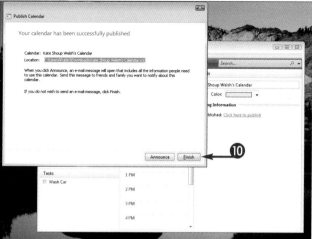

● The Browse for Files or Folders dialog box opens.

⑤ Navigate to the desired folder and click it to select it.

⑥ Click OK.

⑦ If you want Windows to automatically copy changes made to your calendar to the shared version, click the Automatically Publish Changes Made to This Calendar checkbox.

⑧ Click the Notes, Reminders, and/or Tasks checkboxes if you want your published calendar to contain these.

⑨ Click Publish.

⑩ Calendar asks whether you want to announce the publication of your calendar. If so, click the Announce button and follow the prompts to send an e-mail; otherwise, click Finish.

TIPS

Did You Know?

In addition to publishing a calendar, you can export it. When you export a calendar, you create a special Calendar file, with an .ics extension; this file can then be imported into Calendar on another PC, or imported into another application that supports the use of ICS files. To export a calendar, open the File menu in Calendar and click Export.

Attention!

In this task, the calendar is saved in the Public Downloads folder. This enables other people who have a user account on the same computer to access the calendar. Likewise, the calendar will be accessible to people with computers on the same network as the computer.

CALENDAR:
Set an Appointment

Windows Vista's Calendar function is both flexible and easy to use. With it, you can plan your daily activities by entering appointments. An *appointment* can be a one-time event, such as a luncheon or a meeting, or a recurring event — for example, a standing doctor's appointment. In addition to creating appointments for yourself, you can use Windows Calendar to send e-mail invitations to appointments to others. You can also configure Windows Calendar to send you a reminder about any appointments you enter. This

reminder can be sent minutes, hours, or days in advance depending on your needs.

See also>> Calendar

See also>> Calendar: Manage

Calendar: Publish

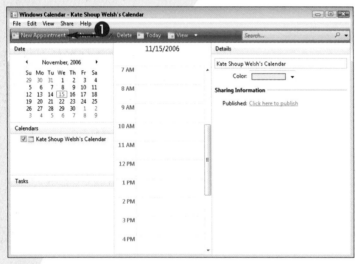

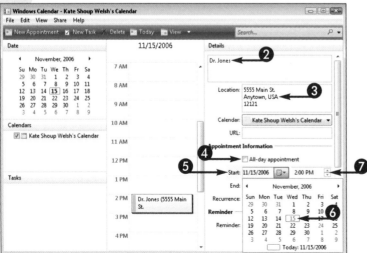

① In the Windows Calendar window, click the New Appointment button.

② At the top of the Details pane, type a description for the appointment.

③ Type the location of the appointment.

Note: *To set an appointment in a calendar other than the one currently displayed, click the down arrow next to the Calendar field and select the desired calendar.*

④ If the appointment will last all day, click the All-Day Appointment checkbox.

⑤ Click the down arrow next to the Start field.

⑥ Click the appointment's start date.

⑦ Type or use the arrows to specify the appointment's start time.

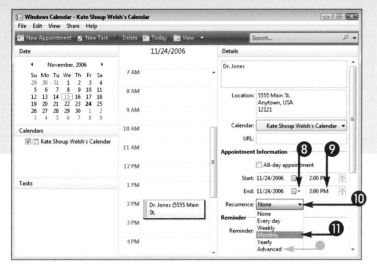

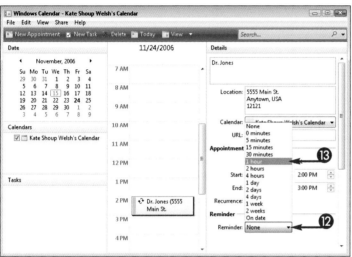

8 If the appointment will end on a different day, click the down arrow next to the End field and click the end date.

9 Type or use the arrows to specify the appointment's end time.

10 If the appointment is recurring, click the down arrow next to the Recurrence field.

11 Click Every Day, Weekly, Monthly, or Yearly.

● Click Advanced if you want to specify an end date for the interval or if the desired interval is not offered in the list.

12 To set a reminder, click the down arrow next to the Reminder field.

13 Specify how many minutes, hours, or days before the appointment the reminder should be sent.

Note: If this is a recurring appointment, Windows may ask whether you want your reminder settings to apply to all appointments in the recurring series. If so, click Change the Series to proceed.

Change It!
Change your calendar's view to Day, Work Week, Full Week, or Month from the View menu.

More Options!
When planning a meeting, use Windows Calendar to send e-mail invitations. First, click the Attendees button. In the dialog box that opens, click one of your contacts in the left window and click the To button; the contact will appear in the right window. When you are finished adding contacts, click OK, and click Invite.

More Options!
To create a new calendar, open the File menu, click New, and select Calendar. Type a name for the calendar and choose a color for the appointments in this calendar. Creating a new calendar enables you to, say, maintain one for work and one for home.

CALENDAR:
Subscribe to a Calendar

iCalendars are special calendars to which you can subscribe, and that can be downloaded to Windows Calendar. An iCalendar might contain the schedule for your favorite sports team or a list of concerts in your area. You can find iCalendars at a calendar-sharing site such as www.icalshare.com.

If you know the location of the calendar to which you subscribe — for example, if you are subscribing to a calendar that another user has stored in your network's Public Downloads folder — you can simply type the path to the folder when prompted.

Alternatively, if you locate a calendar to which you want to subscribe online using a site such as

icalshare.com, you will typically be given the option to click a Subscribe link or something similar. (You will learn how to subscribe to an online calendar in this manner in this task.)

After you subscribe to a calendar, it appears alongside your personal calendar in Windows Calendar.

See also>> Calendar

See also>> Calendar: Publish

1 When you locate the calendar you want to download on a Web site such as icalshare.com, click Subscribe (or a similarly named option).

● The Subscribe to a Calendar window opens, with the selected calendar's Web address already filled in.

2 Click Next.

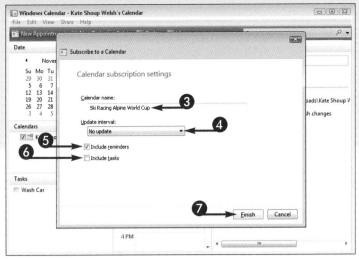

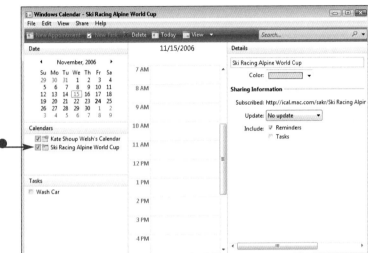

Windows Calendar displays a progress dialog box, indicating the progress of the subscription operation.

3 If you do not like the name provided, type a new name for the calendar.

4 Specify how frequently you want the calendar to be updated: every 15 minutes, every hour, every day, or every week.

5 If you want to be sent reminders about upcoming calendar events, select the Include Reminders checkbox.

6 If you want any tasks included with the calendar to appear in Windows Calendar, select the Include Tasks checkbox.

7 Click Finish.

● The calendar to which you subscribed is added to the Calendar window; click it to view it.

Did You Know?

If you followed the steps in the previous task, "Calendar: Publish a Calendar," to publish your own calendar to your network's Public Downloads folder, other users can follow the steps in this task to access that calendar. They will simply need to enter the network path to the Public Downloads folder in the screen shown in Step **2**.

CARDSPACE:
Create a Personal Information Card

Information Cards, which are created in CardSpace, free users from keeping track of the user names, passwords, and other information required to use certain Web sites and online services. You can send an Information Card to any Web site that supports its use in lieu of entering a user name and password or supplying other pertinent information — after ensuring that the site is reputable, of course.

CardSpace supports the creation and use of two types of Information Cards: personal cards and managed cards. Personal cards include information such as your name, address, phone number, date of birth, and gender. Managed cards are Information Cards issued by trusted businesses and organizations such as a bank, employer, or government agency.

Just as the various cards you carry in your wallet meet different needs — some enabling you to purchase goods and services nearly anywhere, others establishing your identity — so, too, do the different types of Information Cards.

See also>>   **CardSpace**

1 In the Windows CardSpace window, click Add a Card.

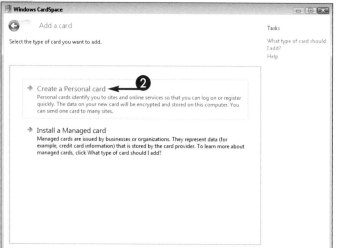

The Add a Card screen opens.

2 Click Create a Personal Card.

The Edit Card screen opens.

3 Type the information you want to include in your card.

4 Click Save.

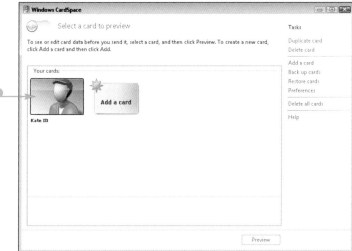

● The card is added to the main CardSpace window.

TIPS

Attention!

You should back up your Information Cards so you can use them on a different computer or recover them if you lose or damage your PC. To do so, click Back Up Cards in the CardSpace window and follow the prompts. To restore a backed-up card, open the folder containing the backup, double-click it, and follow the onscreen instructions.

Attention!

Protect your Information Cards with a PIN — especially if they contain private information or are used for sensitive tasks.

Did You Know?

In order to use a managed card, you must first obtain it from the card's issuer. Then install the card by clicking Add a Managed Card in Step **2** and following the onscreen prompts.

CDS AND DVDS:
Burn Data, Music, and Photos

If your system features a recordable CD and/or DVD drive, you can copy — or *burn* — data files, music files, and digital photographs to one of these discs.

By default, Windows burns CDs and DVDs using the File System format (UDF), but you can instead burn your discs in the Mastered format (ISO). Both enable you to burn files using drag-and-drop. UDF discs, however, copy the file immediately after you drag it. In contrast, ISO discs require that you drag all the files you intend to burn to a staging area before launching the burn operation.

If you are copying lots of files, choose ISO. Likewise, use ISO if your disc is intended for an older version of Windows or for a CD or DVD player. Otherwise, choose UDF. (UDF is compatible only with Windows XP and Windows Vista.)

See also>>

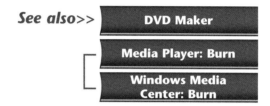

| DVD Maker |
| Media Player: Burn |
| Windows Media Center: Burn |

① Insert a writeable CD or DVD into your computer's recordable CD drive.

● The AutoPlay dialog box opens.

② Click Burn Files to Disc Using Windows.

● The Burn a Disc dialog box opens.

③ Type a name for the disc.

④ Click Next.

Note: If you want to burn an ISO disc rather than a UDF disc, click Show Formatting Options after you type a name for the disc, click Mastered (ISO), and click Next. Be aware that in order to burn an ISO disc, the amount of free space on your computer must be at least equal to the disc's capacity.

● Windows formats the blank disc. (It may take your system several minutes to complete this operation.)

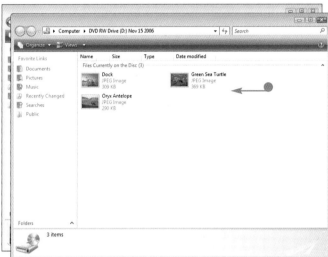

When the formatting is complete, an empty disc folder opens.

5 Click one of the links on the left to open the folder containing the files you want to burn.

6 Click the files to select them.

7 Click the Burn button.

● The files are copied to the disc.

TIP

Did You Know?

There are many types of CDs and DVDs, including the following: CD-ROMs and DVD-ROMs, to which you cannot copy or delete files; CD-Rs and DVD-Rs, which allow you to burn files but not to erase them; and CD-RWs and DVD-RWs, on which files may be burned and erased multiple times. (To erase a file, insert the disc into the drive, double-click the drive in your Computer folder, select the file you want to erase, and press the Delete key on your keyboard.)

COMPLETEPC BACKUP:
Back Up Your PC with CompletePC Backup

When you *back up* your system, you store copies of your files on separate media such as a CD or DVD, an external hard drive, or a tape drive. Doing so ensures that in the event of disaster — natural or technical — you can still access your work.

Windows Vista offers two tools for backing up: Windows Backup and CompletePC Backup. (Note that CompletePC Backup is not included with the Home versions of Windows Vista.) You use the File and Folder Backup Wizard to back up your documents and other files on a regular basis — perhaps even

daily. In contrast, you use CompletePC Backup to back up your system settings. If your computer fails, you can use the backup you made with CompletePC Backup to restore it. You should run a system backup with CompletePC Backup when you first set up your computer, and again every six months or so.

See also>>

In the Backup and Restore Center, click Back Up Computer.

Note: If prompted, type the administrator password or click Continue.

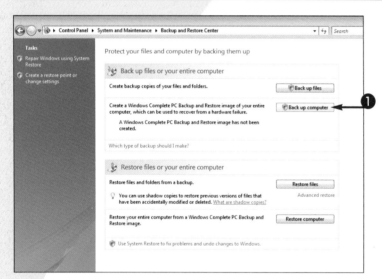

The Windows CompletePC Backup Wizard starts.

❷ Specify where you want Windows Vista to store your backup.

❸ Click Next.

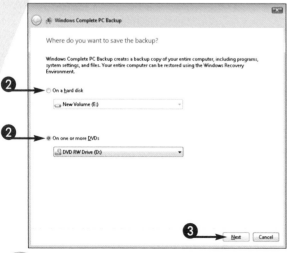

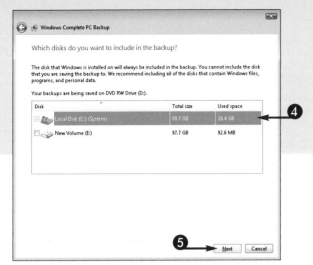

④ Choose the drive you want to back up.

⑤ Click Next.

The Confirm Your Backup Settings screen opens.

⑥ After you confirm the settings, click the Start Backup button.

A dialog box with a status bar appears to indicate the progress of the backup operation.

TIPS

More Options!

Another way to ensure you have access to your system and files is to set *restore points*. That way, in the event your system becomes unstable — perhaps because of a change in your settings or, say, a driver update — you can revert to the system as it was when the restore point was set.

Important!

The media onto which you have stored your backup should be kept in a secure, external, fireproof location, away from the original files. Doing so ensures that in the event of disaster — natural or otherwise — you can still access your work.

COMPUTER FOLDER:
View Free Space and Other Information

Your computer's hard disk houses all the programs and files on your computer — all of which can consume considerable space. If you are planning to install new software on your PC or to burn files to an ISO CD, you will want to check how much free space you have on your hard disc first to ensure you have adequate room.

In addition to enabling you to assess how much free space your computer has at a glance, the Computer folder provides easy access to the hard drive's

Properties dialog box. In this dialog box, you can access tools to increase the amount of free space, as well as to settings for Previous Versions, sharing, and security.

See also>> Disk Cleanup

See also>> Previous Versions

Quotas: Set

1. Click Start.
2. Click Computer.
   - The Computer folder opens.
3. Click the hard drive whose free space you want to check.

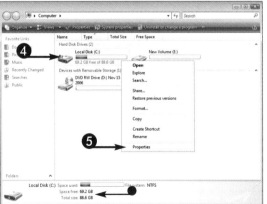

- The total size of your hard disk appears in the Preview pane at the bottom of the Computer folder, along with the available free space.

4. To see additional information about the hard drive and to access tools and options for improving the hard drive's performance, right-click the drive's icon in the Computer folder.

5. Choose Properties.

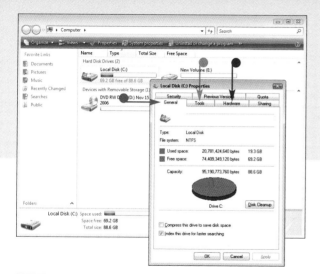

The hard drive's Properties dialog box opens.

● The General tab shows how much free space is available, offers indexing and compression options, and provides access to Disk Cleanup.

● From the Tools tab, check errors, defragment the drive, and back it up.

● Click the Hardware tab to see information about hardware components.

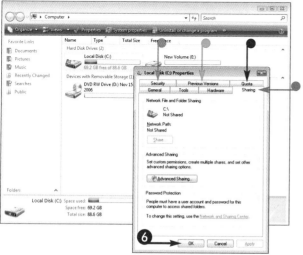

● The Sharing tab indicates the sharing status of the drive and provides access to share-related features.

● Click the Security tab to view and change permissions.

● The Previous Versions tab enables access to previous versions of files and folders, which can be used to restore files that have been damaged or that have been changed or deleted by accident.

● To ensure that a single user does monopolize disk space, click the Quota tab to access space-limiting settings.

⑥ Click OK.

TIP

Did You Know?

If your disk is low on free space, run the Disk Cleanup utility to delete the temporary files that are created as you work in a program, files that are left over from Web browsing, and setup files that remain after the installation of some applications. The utility also empties the Recycle Bin. To run the utility, click the Start button, choose All Programs, click Accessories, select System Tools, and choose Disk Cleanup. Specify whether you want to limit the cleanup operation to your user folder or to apply it to all files on your system, select the drive you want to free up space on, and the types of files you want to delete (temporary files and so on).

COMPUTER NAME:
Identify and Change the Computer Name

Every computer has a name that is used to identify it on a network. This enables the computer to communicate with other machines on the network. The best computer names are both short (no more than 15 characters) and easily recognizable. If you want, you can find and change your computer's name.

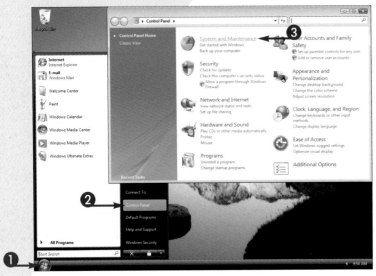

1 Click Start.

2 Click Control Panel.

3 Click the System and Maintenance link.

4 Click the System link.

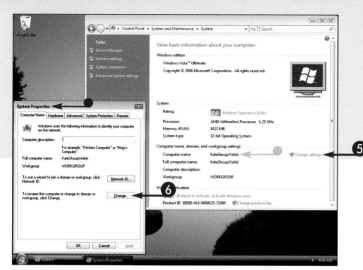

- The computer's name appears under Computer Name, Domain, and Workgroup Settings.

5 Click the Change Settings link.

Note: If prompted, type the administrator password or click Continue.

- The System Properties dialog box opens.

6 On the Computer Name tab, click the Change button.

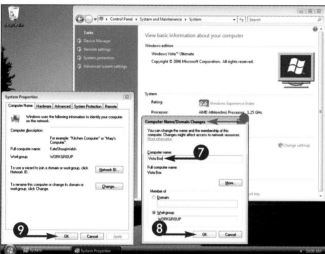

- The Computer Name/Domain Changes dialog box opens.

7 Delete the old computer name in the Computer Name field and type the new one.

8 Click OK in the Computer Name/Domain Changes dialog box to close it.

9 Click OK in the System Properties dialog box to close it.

Important!
If you are connected to a domain, the Group Policy settings implemented by the domain's administrator may prevent you from performing the steps in this task.

Important!
The name you choose for the computer must not include any of the following characters:
< > ; : " * + = \ | ? ,

CONTACTS:
Import and Export Contacts

Windows Vista's Contacts function stores information you enter about people and organizations — phone numbers, fax numbers, e-mail addresses, postal addresses, Web site addresses, personal information, notes, even a photo. But what if you have already entered much of that information in another contacts-management program?

Fortunately, rather than requiring you to enter it by hand, Windows Contacts allows you *import* a file containing all your contact information. To do so, you will want to locate the folder that contains the file with your contacts and determine what type of

file it is: CSV (a generic file format used for exporting and importing information to and from databases or spreadsheets), LDIF (used to import directory information from LDAP-based directory servers), VCF (the most widely used contacts format), or WAB (used by most earlier versions of Windows, including Windows XP).

See also>> 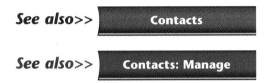 Contacts

See also>> Contacts: Manage

Import Contacts

1 Click Start.

2 Click All Programs.

3 Click Windows Contacts.

The Windows Contacts window opens.

4 Click the Import button on the toolbar.

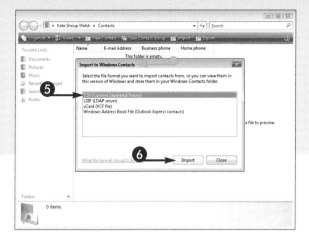

- The Import to Windows Contacts dialog box opens.

⑤ Click CSV, LDIF, VCF, or WAB, depending on what type of file you want to import.

⑥ Click the Import button.

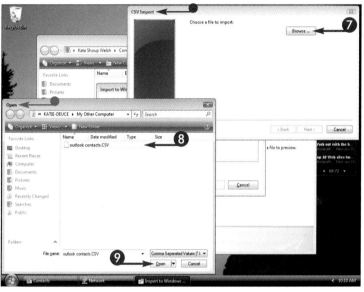

- The Import Wizard starts.

⑦ Click Browse to locate the file you want to import.

- The Open dialog box opens.

⑧ Locate and select the contacts file.

⑨ Click Open.

Important!

If the file you want to import lives on another computer, and if that computer is not accessible to you via a network, you will need to copy the file onto a CD or some other type of removable media, and then transfer it to your Vista system in an easy-to-remember location. (You may need to *export* the file first, using the contacts-management program on the original computer.)

Did You Know?

If you cannot find the contacts file you want to import, use Vista's search tools to locate it.

CONTACTS:
Import and Export Contacts (Continued)

After you select the contacts file you want to import — in this example, a CSV file — Contacts prompts you to specify which fields you want to include. Options include First Name, Middle Name, Last Name, Company, Department, Job Title, and Email Address. Fields also exist to house a contact's business address and home address, business and home phone and fax numbers, mobile phone, and pager, as well as personal information about a contact such as his birthday, anniversary, the names

of his children, his profession, the language he speaks, even his hobbies. If you like, you can change the order of the fields by clicking the Change Mapping button in the Import Wizard.

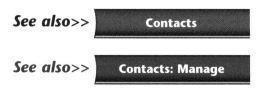

See also>> Contacts

See also>> Contacts: Manage

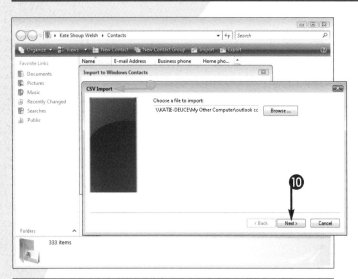

- The Import Wizard displays the path to the file you selected in Steps **7** and **8**.
- **10** Click Next.

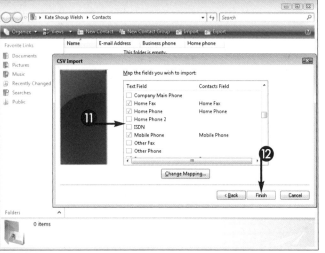

- **11** Select the checkbox next to each field of contact information you want to import.
- **12** Click the Finish button.

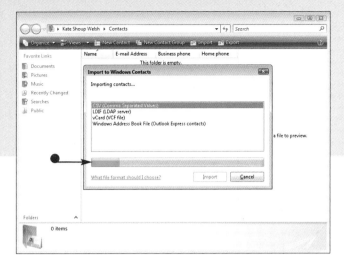

● Windows displays a status bar to indicate the progress of the import operation.

● Your contacts are imported into Windows Contacts.

⑬ Click the Close button.

TIPS

Did You Know?

Windows Contacts enables you to print your contacts. Click the contact (or contacts) you want to print; then click the Print button on the toolbar. In the dialog box that opens, click Selection to print only the selected contacts or All to print your entire list of contacts. Under Print Style, specify how you want the contacts to be printed: in memo form, like a set of business cards, or as a phone list. When you are finished, click Print.

Did You Know?

If you installed Windows Vista by upgrading an XP system, Vista will automatically import all your contacts, converting them from WAB format.

CONTACTS:
Import and Export Contacts (Continued)

In addition to importing contacts files, you can also *export* your contacts to a file. The exported contacts file can then be imported by another contacts-management program, imported by another Windows Vista computer, shared with someone who uses an earlier version of Windows, copied into an Excel spreadsheet, or even used to create an Access database.

Export Contacts

1 Click the Export button in the Windows Contacts window.

● The Export Windows Contacts dialog box opens.

2 Click CSV or vCards, depending on what type of file you want to export.

3 Click Export.

● The Export Wizard starts.

4 Click Browse to locate the folder in which you want to save the exported file.

● The Save As dialog box opens.

4 Click the folder into which you want to save the exported contacts file.

5 Type a name for the exported file.

6 Click Save.

7 Click Next.

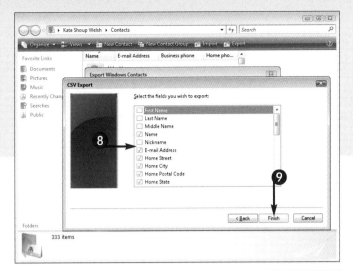

8 Select the checkbox next to each field of contact information you want to export.

9 Click Finish.

Windows displays a status bar to indicate the progress of the import operation.

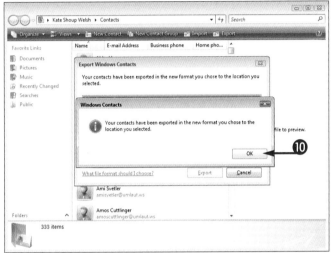

10 When you see a message that indicates the export process is complete, click OK, and then click Close.

Contacts saves your exported contacts file in the location you specified.

TIPS

Did You Know?

To share a single contact with someone who both uses a Windows Vista machine and shares your network, right-click the contact, choose Share, and follow the onscreen instructions. The person with whom you are sharing the file will be able to save the contact in his or her own Windows Contacts program. To share a contact's file with someone using a Vista machine outside your network, send it as an e-mail attachment. For people who use an earlier version of Windows or a different OS altogether, right-click the contact and choose Send Contact (vCard). Windows converts the contact to a VCF file and attaches it to a blank Windows Mail e-mail message.

Did You Know?

To share your contacts with someone who does not use Windows Vista, choose vCard in Step **2**. (Note that any photos you have attached to your contact will not transfer over; likewise, some information entered into the contacts' Family and Notes tabs may be lost.)

CONTACTS:
Manage Contacts

The more you use Windows Contacts to store details about people with whom you communicate, the more vital it is that you manage your entries to keep them up-to-date and viable. Indeed, unless you manage your contacts, you may discover multiple entries, unwanted or outdated entries, or missing key contact information.

Your best option is to review and manage your contacts often to prevent this situation altogether. Fortunately, Windows Contacts provides several tools

to help you manage this information — tools that become increasingly important as your list of contacts grows. In addition to enabling you to easily add and edit contacts, Windows Contacts allows you to delete unwanted entries.

See also>> | **Contacts**

See also>> | **Contacts: Import Export**

Add a Contact

1 In the Contacts window, click New Contact.

● The new contact's Properties window opens.

2 Type your contact's information — as much or as little as you want — on the various tabs.

3 Click OK to close the contact's Properties window.

Edit a Contact

1 Double-click the contact you want to edit.

● The contact's Properties window opens.

2 Edit the contact's information as needed, adding or removing information from the various tabs.

3 Click OK to close contact's Properties window.

● The contact's information is updated.

Organize Contacts

1 To create a new folder for certain contacts, click the Organize button on the toolbar.

2 Click New Folder.

TIPS

Attention!
To add an e-mail address to your contact information, type it in the E-mail field on the Name and E-mail tab and click Add. To set this new e-mail address as the default address for this contact, click it in the list of available e-mail addresses and click Set Preferred.

Did You Know?
Using Windows Contacts, you can create a contact for yourself, which you can use like a virtual business card. Simply create it as you would any other contact. Then, after you save it, right-click it and choose Set as My Contact.

CONTACTS:
Manage Contacts (Continued)

You can create folders to organize your contacts. For example, you might put all your contacts from a certain company in one folder. If you are having trouble locating one of your contacts, use Windows Contacts' Search function to locate it. At times, certain contacts may need to be deleted — for example, if you have a duplicate contact, or if you

are no longer in touch with a contact; doing so is a snap.

See also>> 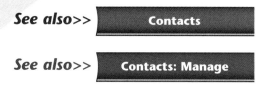 Contacts

See also>> Contacts: Manage

③ Type a name for the folder, pressing Enter when you finish.

④ To move a contact into a folder, click the contact to select it; then, while you are holding the mouse button, drag it to the folder. Finally, drop it by releasing the mouse button.

Find a Contact

① To find a contact, type the contact's name in part or in full in the Contacts window Search box.

● As you type, Contacts filters your contacts to display ones that match.

② To close the search, click the Close button next to the Search field.

Delete a Contact

① To delete a contact, click the contact you want to delete.

② Click the Delete button on the toolbar.

● The Delete File dialog box opens.

③ Click Yes to delete the contact.

● The contact is deleted.

TIPS

More Options!
If typing the contact's name in the Search field does not yield the desired result, click Advanced Search for more search options.

Did You Know?
To sort your contacts, click a column heading. For example, click Name to sort your contacts by name. To add more headings by which to sort, right-click the heading of any existing column and choose a heading for a new column from the list that appears.

Did You Know?
If you have trouble putting names to faces, add a digital photo to each of your contacts. Double-click the contact to which you want to add a photo, click the Name and E-mail tab, click the arrow next to the space where the contact's photo will go, and click Choose Picture. Locate the photo on your hard drive, click it to select it, and click Open.

CONTENT ADVISOR:
Set Internet Explorer 7 Parental Controls

Although the Internet can be both educational and entertaining, it can also expose users, especially children, to inappropriate — even dangerous — content. To restrict what types of Internet Web sites and other resources your children (or anyone who shares your computer) can access, enable Internet Explorer 7's Content Advisor tool.

You can restrict content using four main criteria: language, nudity, sex, and violence. Content Advisor uses ratings provided voluntarily by Web sites to block or allow certain content, depending on the settings you choose. (Web sites that are unrated are blocked by default when Content Advisor is enabled.)

Once you enable the parental controls, anyone who tries to access the types of material that you filter out through Content Advisor cannot do so. Moreover, no one can modify the settings without the supervisor password that you set when you activate the tool. In addition, users cannot turn off Content Advisor without the password.

See also>>

> **Content Advisor**

> **Internet Options**

Set the Supervisor Password

1 Click Start.

2 Click Internet.

The Internet Explorer window opens.

3 Click Tools.

4 Click Internet Options.

> *Note: If prompted while you perform the steps that follow, type the administrator password or click Continue.*

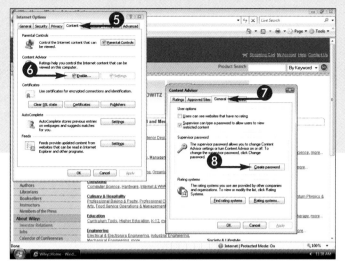

5 In the Internet Options dialog box, click the Content tab.

6 Under Content Advisor, click Enable.

7 In the Content Advisor dialog box, click the General tab.

8 Click Create Password.

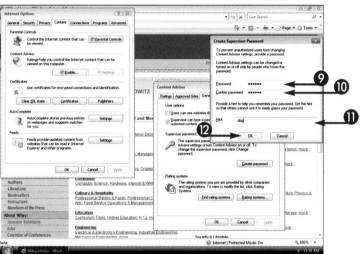

9 In the Create Supervisor Password dialog box, type the password you want to use for Content Advisor.

10 Type the same password a second time to confirm it.

11 Type a password hint.

12 Click OK.

Windows informs you that your supervisor password has been created.

TIPS

Attention!

After you set your supervisor password, be sure to write it down. If you lose your password, you will not be able to change Content Advisor settings or override Web site blocks. That said, you should not store the written password where your children can find it. Also, make it a point to use a difficult password to limit the chances that a child can guess what it is. Passwords of more than six characters that combine a random mix of alphanumeric characters work the best.

Did You Know?

To change your supervisor password, click the Change Password button in the General tab of the Content Advisor dialog box and follow the onscreen instructions.

CONTENT ADVISOR:
Set Internet Explorer 7 Parental Controls (Continued)

After you set your supervisor password, Content Advisor is enabled with the default settings in place. These default settings apply maximum restrictions, blocking all content that does not meet or exceed the most conservative ratings criteria as well as content that is unrated.

You can easily change these settings from within the Content Advisor dialog box. In addition, you can create a list of Web sites that can always be blocked — as well as Web sites that can always be viewed, regardless of their rating. Also, if you do not like

Content Advisor's ratings system, you can change it to suit your purposes.

To change these settings, start in the Internet Options dialog box. (Open it by clicking Tools and clicking Internet Options.)

See also>>

> **Content Advisor**

> **Internet Options**

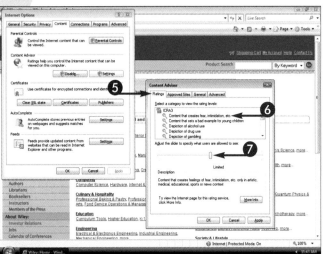

Change Content Advisor Settings

① In the Internet Options dialog box, click the Content tab.

② Under Content Advisor, click Settings.

Note: If prompted, type the administrator password or click Continue.

The Supervisor Password Required dialog box opens.

③ Type your supervisor password.

④ Click OK.

The Content Advisor dialog box opens.

⑤ Click the Ratings tab.

⑥ Click a category in the Select a Category to View the Rating Levels list.

⑦ Click in the slider box to set the desired limit.

⑧ Repeat Steps **6** and **7** for the remaining categories in the list.

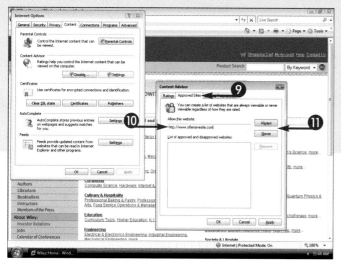

❾ Click the Approved Sites tab.

❿ Under Allow This Website, type the URL for a site you want to allow or block.

⓫ Click Always or Never to allow or block the site, respectively.

The site is added to the list of approved or disallowed sites.

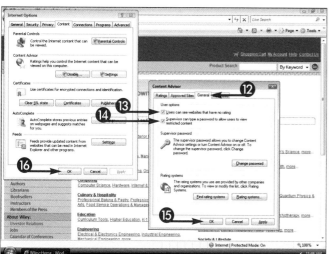

⓬ Click the General tab.

⓭ To allow unrated sites, click the Users Can See Websites That Have No Rating checkbox to select it.

⓮ If you want to be able to override Content Advisor in order to view blocked content, click the Supervisor Can Type a Password to Allow Users to View Restricted Content checkbox to select it.

⓯ Click OK to close the Content Advisor dialog box.

⓰ Click OK to close the Internet Options dialog box.

More Options!

In addition to setting up parental controls for Internet Explorer 7, you can also establish parental controls for your entire Vista machine. These include limiting access to certain games and programs and restricting the amount of time a user spends logged in. You can even generate reports to assess how much a particular user is using the PC.

DATE AND TIME:
Change Your System Date, Time, and Time Zone

If you relocate, you may need to adjust your time and time zone settings in Windows. That way, when you create and modify files on your computer, the time and date information that is automatically recorded will be accurate.

You can quickly match the Windows date and time to your new time and time zone through the Date and Time dialog box. Once you set it, the time should stay up-to-date until you reset it again. This is particularly true if you use the synchronization option that is available from the Internet Time tab.

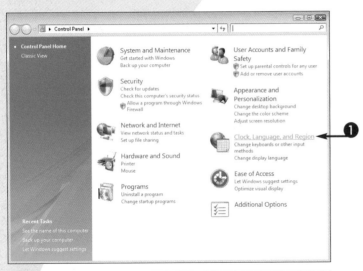

1 In the Control Panel window, click Clock, Language, and Region.

The Clock, Language, and Region window opens.

2 Under Date and Time, click the Set the Time and Date link to open the Date and Time dialog box.

Note: Another way to open the Date and Time dialog box is to double-click the clock on your taskbar (assuming it is visible).

Note: If prompted, type the administrator password or click Continue.

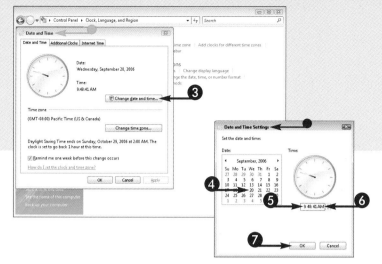

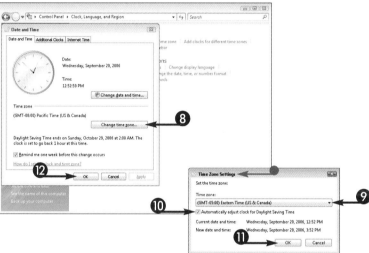

- The Date and Time dialog box opens.

3 Click the Change Date and Time button.

- The Date and Time Settings dialog box opens.

4 Click today's date in the calendar on the left.

5 Double-click the hour and click the up or down arrow alongside the field to increase or decrease the value.

6 Repeat Step **5** for minutes, seconds, and AM/PM.

7 Click OK.

8 Click the Change Time Zone button.

- The Time Zone Settings dialog box opens.

9 Click here and select your time zone from the list that appears.

10 If your area observes daylight saving time, click the Automatically Adjust Clock for Daylight Saving Time checkbox to select it.

11 Click OK to close the Time Zone Settings dialog box.

12 Click OK to close the Date and Time dialog box.

Did You Know?

You can set up Windows to synchronize the time that it displays with Internet-based time servers. To do so, click the Internet Time tab in the Date and Time dialog box, click Change Settings, and, in the Internet Time Settings dialog box, select a server. Options include time.windows.com or time.nist.gov. Click Update Now, and click OK.

More Options!

If you frequently communicate with others in different time zones, you can set up as many as two additional clocks to keep track of the time in those zones. Click the Additional Clocks tab in the Date and Time dialog box and, for each clock you want to set up, choose a time zone and type a name. When you finish, click OK.

DEFAULT PROGRAMS CENTER:
Set Windows Default Programs

A *default program* is the program that Windows launches when you open a certain type of file. For example, opening an HTML file automatically launches Internet Explorer; likewise, double-clicking an image file starts the Windows Photo Gallery by default.

Suppose, however, that you have installed a new program that you want to use for certain types of files. For example, maybe you downloaded special software for listening to music. If you like, you can configure Windows Vista to launch that new program by default any time you open a music file. You do this within Windows Vista's Default Programs window. The Default Programs window also enables you to specify which programs should be used to launch programs on certain types of media such as CDs and DVDs.

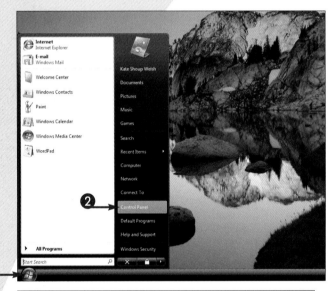

1 Click Start.

2 Click Control Panel.

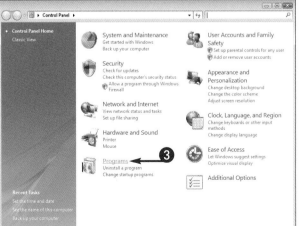

The Control Panel window opens.

3 Click Programs.

The Programs window opens.

4 Click Default Programs.

● The Default Programs window opens.

● Click Set Your Default Programs to choose the program Windows runs by default when you launch a certain type of file, such as a music file.

● Click Associate a File Type or Protocol with a Program to fine-tune your default program settings — for example, if you want JPG image files to open with Windows Photo Gallery but BMP files to open with another type of image program.

● Click Change AutoPlay Settings if you want a certain program to launch when you insert certain media, such as CDs containing music files.

● Click Set Program Access and Computer Defaults to configure default programs for certain activities, such as sending an e-mail or browsing the Internet, for everyone who uses your computer.

More Options!

Setting a default program for a certain file type does not preclude you from using another program to open that type of file. To do so, right-click the file you want to open and choose Open With. In the dialog box that appears, select the program you want to use and click OK. (If you decide you want the selected program to become the new default, select the Always Use the Selected Program to Open This Kind of File checkbox in the Open With dialog box.)

More Options!

The selections you make after clicking Set Your Program Defaults apply to your user account only. To apply the changes to all user accounts, choose Set Default Programs for This Computer.

DEVICE MANAGER:
Access Device Driver Information

A *driver* is a special type of software that Windows uses to communicate with a piece of hardware. You can use the Driver tab available for many hardware components in Device Manager to check the version of your most recent driver.

This driver information is useful if you have problems with a hardware device. When you call a technical support line, you may also be asked to provide details about the driver version that you currently use for a particular hardware device.

Likewise, accessing this driver information is helpful if you are unsure whether you have the most recent driver for a piece of hardware. If, for example, the

Driver tab reveals that the driver for your display adapter was last updated in December 2004, but the display adapter manufacturer's Web site indicates that a new driver was made available in January of 2007, you will know you should download and install the newly available driver.

See also>>

Device Manager

Device Manager: Remove

Device Manager: Troubleshoot

① In Control Panel, click System and Maintenance.

② Click Device Manager to open the Device Manager window.

Note: *If prompted, type the administrator password or click Continue.*

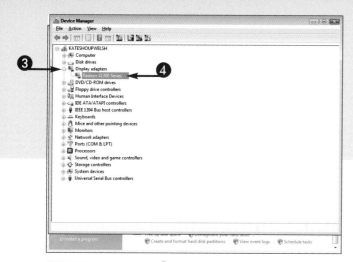

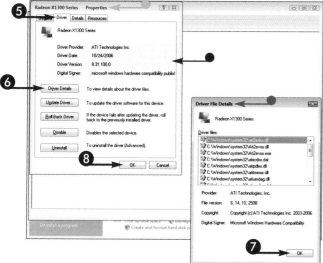

The Device Manager window opens.

③ Click the plus sign next to the category of the device whose driver you want to see.

④ Double-click the device whose driver you want to see.

● The device's Properties dialog box opens.

⑤ Click the Driver tab.

● Information about the driver, including its version number, appears here.

⑥ For more information about the driver, click the Driver Details button.

● The Driver File Details dialog box opens, displaying additional details about the driver.

⑦ Click OK to close the Driver File Details dialog box.

⑧ Click OK to close the device's Properties dialog box.

TIPS

More Options!

Visit the device manufacturer's Web site to see what symptoms may occur if a new driver is incompatible with your setup, as well as what you can do to adjust the setup. Your best bet may be to roll back to the previous driver version. To do so, click Roll Back Driver in the device's Driver tab in Device Manager. If, after rolling back a driver, your system still experiences problems, restart your computer. If the problem *still* remains, run Windows Update to see if there are any drivers, patches, or other software available for your computer that might resolve the issue.

More Options!

You can update a driver from within Device Manager. Simply click Update Driver in the Driver tab of the device's Properties dialog box.

DEVICE MANAGER:
Remove a Device

When you no longer use a particular device, it is a good idea to first physically uninstall the hardware and then to disable or remove the support for it in Device Manager. When you do so, Windows no longer loads support for the device as it determines which hardware is connected when the operating system loads.

There are other times when you may want to remove a device in Device Manager. For example, this may be necessary when you replace a chipset — such as video, audio, networking, or a modem — that is already integrated into your motherboard with a

separate, dedicated adapter. Another situation in which you might want to remove a device in Device Manager is when you want to force Windows to reload the driver when you are troubleshooting a problem with a device.

See also>> **Device Manager**

See also>> **Device Manager: Access**

Device Manager: Troubleshoot

❶ In Control Panel, click System and Maintenance.

❷ Click Device Manager.

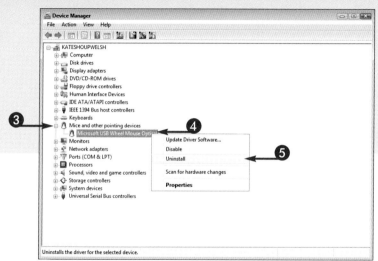

The Device Manager window opens.

Note: *If prompted, type the administrator password or click Continue.*

③ Click the plus sign next to the category of the device whose driver you want to see.

④ Right-click the device you want to remove.

⑤ Choose Uninstall.

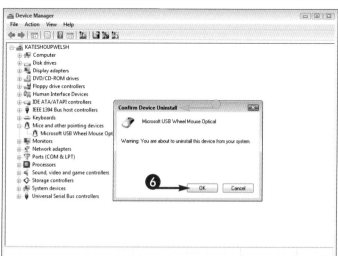

● The Confirm Device Uninstall dialog box appears.

⑥ Click OK.

Windows removes support for the device.

Note: *You may need to restart Windows to apply the change.*

Did You Know?

After you make a change in Device Manager, such as removing support for a device, and then restart your system, always check Device Manager again to ensure that everything appears as it should (for example, that the device no longer appears).

More Options!

If you want to disable rather than remove all support for a piece of hardware, click Disable rather than Uninstall in Step **5**.

Attention!

If you uninstall a device in Device Manager without physically removing the hardware, Windows will likely detect the device as brand new when it restarts and then reload support for it. If your objective is to force Windows to reload the driver, then you want to take this approach.

DEVICE MANAGER:
Troubleshoot Issues

Device Manager makes it easy to locate and identify problems through special icons that it displays next to problem devices. For example, a downward-pointing arrow on the icon for a device listed in Device Manager indicates that support for the device is disabled. This can occur when Windows cannot work with the driver for the device, cannot locate the correct driver, or if you have purposely disabled a

device. (This last case probably is not a problem you need to fix.)

See also>> Device Manager

See also>> Device Manager: Access

Device Manager: Remove

Troubleshot a Disabled Device

❶ Click Start.

❷ Click Control Panel.

❸ In Control Panel, click System and Maintenance.

④ **Click Device Manager.**

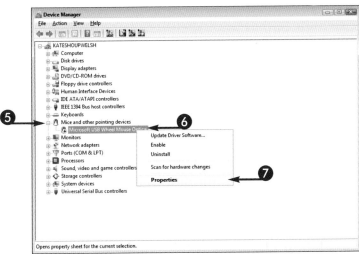

The Device Manager window opens.

Note: If prompted, type the administrator password or click Continue.

⑤ Click the plus sign next to a device category to display the listing for a specific component.

⑥ If a device in the category displays a downward-pointing arrow, right-click the device.

⑦ Choose Properties.

Try This!
It does not hurt to consult Device Manager regularly regardless of how well your system performs to identify potential problems and correct them before they develop into crises.

Caution!
Do not assume that anything you download from a manufacturer's Web site — including drivers — is safe. Always scan downloaded software for viruses, regardless of the source.

DEVICE MANAGER:
Troubleshoot Issues (Continued)

A yellow exclamation point usually means that Windows cannot find the driver for the device, or has a problem with the current driver. You can usually resolve this issue by reinstalling the proper driver.

Speaking of drivers, when using Device Manager to troubleshoot, look for old driver versions; these might be ready for updates. Also look for entries that *should* be listed — such as a new device that you have installed — but are not.

See also>> **Device Manager**

See also>> **Device Manager: Access**

Device Manager: Remove

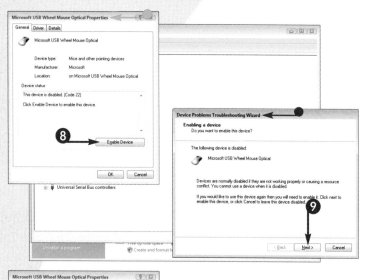

● The device's Properties dialog box opens.

⑧ In the General tab, click the Enable Device button.

● The Device Problems Troubleshooting Wizard opens.

⑨ Click Next.

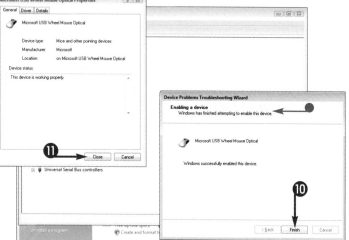

● The Device Problems Troubleshooting Wizard enables the device.

⑩ Click Finish.

⑪ Click Close in the device's Properties dialog box to close it.

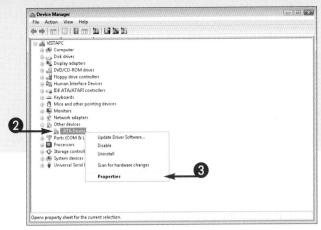

Troubleshoot a Non-working Device

1 Repeat Steps **1** to **5** from the previous page to display a component in the Device Manager window.

2 If a device displays a yellow exclamation point, right-click it.

3 Click Properties.

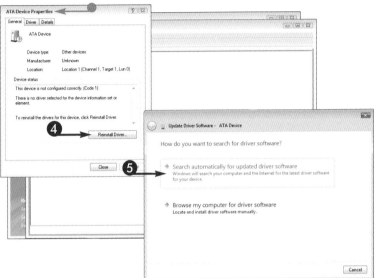

● The device's Properties dialog box opens.

4 Click Reinstall Driver in the General tab.

5 Choose how you want Windows to search for the driver.

Windows reinstalls the driver.

Note: If Windows cannot locate the driver, insert the CD or other disk that came with your hardware.

Important!

When you replace one piece of hardware with another, carefully examine the accompanying documentation for warnings. For example, when you install certain types of video adapters to replace a motherboard-integrated video chipset, you may achieve better results when you disable the onboard video in Device Manager and then restart your system in Safe mode to prepare to install the new driver.

DISPLAY PROPERTIES:
Configure Display Properties

You can modify your display properties to change the appearance of your desktop as well as how applications look when you open them. One common change users make to their desktop is the screen resolution, or the overall size of the Windows desktop in relation to its content. The higher the screen resolution, the smaller the windows appear. For example, the windows in a screen with a resolution of 800×600 are much larger than in a screen with a resolution of 1024×768 or higher. A larger monitor often requires a higher screen resolution.

You can also change the number of colors that can appear in Windows. While some monitors and video adapters — also called *graphics cards* — can distinguish between many thousands of colors, others can draw millions of colors. The number of colors that can display depends on your monitor and video adapter, as well as their drivers.

See also>>

Background

Themes

① Right-click a blank area of your desktop.

② Click Personalize.

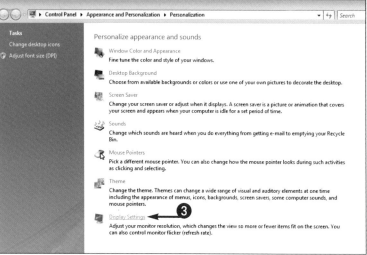

The Personalization window opens.

③ Click the Display Settings link.

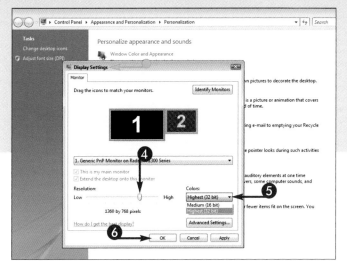

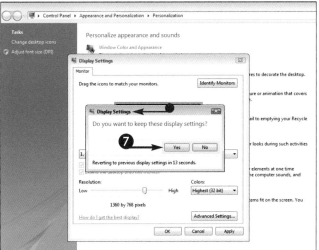

● The Display Settings dialog box opens.

④ Drag the Resolution slider to increase or decrease the resolution.

⑤ Open the Colors list and choose the color level you want.

⑥ Click OK.

● Windows automatically changes the resolution, and a dialog box appears, asking if you want to keep these settings.

⑦ Click Yes to keep the settings or No to revert back to the previous settings.

If you keep your settings, then the monitor changes to the new screen resolution. (If you choose nothing, Windows momentarily reverts to its original settings in case the dialog box is not readable.)

More Options!

If you were able to make changes to your display settings in the past, but you now cannot, this could mean that you have a corrupted video driver. You can update the driver either through Device Manager or through Windows Update.

Try This!

If you cannot change settings immediately after you update a driver, then you may want to use the Roll Back Driver option in Device Manager to revert to the previous settings

Did You Know?

You may be very limited in terms of screen resolution and color settings if your display is provided by a video chipset that is integrated directly into your motherboard. In order to make custom changes, you may need to install a separate video adapter.

DVD MAKER:
Burn a Movie to DVD

If your PC has a DVD burner, you can use DVD Maker to burn films you create using Windows Movie to DVD, as well as burn slide shows composed of pictures, and audio. DVD Maker acts like a wizard of sorts, guiding you through the DVD-creation process.

Single-sided/single-layered DVDs can contain 60 minutes of video material, while single-sided/double-layered DVDs can hold 120 minutes.

You can view the contents of your DVD on your television using any standard DVD player or on your computer, provided you have DVD playback software installed. (You can configure the aspect ratio of your DVD — 16:9 for a widescreen or 4:3 for a standard screen.)

See also>>

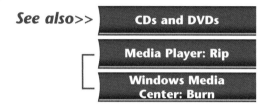

| CDs and DVDs |
| Media Player: Rip |
| Windows Media Center: Burn |

① Click Start.

② Click All Programs.

③ Click Windows DVD Maker.

④ Insert a blank recordable or rewriteable DVD into your DVD burner.

● The Add Pictures and Video to the DVD screen opens.

⑤ Click Add Items.

● The Add Items to DVD dialog box opens.

⑥ Locate and select the files you want on your DVD.

⑦ Click Add.

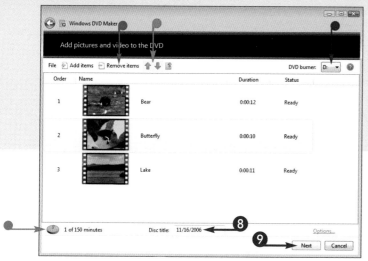

The clips you selected appear in the Add Pictures and Video to the DVD screen.

● To remove a clip, select it and click Remove Items.

● To move a clip, select it and then click the up or down arrow.

● If multiple DVD burners are installed on your computer, choose the burner you want to use.

● View the amount of space remaining on the DVD here.

⑧ Type a title for your DVD.

⑨ Click Next.

● The Ready to Burn Disc screen opens.

⑩ Click a DVD menu style to select it.

⑪ To add text to your menu, click Menu Text.

TIP

More Options!

To access various DVD-related settings, click the Options link in the lower-right corner of the Add Pictures and Video to the DVD screen. The DVD Options dialog box opens; here you can choose DVD playback settings such as whether a DVD menu is displayed or whether the DVD plays in a continuous loop. You can also choose the aspect ratio for the DVD, as well as the video format (in general, NTSC applies if the DVD will be played in North, South, or Central America, Japan, South Korea, the Philippines, or the U.K.; if the DVD will be played elsewhere, PAL is likely the correct choice), the burner speed, and more.

DVD MAKER:
Burn a Movie to DVD (Continued)

DVD Maker detects natural stopping places in your movie or slide show's action, using this information to divide your video into scenes. To add a professional touch to your DVDs, you can use DVD Maker to create and customize the menus to be displayed when the DVD is played.

See also>>

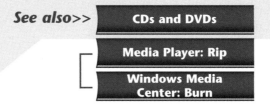

The Change the DVD Menu Text window opens.

⑫ Choose a font for the menu text.

⑬ Type a title for the disc. This title will appear on the menu.

⑭ Type the text you want the viewer to select to play the DVD.

⑮ Type the text you want the viewer to select to view the scenes on the DVD.

⑯ Type the text you want the viewer to select to view notes about the DVD.

⑰ Type any notes about the DVD.

⑱ Click Change Text.

⑲ In the Ready to Burn screen, click Customize Menu.

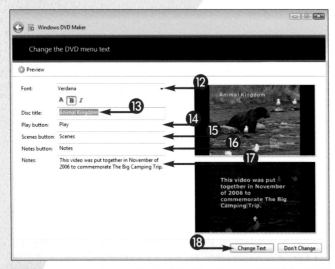

The Customize the Disc Menu Style window opens.

● Change the menu's font here.

● Click here to choose a video clip to run in the menu's foreground.

● Click here to choose a video clip to run in the menu's background.

● Click here to choose an audio clip to run while the menu is displayed.

● Click here to choose a different button style.

● To save your custom DVD menu settings as a new menu style, click Save as New Style.

20 Click Change Style.

21 Click Burn.

● You can preview your DVD before you burn it by clicking the Preview button in the Ready to Burn Disc screen.

DVD Maker displays a progress dialog box as it burns the movie to DVD. (Note that the burn process may take some time.)

Try This!

You can use DVD Maker to burn a slide show of photographs to DVD. Click Add Items and choose your photos. DVD Maker stores them in a special folder in the Add Pictures and Video to the DVD screen; double-click the folder to view the photos, and use the up and down arrow buttons to rearrange them. To add music to the slide show and adjust various slide show settings, click the Slide Show button in the Ready to Burn Disc screen.

EASE OF ACCESS CENTER:
Set Accessibility Options

The Ease of Access Center serves as a centralized repository for Windows Vista's sensory and dexterity settings. These include Magnifier, which expands an area of the desktop to make it easier to read; Narrator, which reads onscreen items, such as dialog box options, aloud; and On-Screen Keyboard, which allows a user to type text on the screen rather than with a keyboard. Some of these features may assist you even if you do not have a physical limitation but want to do something in a different way.

If you are not sure whether Windows Vista's accessibility features would be useful to you, complete the Ease of Access Center's questionnaire; it is designed to help you determine which, if any, of the accessibility features might be of help.

See also>>   **Ease of Access Center**

① In the Control Panel window, click the Ease of Access link.

② Click Ease of Access Center.

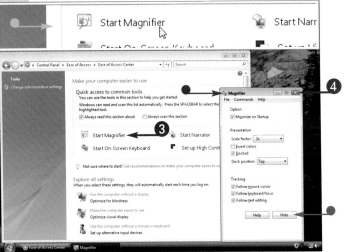

The Ease of Access Center opens.

③ Click Start Magnifier.

● Windows magnifies the cursor location, showing the magnified view in its own pane.

● Use the Magnifier dialog box to adjust Magnifier settings.

● To use Magnifier without the dialog box displayed, click the Hide button.

④ To turn off Magnifier, click the Magnifier dialog box's Close button.

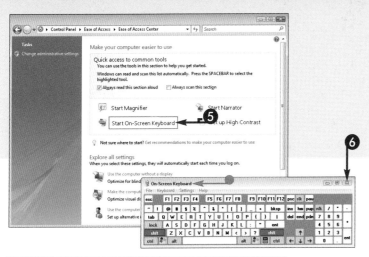

5 Click Start On-Screen Keyboard.

● On-Screen Keyboard opens.

6 To turn off On-Screen Keyboard, click the keyboard's Close button.

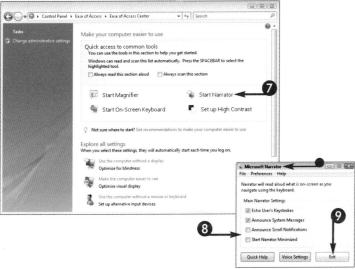

7 Click Start Narrator.

Narrator starts. As you move your cursor, Narrator verbally indicates the name of the setting, button, window, or other item over which the cursor is hovering.

● The Microsoft Narrator dialog box opens.

8 Adjust the settings in the Narrator dialog box as needed.

9 To close Narrator, click Exit.

TIP

More Options!

If you are not certain which, if any, of Windows Vista's accessibility functions will be helpful to you, click the Get Recommendations to Make Your Computer Easier to Use link in the Ease of Access Center window. Answer the questions (they relate to eyesight, hearing, dexterity, speech, and reasoning), and click Next to move through the series of screens. When you finish, Windows Vista will list those technologies in the operating system that may prove useful, as well as provide a link to more information about assistive technologies online.

EDIT:
Cut, Copy, and Paste

You can perform the same basic text-editing functions in virtually every application you use in Windows. The editing tools, found in the Edit menu in most programs, include Cut, Copy, and Paste commands. Cut allows you to select and remove material — such as text — from one place to move it to another. Copy allows you to select and copy material without removing it. Paste allows you to paste into place the material that you have copied or cut.

Windows allows you to cut and paste, as well as copy and paste, from one open window to another. For example, you can copy and paste sentences from a Web page into a Notepad or WordPad document. You can use the same technique to copy or cut and paste between two open Microsoft Office files, as well as two instant-messaging chat windows.

See also>>

Notepad

WordPad

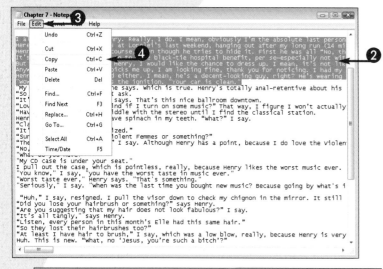

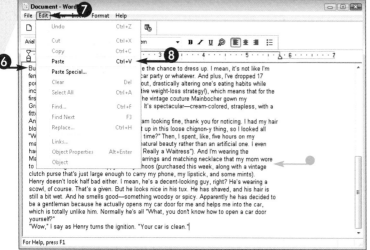

Copy and Paste

1 Open the file that contains the material you want to copy.

This example uses a Notepad text file.

2 Select the text you want to copy.

3 Click Edit.

4 Click Copy.

5 Open the program and file in which you want to paste the material from the first file.

This example uses a WordPad text file.

6 Position your cursor where you want to paste the text.

7 Click Edit.

8 Click Paste.

● The material that you copied from the first window is now pasted in the second window.

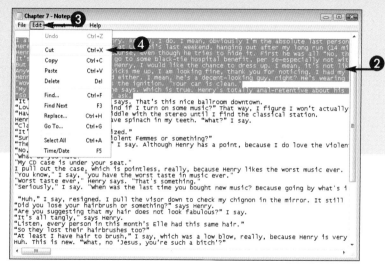

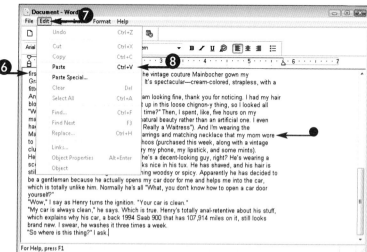

Cut and Paste

① Open the file that contains the material you want to cut.

This example uses a Notepad text file.

② Select the text you want to cut.

③ Click Edit.

④ Click Cut.

The selected text disappears from the open file window.

⑤ Open the program and file in which you want to paste the material from the first file.

This example uses a WordPad text file.

⑥ Position your cursor where you want to paste the text.

⑦ Click Edit.

⑧ Click Paste.

● The material that you cut from the first window is now pasted into the second window.

TIPS

More Options!

The Copy, Cut, and Paste functions can be executed using keyboard shortcuts, which are usually the same between different programs in Windows. To copy, use Ctrl+C; to cut, use Ctrl+X; and to paste, use Ctrl+V. (By the way, if you cut or paste in error, or make any other mistakes while working with a program, press Ctrl+Z to undo your blunder.)

Did You Know?

If you use Microsoft Office, then every bit of text that you cut or copy and paste is copied into the Office Clipboard, which is a cut-and-paste buffer. You can then retrieve the text to use elsewhere in the same Windows session.

ENCRYPTING FILE SYSTEM:
Encrypt Files and Folders

You can use the Encrypting File System, or EFS, in Windows to secure any files or folders that you store on your drive. With EFS, you choose which files you want to encrypt. When you encrypt an entire folder, you automatically encrypt all of the files and sub-folders within it. (Note that files and folders not stored on an NTFS drive cannot be encrypted, nor can compressed files and folders or certain other types of files such as system files that support your operating system.)

When you encrypt a folder or file, Windows issues a certificate with an associated file encryption key. EFS

uses this key to encrypt and decrypt your data. Even after you encrypt a file, you work with it as you normally would. Windows does all this encryption and decryption work behind the scenes for you.

To further secure your system, use EFS in conjunction with BitLocker, which encrypts the operating system drive. BitLocker can also help protect the EFS encryption keys stored with the operating system.

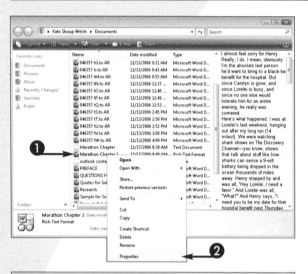

① Right-click the file or folder you want to encrypt.

② Click Properties.

● The file's Properties dialog box opens.

③ Click the General tab.

④ Click Advanced.

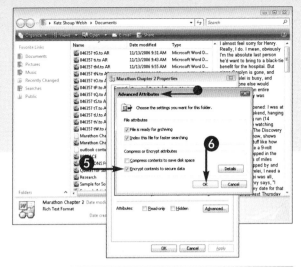

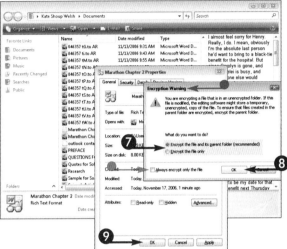

● The Advanced Attributes dialog box opens.

5 Click the Encrypt Contents to Secure Data checkbox to select it.

6 Click OK to close the Advanced Attributes dialog box.

● The Encryption Warning dialog box opens.

7 Click an encryption option.

Click the first option to encrypt both the file and the folder in which it resides.

Click the second option to encrypt the file only.

● If you always want to encrypt the file only, select the Always Encrypt Only the File checkbox.

8 Click OK to close the Encryption Warning dialog box.

9 Click OK to close the file's Properties dialog box.

Caution!

You *must* back up your encryption keys and store the backup file on removable media such as a USB Flash drive, a CD, or a DVD. (You should also password-protect the backup file and store it in a safe place.) Otherwise, if your keys are deleted or corrupted, your data will be virtually impossible to recover. To back up the keys, use the Certificate Export Wizard: Click the Details button in the Advanced Attributes dialog box and click Back Up Keys.

Did You Know?

To decrypt an encrypted file or folder, clear the Encrypt Contents to Secure Data checkbox in the Advanced Attributes dialog box.

FAX AND SCAN:
Scan a Document

There are many reasons to scan documents — for example, to keep an electronic repository of your important papers. Once a document has been scanned, you can fax it, e-mail it, print it, or simply stow it on your system.

You can save your scanned documents as JPG or TIFF image files. Choose JPG if file size is a concern; select TIFF for higher-quality scans or, if you are using an automatic feed scanner, for saving multiple scanned pages as a single file. You can also set, among other properties, the scan's resolution and

color depth. For black-and-white documents, a resolution of 75 dots per inch (DPI) and an 8-bit color depth are sufficient. For color documents, choose 150 DPI and 16-bit color.

See also>> Fax and Scan

See also>> Fax and Scan: Send

Fax and Scan: Set Up

1 Place the document you want to scan in your scanner.

2 Click Start.

3 Click All Programs.

4 Click Windows Fax and Scan.

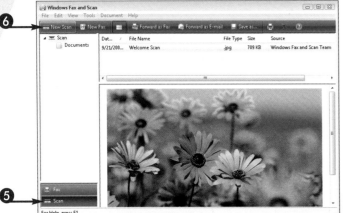

The Windows Fax and Scan window opens.

5 If necessary, click the Scan button to switch to Scan view.

6 Click the New Scan button.

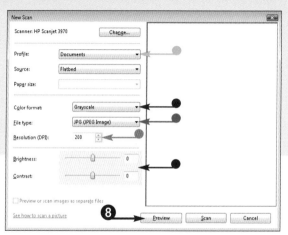

The New Scan window opens.

Note: *The settings shown in this window may differ by scanner.*

⑦ Adjust the settings for the scan.

● Indicate whether you plan to scan an image or a document.

● Specify whether the scan should be color, grayscale, or black and white.

● Choose the scan file's format — BMG, GIF, JPG (the default), PNG, or TIF.

● Set the scan's resolution, in dots per inch (DPI). (Note that a higher value here yields a crisper scan.)

● Adjust the scan's brightness and contrast.

⑧ Click Preview.

● Fax and Scan displays a preview of the scanned document.

⑨ Click Scan.

Windows scans, names, and saves the document in Windows Fax and Scan.

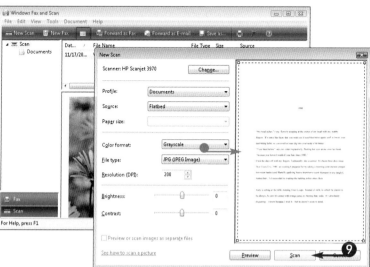

TIPS

Did You Know?
Although it is possible to scan photographs or other images using Windows Fax and Scan, the program is more suited to scanning documents. To scan photos, use Windows Photo Gallery.

More Options!
To combine scan and fax operations, in Fax view, click File, click New, and click Fax from Scanner, and repeat Steps **7** to **9**. Then, in the New Fax window, enter the recipient's fax number and click Send.

More Options!
You can configure Fax and Scan to automatically forward all your scans to the folder and/or e-mail address of your choice. In Scan view, click Tools, click Scan Routing, and follow the onscreen instructions.

FAX AND SCAN:
Send a Fax

In addition to using Fax and Scan to scan documents, you can also use the program to send, receive, organize, and view faxes.

To use Fax and Scan, you must have installed on your computer a scanner (or multifunction device with scanning capabilities). You must also have a fax modem installed, connected to an analog phone line; alternatively, you must be connected to a network with a fax server. (How you send or receive faxes is the same regardless of whether you use a fax modem or a fax server.) You must also create a fax account in Windows Fax and Scan to enable your computer to send and receive faxes.

If you have stored the fax number for your fax's recipient in Windows Contacts, you can retrieve it from within Fax and Scan. If not, you can simply type the recipient's fax number in the To field.

See also>> **Fax and Scan**

See also>> **Fax and Scan: Scan**

Fax and Scan: Set Up

① Click Start.

② Click All Programs.

③ Click Windows Fax and Scan.

The Windows Fax and Scan window opens.

④ Click the Fax button to switch to Fax view.

⑤ Click the New Fax button.

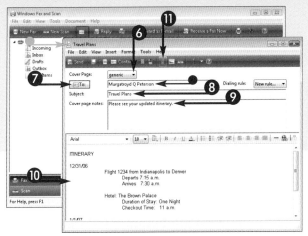

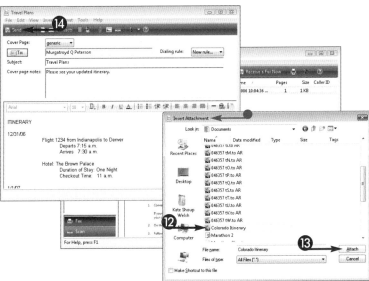

- The New Fax window opens.

6 Click here to choose a cover page (if any).

7 If the recipient's fax number is listed in Windows Contacts, click the To button to retrieve it.

- You can also type the recipient's fax number here.

8 Type a subject for your fax.

9 Optionally, type a note for the recipient.

10 Type the text for your fax directly into the New Fax window.

11 Alternatively, click the Attach button to attach a file to your fax.

- The Insert Attachment dialog box opens.

12 Locate and select the file you want to attach.

13 Click Attach to close the Insert Attachment dialog box.

14 Click Send.

Fax and Scan sends the fax.

Did You Know?

If Fax and Scan uses a fax server, or uses a fax modem but has been configured to automatically answer incoming calls, faxes will simply appear in your Inbox. If, however, you set up the program to *never* answer incoming calls, you will need to receive faxes manually from within the Fax Status Monitor window. To open this window, click the Fax button to switch to Fax view, click Tools, and click Fax Status Monitor. Then, next time your phone rings, pick it up; if you hear the telltale whine of a fax transmission, click Answer Now in Fax Status Monitor.

FAX AND SCAN:
Set Up Your System to Use Fax and Scan

Before you can use Windows Fax and Scan to send and receive faxes, you may need to enable the program on your PC. To do so, click Programs in Control Panel, click Turn Windows Features On or Off under Programs and Features, click the Windows Fax and Scan checkbox to select it, and click OK.

With the program enabled, you must create a fax account. When you do, among other things you specify whether you plan to fax via a fax modem or using a fax server.

If you plan to fax via fax modem, you must also configure your PC to specify how you want to handle incoming faxes. (You can skip this step if your fax account uses a fax server because your incoming faxes will arrive via your network, not via a phone line.)

See also>> **Fax and Scan**

See also>> **Fax and Scan: Send**

Create a Fax Account

① In Windows Fax and Scan, click the Fax button to switch to Fax view.

② Click Tools.

③ Click Fax Accounts.

● The Fax Accounts dialog box opens.

④ Click Add.

The Fax Setup Wizard starts.

⑤ Choose a fax option.

If your PC has a fax modem and is connected to an analog phone line (the kind most people use at home), click Connect to a Fax Modem and follow the onscreen instructions.

To send and receive faxes via a fax server on your network, click Connect to a Fax Server on My Network and follow the onscreen instructions.

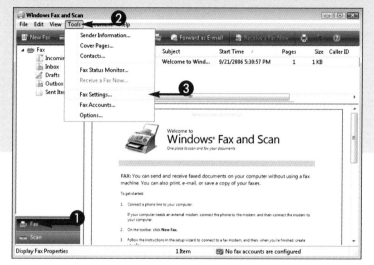

① In Windows Fax and Scan, click Fax to switch to Fax view.

② Click Tools.

③ Click Fax Settings.

● The Fax Settings dialog box opens.

④ Click the General tab.

⑤ Click the Allow the Device to Send Faxes checkbox to select it.

⑥ Click the Allow the Device to Receive Fax Calls checkbox to select it.

● Click to select Manually Answer if your fax line and your phone line are one in the same.

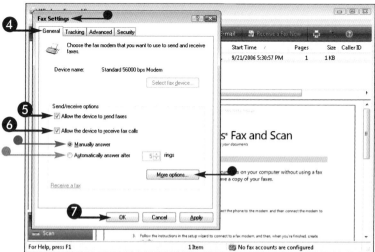

● Click to select Automatically Answer After — Rings (and choose how many rings) if you have a dedicated phone line for your fax.

● To automatically print every fax you receive or save a copy of every incoming fax in a particular folder, click More Options and adjust the settings as needed in the dialog box that apears.

⑦ Click OK.

TIPS

Attention!

In order to send and receive faxes with a fax server, your computer must be connected to the same network as the fax server. You also need the appropriate permissions to use the fax server as well as a fax server account — this is different from your Fax and Scan account. (Contact your system administrator for details on obtaining a fax server account.)

More Options!

You can configure other fax-related PC properties from the Fax Settings dialog box. For example, you can instruct Windows to notify you when incoming and outgoing faxes have been successfully sent (or not), and to display a progress bar during the send or receive operation.

FILE AND FOLDER BACKUP:
Make Backups Automatic

Any number of disasters can befall your computer, including theft, loss, breakage, and so on. To mitigate your losses if such an event occurs, you should back up your computer. When you do, Windows creates a copy of your computer's files and folders. This backup is then stored on a CD or DVD or on an external hard drive, separate from the computer itself. In the event your system becomes damaged or lost, you can use your backup file to restore your system.

Although you can back up your computer manually — and you should anytime you add a lot of new files to

your computer at once (for example, after transferring a batch of photos from your digital camera) — chances are you will not always remember to do so. Instead, configure your system to run backups automatically, on the schedule you specify.

You set up automatic backups with the File and Folder Backup Wizard, accessible via the Backup and Restore Center.

See also>> **Backup and Restore**

1 In the Backup and Restore Center, click Back Up Files.

Note: If prompted, type the administrator password or click Continue.

● The Where Do You Want to Save Your Backup window opens.

2 Choose where you want to store the backup file.

3 Click Next.

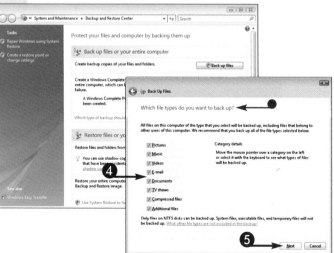

● The Which File Types Do You Want to Back Up screen opens.

4 Select the types of files you want to include in the backup.

5 Click Next.

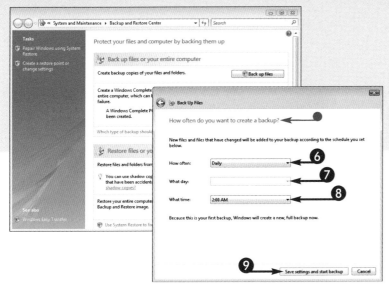

● The How Often Do You Want to Create a Backup screen opens.

⑥ Choose whether you want the backup to occur daily, weekly, or monthly.

⑦ If you chose Weekly or Monthly in Step **6**, indicate on what day of the week or month the backup should occur.

⑧ Specify the time at which the backup should occur.

> *Note: Backing up can be time-consuming, so choose an "off" time — but be sure the computer will be left on.*

⑨ Click Save Settings and Start Backup.

● A progress dialog box opens to show the status of the backup operation.

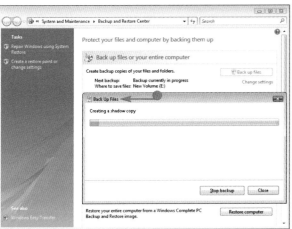

More Options!

To change the automatic backup settings, click the Change Settings link under the Back Up Files button in the Backup and Restore Center and follow the onscreen instructions. (This link appears only if your computer is configured to perform automatic backups.)

Important!

How frequently you back up depends on how often you create new files or change existing ones. If you do so every day, then you might want to back up every day to ensure nothing is lost.

Did You Know?

Even if automatic backups are enabled, you may occasionally want to run a backup manually — for example, after transferring a large number of videos from your video camera to your PC. To perform a manual backup, simply click the Back Up Files button. If automatic backups are indeed enabled, Windows will perform the backup operation instead of launching the File and Folder Backup Wizard.

FILE AND FOLDER MANAGEMENT:
Copy and Move Files and Folders

Like a filing cabinet, Windows uses *folders* to store and organize files. Windows Vista includes several built-in folders, including the Documents, Pictures, Music, and Videos folders. By default, documents are stored in the Documents folder, pictures are stored in the Pictures folder, and so on. There may be times, however, when you want to copy or move a file into a different folder. For example, you might want to move a document from your Documents folder to one of your Public folders.

When you *copy* a file (or a folder), you make a duplicate of it, so that there are two versions of it. When you *move* a file or folder, you remove it from the original location and place it in a new location.

In addition to copying files and folders within Windows' built-in folders, you can also copy them to other drives, such as a recordable CD or DVD drive.

See also>> **Folders: Create**

① Click Start.

② Click Documents.

Note: *Documents is chosen for the sake of example; sharing other types of folders involves the same set of steps as outlined here.*

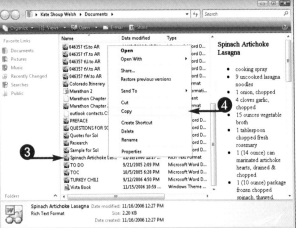

The folder opens.

③ Locate the file or folder you want to copy or move and right-click it.

④ Click Copy or Cut.

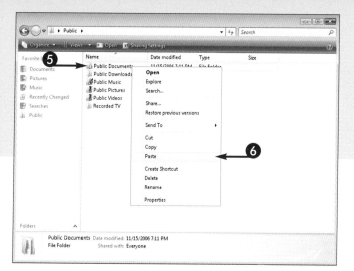

⑤ Right-click the folder in which you want the file or folder to appear.

⑥ Click Paste.

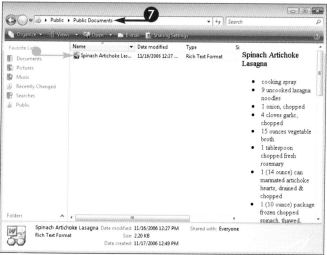

⑦ Open the folder into which you copied or moved the file or folder.

● The file or folder appears in the new location.

TIPS

More Options!
You can move or copy multiple selected files in a single operation. For consecutively listed files and folders, click the first and last item in the list while holding down the Shift key. To select non-consecutive items, hold down the Ctrl key and click the desired files and folders. To select all items in a folder, click Organize and click Select All. To clear your selection, click a blank area of the folder window.

More Options!
A quicker way to copy or move files and folders is to hold down the right mouse button, drag the file or folder to its new location, and choose Copy Here or Move Here from the menu that appears when you release the mouse button.

FILE AND FOLDER MANAGEMENT:
View and Set File and Folder Properties

Each file and folder in Windows includes a selection of properties that determine specific characteristics for the file or folder. You can customize the way a file or folder appears and works through its properties.

The properties for files differ in some respects from the properties for folders, but both include the file or folder's name, the path, the size, the date that it was created, and whether it is read-only (that is, it can be read but not modified).

In some situations, it is useful — or even necessary — to view and modify certain file and folder properties. For example, you can turn off a file's read-only attribute if you need to modify the file.

See also>> **File and Folder Management: Copy**

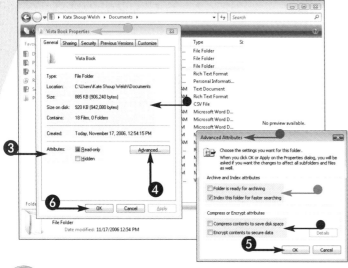

View and Set Folder Properties

1 Right-click the folder whose properties you want to view or change.

2 Choose Properties.

● The folder's Properties dialog box opens to the General tab.

● View folder information here.

3 To configure the folder as read-only, select Read-Only. To hide the folder, select Hidden.

4 Click Advanced.

● The Advanced Attributes dialog box opens.

● Click to archive or index the folder.

● Click to compress or encrypt the folder.

5 Click OK.

6 Click OK.

Note: When prompted, specify whether you want to apply your changes to this folder only or to all subfolders and files within the folder and click OK.

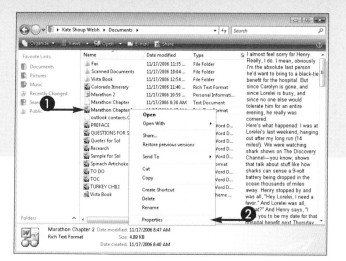

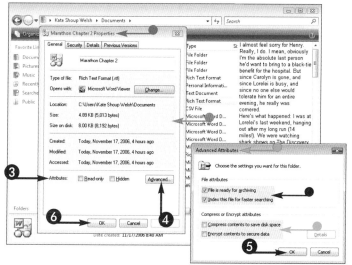

View and Set File Properties

F

① Right-click the file whose properties you want to view or change.

② Choose Properties.

● The file's Properties dialog box opens to the General tab.

● View file information here.

③ To configure the file as read-only, select Read-Only. To hide the file, select Hidden.

④ Click Advanced.

● The Advanced Attributes dialog box opens.

● Click to archive or index the file.

● Click to compress or encrypt the file.

⑤ Click OK.

⑥ Click OK.

TIPS

Did You Know?
If you are having trouble modifying a file on your hard drive, it might be read-only. To change it, uncheck the Read-Only checkbox to allow modifications.

Customize It!
If you do not like the icon for a folder, change it. Right-click the folder and click Properties. Click the Customize tab and then click the Change Icon button. Select an icon from the list and click OK; click OK again to apply the change.

More Options!
To set additional folder options, click Appearance and Personalization in Control Panel and choose Folder Options. Then, in the Folder Options dialog box, you can, among other things, specify whether you want to single-click or double-click a file to open it.

FILE AND FOLDER SHARING:
Share Folders and Files

One way to share folders and files is to burn them onto a CD or DVD and hand the disc off to the recipient. Another is to use e-mail to send a file as an attachment. If your computer is part of a network, however, you can use the network to share files and folders on your hard drive with others. One way to do so is to place files and folders you want to share in your Public folder, where all users who have an account on your computer can access them. You can also configure Windows to allow others on your network to open files in your Public folder and, if you like, change these files or create new ones.

Note that allowing or restricting access to your Public folder from others on the network is an all-or-nothing proposition; that is, you cannot allow some people to access your folder but prevent others. Likewise, you cannot allow them to view certain files or folders within the Public folder but not others.

See also>>

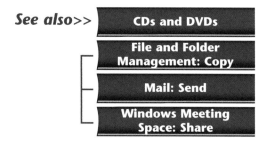

CDs and DVDs
File and Folder Management: Copy
Mail: Send
Windows Meeting Space: Share

Share Via the Public Folder

① Click Start.

② Click Documents.

Note: Documents is chosen for the sake of example; sharing other types of folders involves the same set of steps as outlined here.

The folder opens.

③ In the Navigation pane, click Public.

④ Click Sharing Settings.

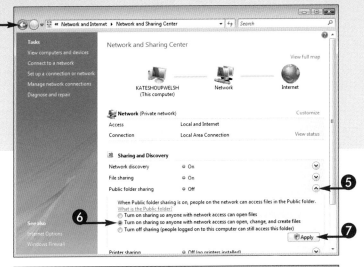

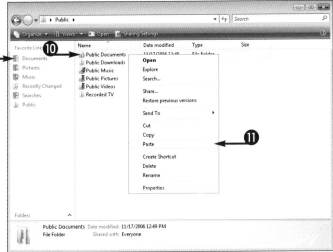

The Network and Sharing Center opens.

5 Click the down arrow next to Public Folder Sharing. (It changes to an up arrow after you click it.

6 Click a sharing option.

The first option allows others on your network to open — but not alter — files in your Public folder.

The next option allows others on your network to open, change, and create files in your Public folder.

The last option turns off sharing.

Note: This applies only to others on your network, not to other users with an account on your machine.

7 Click Apply.

8 Click the Network and Sharing Center window's Back button twice to return to the folder you opened in Step **2**.

9 In the folder, right-click a file you want to share and choose Copy or Cut.

10 Right-click the Public folder or any of its subfolders.

11 Click Paste.

TIP

Caution!

If you do allow others on your network to alter the files in your Public drive, be aware that any changes they make will override the original document you supplied. If it is important to you to keep your files as is, but you want to share them with others, opt for the Turn On Sharing So Anyone with Network Access Can Open Files setting.

FILE AND FOLDER SHARING:
Share Folders and Files (Continued)

In addition to using the Public folder to share your files and folders with others on your network, you can also configure your computer to share files and folders within another folder that you specify. To do so, you set *sharing permissions*. These specify who can access the shared files and folders and what, if any, changes they can make.

Setting sharing permissions on certain files and folders rather than sharing via your Public folder offers a bit more flexibility. In particular, this approach enables you to specify which individuals

may have access to your shared items, regardless of whether they have a user account on your computer or use a different computer on your network.

See also>>

| CDs and DVDs |
| File and Folder Management: Copy |
| Mail: Send |
| Windows Meeting Space: Share |

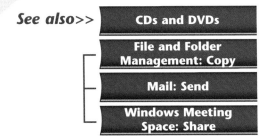

Set Sharing Properties

1 Click Start.

2 Click Documents.

Note: Documents is chosen for the sake of example; sharing other types of folders involves the same set of steps as outlined here.

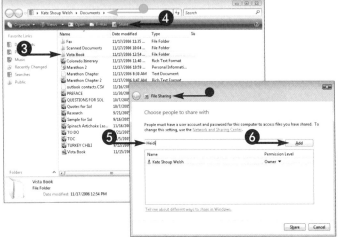

● The folder opens.

3 Locate and click the folder or file you want to share.

4 Click the Share button.

● The File Sharing dialog box opens.

5 Type the user name of the person with whom you want to share the selected file or folder.

6 Click Add.

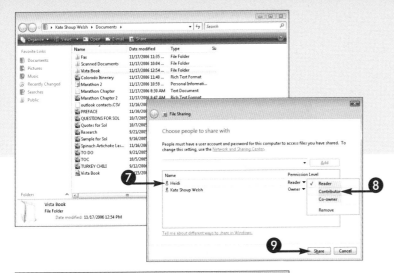

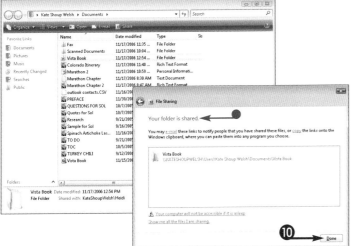

The name of the user is added to the list.

7 Click the user's name.

8 Click a permission level.

Reader allows the selected user to view files in the shared folder, but not change them.

Contributor enables the selected user to view, change, and add files, as well as delete any files she adds to the shared folder.

Co-owner enables the selected user to view, change, add, and delete all files in the shared folder.

9 Click Share.

Note: *If prompted, type the administrator password or click Continue.*

● Windows confirms that the folder is shared.

10 Click Done.

Attention!

In order for the users with whom you have shared your file or folder to access it, you must send them the folder or file's location on the network. The easiest way to do so is to click the E-mail These Links option in the confirmation screen; this opens a Windows Mail message containing a link to your shared files.

Caution!

Although you can share entire hard drives, such as your C: or D: drive, it is usually better to share only selected files and folders on your computer. When you share your entire drive, you make your computer more vulnerable to certain types of spyware and computer viruses.

FOLDERS:
Create a New Folder

Windows Vista includes several built-in folders: Documents, Pictures, Music, Videos, and so on. If you find it difficult to find the files you need in these folders, you can create subfolders within them and copy or move files — or even other folders — among them. For example, you might create a subfolder for one of your clients in your Documents folder to contain any correspondence or other documents pertaining to that client.

When you create a new folder, it is named New Folder by default, but you can give it a more descriptive title. This title should help you to identify what the folder contains. (Note that two subfolders within the same folder cannot have the same name. If you try to use the same name for a second folder, Windows will likely add -1 or -2 to the name.)

See also>> **File and Folder Management: Copy**

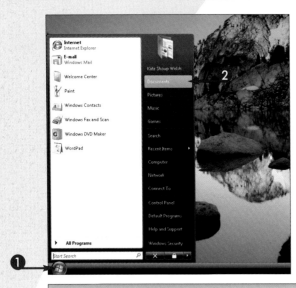

① Click Start.

② Click Documents.

Note: Documents is chosen for the sake of example; sharing other types of folders involves the same set of steps as outlined here.

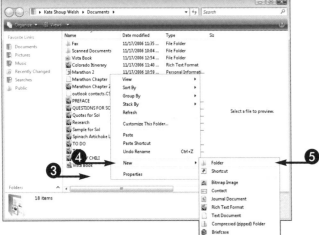

The folder opens.

③ With the folder in which you want to create a new folder open, right-click a blank area.

④ Click New.

⑤ Click Folder.

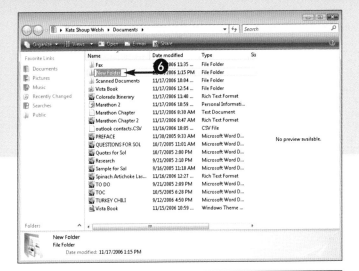

The new folder is created, with the default name New Folder selected.

6 Type a new name for the folder and press Enter.

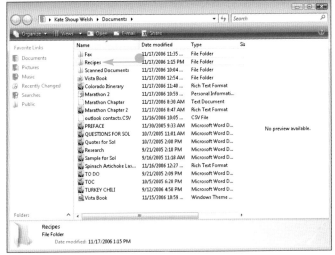

● Your newly named folder is ready for use.

TIPS

Did You Know?
You can move and copy files and folders into folders you create just as you would into any other folder.

Try This!
You can always rename a folder to better reflect what it contains. Simply right-click the folder name, choose Rename, and then type a new name.

Remove It!
Deleting a folder also deletes all its contents. To delete a folder (or a file), right-click it and select Delete from the menu that appears. When you delete a file or folder, it is in fact moved to the Recycle Bin, where it remains until the Recycle Bin is emptied. (Note that you cannot delete any of Windows' built-in folders, such as the Documents folder.)

FONTS:
Add a Font

The word "font" refers to numbers, symbols, and characters with a certain typeface. TrueType fonts make up the majority of the available fonts in Windows. These fonts can be scaled to a variety of sizes.

Although Windows has a number of fonts installed, you can add more. More than 100,000 free fonts, try-before-you-buy shareware fonts, and purchase-only digital fonts are available on the Web, as well as on discs at stores that sell software. If you regularly create your own published works, such as catalogs, brochures, and Web pages, then you

will want to augment your font collection to include popular typefaces that are not already available in Windows. For help locating fonts for your Vista system, visit Microsoft's Typography Web site (www.microsoft.com/typography).

After you find a font you like, you must first download it (precise steps vary; see the help information at the font's source) and then install it.

See also>> **Fonts: Manage**

① After downloading a new font to your system, click Appearance and Personalization in Control Panel.

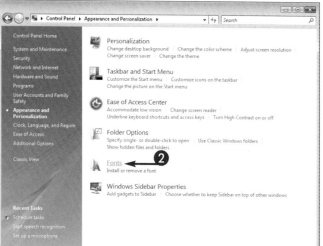

The Appearance and Personalization window opens.

② Click Fonts.

170

The Fonts window opens.

③ Click File.

④ Click Install New Font.

Note: If the File menu option is not visible, click Organize, click Layout, and click Menu Bar.

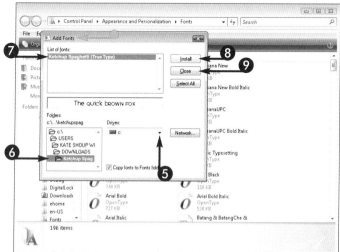

● The Add Fonts dialog box appears.

⑤ Click here and select the drive where the new font was saved.

⑥ Locate and click the folder where the newly downloaded font is stored.

⑦ Select the font you want to install.

⑧ Click Install.

Note: If prompted, type the administrator password or click Continue.

Windows installs the new font, which appears in the Fonts window.

⑨ Click Close.

Note: If you do not see a font that you have just installed in the Fonts window, click View and click Refresh.

F

Remove It!
To remove an installed font, locate the font you want to remove in the Fonts window, right-click it, and click Delete.

Did You Know?
Many fonts come in a ZIP archive, which ends with the .zip file extension. You must unzip these files before you can install them.

Did You Know?
Vista makes use of a technology called ClearType, which renders onscreen text easier to read — especially on LCD screens. It works by smoothing the appearance of each letter. Certain fonts in Vista are designed specifically to work with ClearType, which is enabled by default: Constantia, Cambria, Corbel, Candara, Calibri, and Consolas.

FONTS:
Manage Installed Fonts

If you often install new fonts on your computer, then you probably have dozens if not hundreds of additional fonts that require some management.

Every font that you install takes up a certain amount of hard disk space, and it can also affect available desktop resources when you open documents and other files that use this font. Although Windows does not limit the number of fonts that you can add to your computer, most people use only a few fonts on a regular basis.

If you rarely use a font, then you may want to remove it from your system. This saves disk space and shortens the list of possible fonts that appear in the font lists of word processors and other programs that use them. You can manage your fonts through the Fonts option in the Control Panel.

See also>>   **Fonts: Add**

① In the Control Panel window, click Appearance and Personalization.

The Appearance and Personalization window opens.

② Click Fonts.

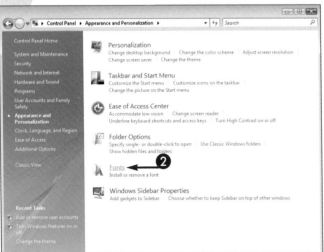

The Fonts window opens, displaying all the fonts installed on your system.

③ Right-click the font you want to remove.

Note: To select multiple fonts, click the first font and then press and hold your Ctrl key while you click additional fonts. Then right-click any of the selected fonts.

④ Click Delete.

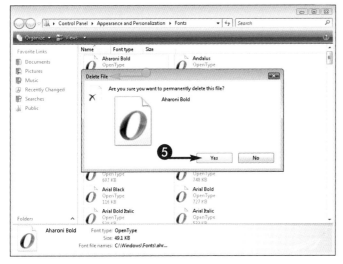

● A dialog box appears, asking you to confirm the deletion.

⑤ Click Yes.

Windows deletes the selected fonts from the Fonts folder.

TIPS

Caution!
You may not be able to delete fonts that were originally installed on your computer through Windows or through programs such as Microsoft Word.

Try This!
To see how a font listed in the Fonts window looks, double-click it.

FTP:
Using FTP in Internet Explorer

You may sometimes need to visit a File Transfer Protocol, or FTP, site to upload or download files. Although many people use dedicated FTP software to access FTP sites, you can in most cases use your Microsoft Internet Explorer Web browser. No special software or browser add-ons are needed. You simply need the address of the FTP server. (If the server requires a user name and password to access the site, then you need this information as well. Otherwise, you can log in as an anonymous user. Internet Explorer will prompt you if a user name and password are required.)

Once you have opened the FTP site in Internet Explorer, Vista enables you to view it in Windows Explorer, a special window that enables you to easily copy files and folders from the FTP site onto your computer and vice versa.

See also>> Internet Explorer 7

See also>> Internet Explorer 7

① In the Internet Explorer window, click in the Address bar to select the existing URL and type or paste the FTP site address over it.

② Click the Go arrow or press Enter.

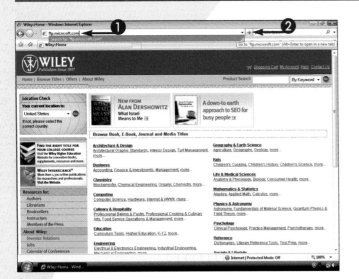

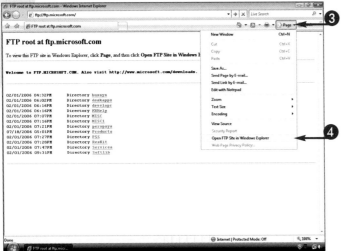

The FTP site opens.

③ Click Page.

④ Choose Open FTP Site in Windows Explorer.

Note: If the FTP site requires you to log in, click File and choose Login As. The Log On As dialog box opens; type your user name and password and click Log On.

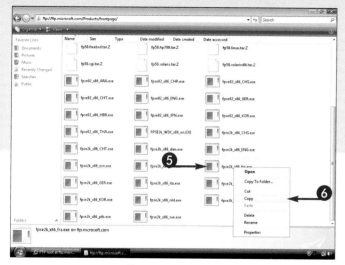

The FTP site is displayed in Windows Explorer.

5 On the FTP site, locate the file or folder that you want to download and right-click it.

6 Click Copy.

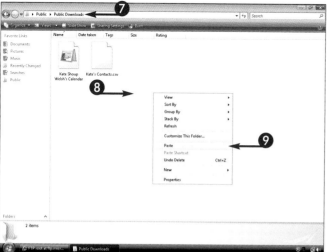

7 Navigate to the folder into which you want to paste the copied file and open it.

8 Right-click in a blank area.

9 Click Paste.

Internet Explorer downloads the file from the FTP site to the specified location.

TIPS

Attention!
If you cannot access an FTP site, it may require a user name or password. To obtain this information, contact the site administrator.

Caution!
Even if the FTP site from which you download files is a trusted site, you should still use caution when opening any files from an outside source. If you have a virus scanner, use it to scan the file before you open it.

Did You Know?
In addition to downloading files from FTP sites, you can upload files to them — although certain permissions, a user name, and a password, are usually required. Once you are set up and signed in, simply copy the files you want to upload and paste them in a folder on the FTP site.

GADGETS:
Add Gadgets

Windows Vista includes numerous *gadgets* — mini programs that offer information such as news headlines, weather conditions, exchange rates, and stock movement, or that offer access to frequently used tools such as Calendar, Contacts, and a clock.

By default, the Windows Sidebar includes a clock gadget, a slide-show gadget that cycles through the images in your Pictures folder, and a news feed gadget, which streams headlines directly onto your desktop. That is not to say, however, that those are the only gadgets available to you. You can easily add more gadgets to the Sidebar or close those you do not want.

See also>>

Gadgets

Windows Sidebar

① Right-click the Sidebar.
② Click Add Gadgets.

A window listing the available gadgets opens.

③ Right-click the gadget you want to add to your Sidebar.
④ Click Add.
⑤ Click the Gadget window's Close button.

176

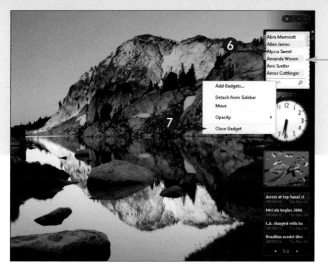

● The gadget appears on the Windows Sidebar.

6 To remove a gadget, right-click it.

7 Click Close Gadget.

● A confirmation dialog box opens.

8 Click Close Gadget.

The gadget is removed.

TIPS

Try This!
You are not required to keep your gadgets on Windows Sidebar. If you prefer, you can detach them and move them elsewhere on your desktop. To detach a gadget from the Sidebar, right-click it and choose Detach from Sidebar. Windows places the gadget on your desktop; drag it to place it where you want. Reattach the gadget by right-clicking it and choosing Attach to Sidebar.

Try This!
If your Sidebar is not currently displayed, open it by clicking the Start button, clicking All Programs, and clicking Windows Sidebar.

Did You Know?
You are not limited to the gadgets included with Windows Vista. Others are available online; see Microsoft's Web site for details.

GROUPS:
Add Users to Groups

Suppose several people have user accounts on your computer, and you want all of them to have the same level of access to specific resources such as files, printers, network services, and so on. You *could* grant the same permissions to each user account one at a time. A more efficient approach, however, is to add each user to a user group that is preconfigured with the desired permissions. A user can belong to as many groups as necessary. (Note that only users with an administrator account can add users to user groups.)

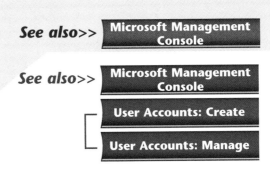

See also>> Microsoft Management Console

See also>> Microsoft Management Console

User Accounts: Create

User Accounts: Manage

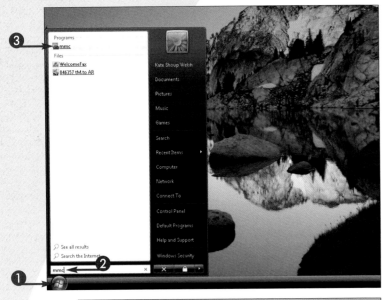

① Click Start.

② Type **mmc** in the Search box.

The Start menu displays a list of programs that match what you typed.

③ Click the mmc link in the Start menu.

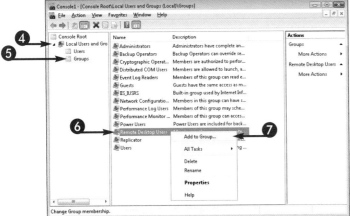

The Microsoft Management Console opens.

④ Click the Local Users and Groups folder.

⑤ Click the Groups folder.

⑥ Right-click the group to which you want to add user accounts (here, Remote Desktop Users).

⑦ Click Add to Group.

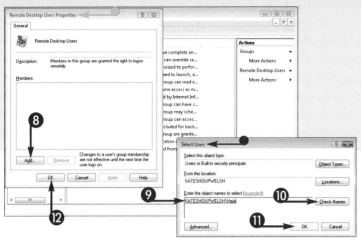

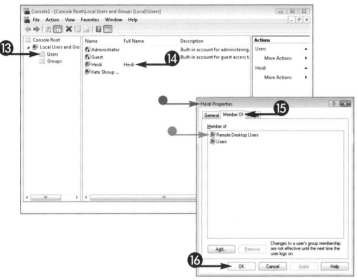

- The group's Properties dialog box opens.

8 Click Add.

- The Select Users dialog box opens.

9 In the Enter the Object Names to Select field, type the name of the user account you want to add to the group.

10 Click Check Names.

11 Windows verifies that the account name you entered is valid; click OK to close the Select Users dialog box.

12 Click OK to close the group's Properties dialog box.

13 To verify that the user is in fact a member of the group, click the Users folder in the Microsoft Management Console.

14 Double-click the user's account.

- The user account's Properties dialog box opens.

15 Click the Member Of tab.

- The user is indeed a member of the group (here, Remote Desktop).

16 Click OK.

TIPS

Attention!

If you do not see Local Users and Groups listed in the Microsoft Management Console, it is probably because that snap-in has not been enabled. (A *snap-in* is a tool designed to help manage a computer.) To enable it, click File in the Microsoft Management Console and click Add/Remove Snap-in. In the window that opens, click Local Users and Groups in the left pane and click Add. Click Local Computer in the dialog box that appears, click Finish, and click OK.

Caution!

For security reasons, avoid adding users to the Administrator group unless absolutely necessary.

HELP AND SUPPORT CENTER:
Access Help and Other Information for Windows

When you run into a problem with Windows Vista, the Windows Vista Help and Support Center is your first and fastest avenue for expert assistance and step-by-step instructions.

The Help and Support Center allows you to access help information in several ways. Perhaps the easiest is to type a keyword or phrase, such as **audio** or **user account**, in the Search field. Windows Help

returns a list of links to help articles matching your search criteria; if your computer is connected to the Internet, your search results and available help articles will include online resources.

Note that while the Help and Support Center is a great way to get help with Vista, it cannot help you with a program that is not part of Windows.

Search for Help

❶ Click Start.

❷ Click Help and Support.

● The Help and Support Center opens.

❸ Type a search word or phrase and press Enter.

Windows displays a list of links to help articles that pertain to the word or phrase you typed.

❹ Click the link that looks most promising.

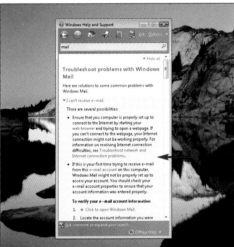

5 If necessary, click Show All to see the article in full.

● The full article text is displayed.

TIPS

Did You Know?
Some help topics offer Guided Help. Rather than simply describing how to complete a task, Guided Help actually performs the steps for you. Alternatively, Guided Help can show you each step — clicking buttons, opening menus, and so on. You know if a help topic includes Guided Help if you see a blue compass icon.

More Options!
To save you time, most Windows-compatible programs offer built-in help systems. To access it, click the Help menu and choose View Help, Help Topics, or a similar phrase (the precise terminology varies); alternatively, press the F1 key on your keyboard. Help is also available from within certain dialog boxes and screens, indicated by a question mark icon or a text link.

HELP AND SUPPORT CENTER:
Access Help and Other Information for Windows (Continued)

Another way to get help is to browse the help articles in the Help and Support Center. To do so, you click one of the links in the Find an Answer section of the Help and Support Center. Links include Windows Basics, which directs users to information about getting started with computers in general and with Windows in particular; Maintenance, which directs users to information about Windows' maintenance

tools, security settings, and so on; Windows Online Help, which launches Microsoft's online Vista support site; Table of Contents, which directs users to a list of help topics broken down by category; Troubleshooting, which directs users to pointers on diagnosing computer problems; and What's New, which directs users to information about new features in Windows Vista.

Browse for Help

❶ In the Help and Support Center, click a link in the Find an Answer section (here, Table of Contents).

Windows Help displays a table of contents.

❷ Click a link that relates to what you need help with (here, Security and Privacy).

Windows lists a series of links to relevant articles.

③ Click the link to the article that looks most promising (here, Understanding Security and Safe Computing).

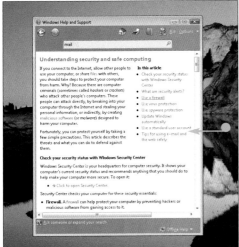

● The full article text is displayed.

y

Did You Know?

Not all the browse-able Help categories act like the Table of Contents category. Clicking certain links in the Find an Answer section direct you straight to an article rather than requiring you to winnow down your article options. Other links direct you to actual tools in Windows rather than to Help articles.

More Options!

You can also get help from others via the Help and Support Center by starting a Remote Assistance session with a more knowledgeable user, by posting a question in a Windows newsgroup, or by contacting Microsoft Customer Support online.

INTERNET EXPLORER 7:
Search the Web with Internet Explorer 7

Internet Explorer 7 offers many of the same features as earlier versions of the Web browser — for example, the Address bar, the Back and Forward buttons, the Favorites button, and so on.

One new feature, however, is Internet Explorer's Toolbar Search box, found in the browser's toolbar. You can use this box as you would a Search box in a search engine: Simply type a keyword or phrase and press Enter. Windows launches Windows Live Search, which has replaced MSN Search as Microsoft's Internet search engine.

See also>>

1 Click Start.

2 Click Internet.

Windows launches Internet Explorer 7.

3 Type a keyword or phrase in the Toolbar Search box and press Enter.

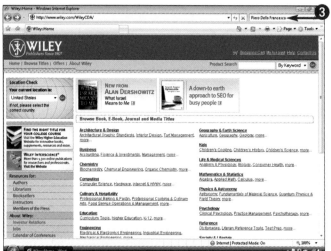

Internet Explorer 7 opens Microsoft's Live Search page with the results of your search displayed.

④ If your search failed to yield the results you need, click the down arrow to the right of the Toolbar Search box.

⑤ Choose Find More Providers.

Internet Explorer 7 displays a page listing several alternative search providers.

⑥ Click the search engine you want to add to your list of available search providers.

More Options!
Another way to search the Web is to use Internet Explorer 7's Address bar. Just type **Find**, **Go**, or **?** followed by a keyword or phrase and press Enter, or press Alt+Enter to display the search results in a new tab.

Try This!
To open a link on your search results page in a new tab, press your Ctrl key when you click it.

More Options!
You are not limited to selecting Web search engines as search providers. You can also choose search providers that relate to shopping (such as Amazon), sports (such as ESPN), travel (such as Expedia), news (such as USA Today), and more.

If you are partial to a different search engine, such as Google, you can add it to your list of search providers; that way, if Live Search fails to deliver helpful results, you can run the search again using the other provider. Alternatively, you can configure Internet Explorer 7 to use the other provider by default.

If your search still does not yield useful results, use a more specific keyword or phrase. For example, instead of using the keyword **motorcycles**, try **Triumph Bonneville**. To search for a specific phrase, surround it with quotation marks; that way,

the search will return only those pages containing the exact phrase. Finally, to exclude pages with a certain word from your results, precede the word with a minus sign. For example, if your keyword is **battery**, but many of your results pertain to New York's Battery Park, you could add **–park** (note that there is no space between the minus sign and the word) to the search string to omit those results.

See also>>

Internet Explorer 7

Quick Tabs

● The Add Search Provider dialog box opens.

● If you know you want this provider to be the default search engine for the Toolbar Search box, click to select the Make This My Default Search Provider checkbox.

7 Click Add Provider.

8 Click the down arrow to the right of the Toolbar Search box.

9 Choose the provider you just added from the list.

Internet Explorer 7 opens the search provider's page with the results of your search displayed.

⑩ If you decide you want this search provider to be the default provider, but you did not indicate this in the Add Search Provider dialog box, click the down arrow to the right of the Toolbar Search box.

⑪ Click Change Search Defaults.

● The Change Search Defaults dialog box opens.

⑫ Click the search provider you want to serve as the default.

⑬ Click Set Default.

⑭ Click OK.

Did You Know?

If you use a public computer, such as one at a library, make it a practice to delete your Internet Explorer browsing history. Click the Tools button, choose Delete Browsing History, and in the Delete Browsing History dialog box, click Delete All to delete temporary files, cookies, history files, form data, and passwords (or click the button alongside each category of files you want to delete). When prompted, click Yes.

Remove It!

If you no longer want to use a search provider with the Toolbar Search box, remove it by clicking the down arrow to the right of the box, clicking Change Search Defaults, clicking the search provider in the list, clicking Remove, and clicking OK.

LOCAL SECURITY POLICY:
Change Local Security Settings

The Local Security Policy is a roster of security settings that you can use to configure Windows for stronger security than the standard Control Panel options allow.

The security settings that you can change through the Local Security Policy include options to enforce password rules. For example, you can tell Windows

to lock users out if they cannot type the correct account password within three attempts, as outlined here. Other password options that enable you to strengthen system security include Minimum Password Length and Password Must Meet Complexity Requirements.

1 Click Start.

2 Type **local security policy** in the Search box.

The Start menu displays a list of programs that match what you typed.

3 Click the Local Security Policy link in the Start menu.

Note: If prompted, type the administrator password or click Continue.

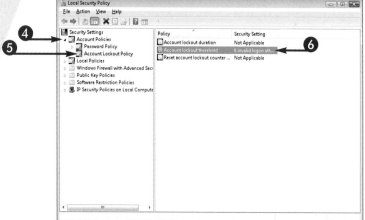

The Local Security Policy window opens.

4 Double-click Account Policies.

5 Double-click Account Lockout Policy.

6 Double-click Account Lockout Threshold.

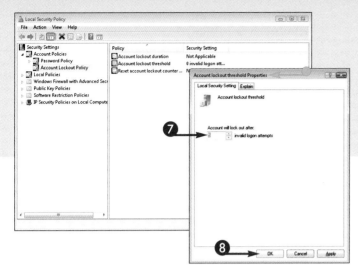

● The Account Lockout Threshold Properties dialog box opens.

7 Using the spin box, specify how many invalid logon attempts must occur for Windows to lock out the user.

8 Click OK.

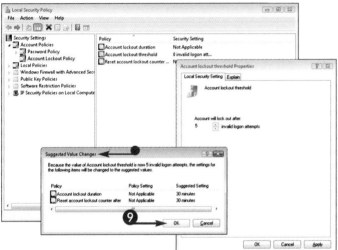

● The Suggested Value Changes dialog box opens, indicating other settings that will be adjusted to accommodate the change (here, Account Lockout Duration and Reset Lockout Counter After).

9 Click OK.

More Options!

To access the Minimum Password Length and Password Must Meet Complexity Requirements settings, open the Local Security Policy window, double-click Account Policies, and double-click Password Policy. Other available settings include Enforce Password History, which prevents users from re-using old passwords for a specified period of time, and Maximum Password Age, which specifies the maximum number of days a user can employ the same password.

More Options!

In addition to changing password-related settings, the Local Security Policy also enables you to configure audit policy settings such as Audit Account Management (this enables you to determine whether someone changed an account name, changed a password, and so on), Audit Logon Events (this reveals whether someone has logged on to your computer), and more. To view the logs of any policies you have audited, use Event Viewer.

MAIL:
Create a Mailing List

If you frequently send e-mails to the same group of people — for example, to your team members at work — you can place those people in a *mailing list*, sometimes called a *group*. That way, anytime you need to send a message to the group, you can simply enter the name of the group in the message's To field instead of adding each name individually.

Not only can you avoid having to enter each name one at a time, but a mailing list protects the privacy of other members in the group because their e-mail addresses are not revealed. Only the name of the group appears in the message's From field.

Although mailing lists are used primarily in Windows Mail, they are in fact created in Windows Contacts. You can easily launch Windows Contacts from within Mail.

See also>> Contacts

Mail

See also>> Mail: Send

① In the Windows Mail window, click Tools.

② Click Windows Contacts.

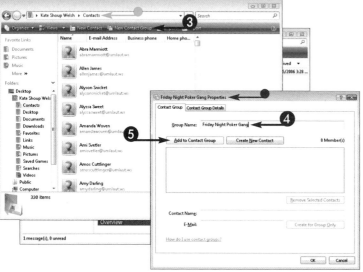

● Windows Contacts opens in its own window.

③ Click New Contact Group.

● The New Contact Group window opens.

④ Type a name for the group.

⑤ Click Add to Contact Group.

M

- The Add Members to Contact Group dialog box opens.

6 While holding down the Ctrl key on your keyboard, click each contact you want to add to the group.

7 Click Add.

- The contacts are added to the group.

8 Click OK.

- The group is added to Contacts.

TIPS

Attention!

These steps assume that each person you want to include in your group is already listed in Contacts. If not, click New Contact in the New Contact Group window to create a contact entry for that person.

More Options!

Optionally, type information about the group — an address, phone number, fax number, notes, and so on — in the New Contact Group dialog box's Contact Group Details tab.

MAIL:
Filter Spams and Scams

Chances are, you sift through dozens of spam e-mails in your Inbox to locate "real" messages — a real time-waster.

Spam can cost you money, too — especially if you use a dial-up Internet connection that charges by the minute. Even broadband users pay for spam indirectly, thanks to the higher rates charged by service providers to cover the costs they incur transmitting spam.

Some spam involves scams. For example, after the attacks of September 11, many spammers sent out requests for donations to bogus charities.

Fortunately, you can use Windows Mail's junk e-mail filter to divert spam from your Inbox into a special Junk E-mail folder. You can also configure the program to block messages from specific people or domains. (The *domain* is the portion of the e-mail address that appears after the @ sign.)

Of course, the best way to minimize spam is to avoid giving out your e-mail address except to reputable sites. Also, never reply to a junk message, even to "unsubscribe."

See also>> **Phishing Filter**

1 In the Windows Mail window, click Tools.

2 Click Junk E-mail Options.

The Junk E-mail Options dialog box opens.

5 Select the level of protection you want.

● If you do not want to block any junk e-mail messages, click No Automatic Filtering. (Note that Windows will continue to block the entries in your Blocked Senders list.)

● Click Low to block only the most obvious spam.

● Click High for maximum junk-mail blockage.

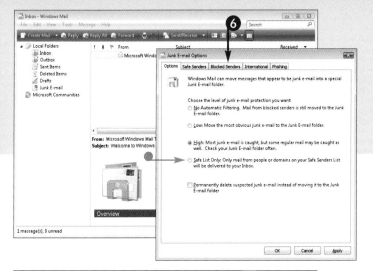

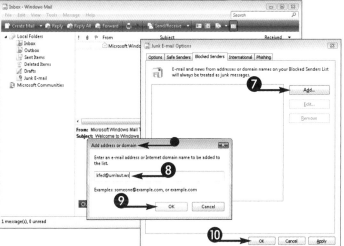

● Click Safe List Only if you want only messages from people or domains on your Safe Senders list to appear in your Inbox. (Choose this option only if you are sure your Safe Senders list includes every single person or domain you want to receive messages from.)

6 To add a sender to the Blocked Senders list, click the Blocked Senders tab.

7 Click Add.

● The Add Address or Domain dialog box opens.

8 Type the e-mail address or domain you want to block.

9 Click OK to close the Add Address or Domain dialog box.

10 Click OK to close the Junk E-mail Options dialog box.

Did You Know?

You should occasionally skim the messages in your Junk E-mail folder to make sure no legitimate messages wound up there by accident. If one does, click it, click Message, choose Junk E-mail, and click Mark As Not Junk to move the message to your Inbox.

Did You Know?

To ensure that messages from a specific sender do not get junked, add the sender to the Safe Senders list. To do so, click a message from the sender, click Message, choose Junk E-mail, and choose Add Sender to Safe Senders List. (Notice that this submenu also enables you to place a sender on your Blocked Senders list.) Alternatively, use the Safe Senders tab in the Junk E-mail Options dialog box.

MAIL:
Participate in a Newsgroup

In addition to functioning as an e-mail program, Windows Mail also acts as a newsreader. A *newsreader* is a program that enables you to download, read, and post newsgroup messages. A *newsgroup* is an online discussion forum for users from all over the world with common interests.

Newsgroups live on special servers called *news servers*. To access them, you usually need to have established a newsgroup account with your Internet service provider (although Windows Mail allows

access to Microsoft Communities newsgroups by default). You also need to have created a newsgroup account within Windows Mail.

See also>> Mail

See also>> Mail: Set Up the Newsreader

Mail: Set Up Account

Read a Newsgroup Post

1. Click Start.
2. Click E-mail.

The Windows Mail window opens on the desktop.

3. Click the newsgroup you want to view in the folder list.

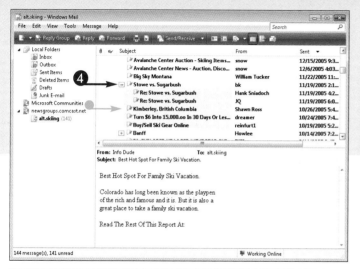

The posts for the selected newsgroup appear.

④ Click the plus sign next to a post.

● The list expands to include responses to the post from other members. (This is called a *thread*.)

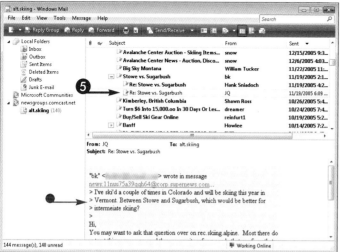

⑤ Click a post to view it.

● The contents of the post appear in the Preview pane.

Note: *You can double-click a post in the message list to open it in its own window.*

Caution!

Composing a newsgroup post is much like composing an e-mail message — and as such, the same etiquette applies. Understand that the recipient might misinterpret comments you made to be witty as offensive. To convey that you are just kidding around, consider using an emoticon. Likewise, avoid using all caps, because many interpret it as shouting. The bottom line: Angering the members of a newsgroup can result in flame wars, which involve an increasingly hostile barrage of posts — an outcome you want to avoid.

MAIL:
Participate in a Newsgroup (Continued)

As with e-mail, participants in newsgroups communicate via messages. Unlike e-mail, however, these messages can be made available to everyone in the newsgroup. As a newsgroup participant, you will likely read posts from others and submit posts yourself. You can submit a post by replying to a post by another member or by creating a brand new post.

Before you submit your first post, spend some time familiarizing yourself with the newsgroup, and post only if you have something pertinent to contribute. Likewise, if you have a question, take a moment to browse the group's Frequently Asked Questions before addressing the group. Finally, avoid posting personal information about yourself or others.

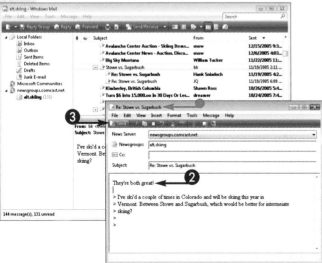

Reply to a Newsgroup Post

1 To reply to a newsgroup post, click the post.

● Click Reply Group to reply to the entire newsgroup.

● Click Reply to reply to the sender only. (The sender will receive your reply in his e-mail Inbox.)

● Click Forward to forward the message to a third party.

● A message window opens.

2 Type your message.

3 Click Send.

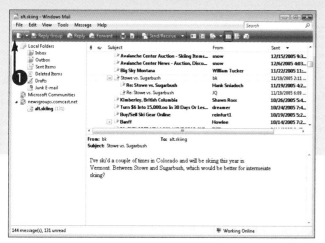

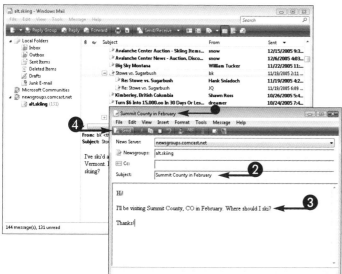

Create a New Post

1 With the newsgroup displayed in Windows Mail, click the Write Message button.

● A new message window opens.

2 Type a subject for your post.

3 Type the body of your message.

4 Click Send.

Your message is posted to the newsgroup.

TIP

Remove It!

If, after you post a message, you change your mind about it, you can cancel it from the newsgroup. To do so, click the message to select it. Then, in the Message menu, choose Cancel Message. (Note that the message is canceled only for those people who have not viewed the newsgroup since you posted it.)

MAIL:
Send and Receive E-mail Messages

Windows Mail makes it easy to send and receive e-mail messages. By default, Windows Mail checks for new messages anytime you start the program and at 30-minute intervals while the program is running.

You can change this interval by clicking Tools in the Windows Mail window and choosing Options. The Windows Mail Options dialog box opens; in the General tab, mark the Check for New Messages Every *x* Minute(s) checkbox and enter a number between 1 and 480 in the *x* box. (While you are there, mark the Play Sound When New Messages

Arrive checkbox to instruct Windows Mail to play a sound when a message arrives in your Inbox.)

If you do not want to wait for Windows Mail to run its automatic check for new messages, you can check for mail manually.

See also>> | Mail

See also>> | Mail: Create Mailing List

Mail: Filter

Check for Mail

❶ Click Start.

❷ Click E-mail.

The Windows Mail window opens.

❸ Click Send/Receive.

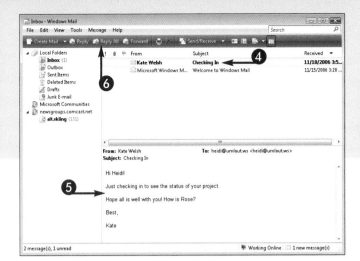

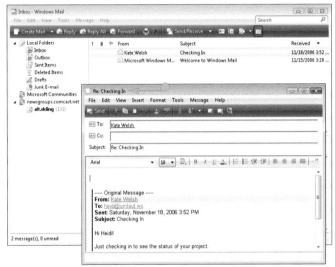

Windows Mail downloads your messages to your Inbox.

Note: In addition to downloading mail, Windows also sends any messages in your Outbox when you click Send/Receive.

4 Click a message in the message list.

5 Read the message's contents.

Note: You can also double-click a message to open it in its own window.

6 To reply to the message, click Reply or Reply All, depending on whether you want to reply to the sender only or to the sender and all other recipients. Alternatively, click Forward to forward the message to a third party.

● Windows Mail opens a Reply, Reply All, or Forward window.

TIPS

Did You Know?

Some messages contain *attachments* — that is, files appended to the message, indicated by a paperclip icon. To open an attachment, double-click the message in the message list, and then double-click the attachment file in the message window's Attach field. Alternatively, to save the attachment to your hard drive, right-click it, choose Save As, choose the folder in which you want to save the file, and click Save. (Caution: Attachments are known carriers of viruses. Open attachments only if they have been sent by a trusted source.)

Did You Know?

If you receive an e-mail from someone you want to add to your Contacts, double-click the e-mail to open it, right-click the sender's name in the From box, and click Add to Contacts.

MAIL:
Send and Receive E-mail Messages (Continued)

Of course, in addition to receiving e-mail messages via Windows Mail, you can also send e-mail messages, be they replies to messages you have received, a forwarded message, or a completely new message.

When composing an e-mail message, keep a few points in mind. First, understand that the recipient might misinterpret your sarcastic repartee as offensive chatter. To convey that you are just kidding around, consider using emoticons, such as the ever-common smiley face composed of a colon and an end parenthesis. Second, sometimes the capability to write and send an e-mail message in an instant is a *bad* thing. If you are angry at the

recipient, give yourself time to cool down before sending a message. Third, keep it short. Your subject line and the body of your message should be clear, concise, and to the point. Finally, avoid spelling and grammatical errors — especially if your e-mail is bound for your boss or a colleague.

See also>>

Mail

See also>>

Mail: Create Mailing List

Mail: Filter

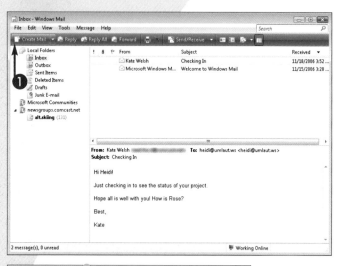

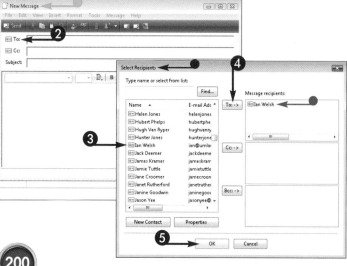

Send a Message

1 In Windows Mail, click Create Mail.

● A New Message window opens.

2 To obtain your recipient's e-mail address from Contacts, click the To button.

Note: *If you know the recipient's e-mail address, you can skip this step and simply type it in the To field.*

● The Select Recipients dialog box opens.

3 Click the recipient's Contacts entry.

4 Click To.

● The recipient's name is added to the Message Recipients pane.

Note: *Repeat Steps 3 and 4 to add as many contacts as needed. To include a contact as a CC or BCC recipient, click the CC or BCC button in Step 4 instead of the To button.*

5 Click OK.

M

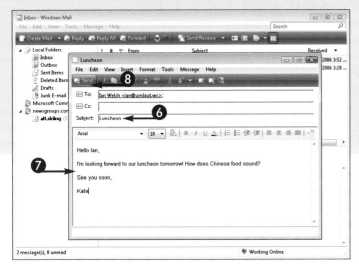

⑥ Type a subject for your message.

⑦ Type your message.

⑧ Click Send.

Note: If you do not have time to finish your message during this session, open the File menu and choose Save. Mail stores the message in the Drafts folder.

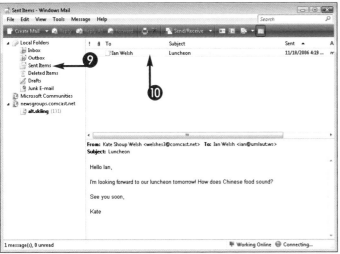

Windows Mail sends the message.

⑨ To verify that the message has been sent, click the Sent Items folder.

⑩ Locate the message in the folder.

More Options!
To attach a file to your message, click the Attach File to Message button (the one with a paperclip on it). Next, locate and select the file you want to attach and click Open.

More Options!
To change the look of your message, adjust the text's style, font, size, and color. Simply select the text and click the appropriate buttons on the Formatting bar (located above the message area).

Did You Know?
To find a specific e-mail message you have saved, use the Search box in the upper-right corner of the Windows Mail window. Type the name of the sender, specific keywords, an e-mail address — anything you remember about the message. As you type, Mail filters your messages, listing only those that match your criteria.

MAIL:
Set Up an Account

In order to use Windows Mail, the mail program included with Windows Vista, you must have signed up with an Internet service provider (ISP) and have set up an e-mail address with that provider. You must also set up your account within Windows Mail.

To set up Windows Mail, you use the Internet Accounts Wizard. Launch it from Mail's Tools menu.

You can set up Windows Mail to handle more than one e-mail account. For example, if you have a personal e-mail account as well as a work account, you can configure Mail to work with both, putting each account in its own folder. Just complete the steps in

this task a second time to add a second account, a third time to add a third account, and so on.

See also>>   **Mail**

See also>>   **Mail: Create Mailing List**

    Mail: Filter

    Mail: Participate

    Mail: Send

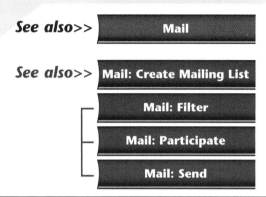

① In the Windows Mail window, click Tools.

② Click Accounts.

The Internet Accounts Wizard starts.

③ Click Add.

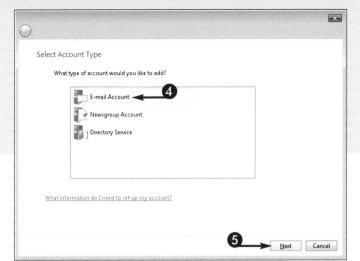

④ Click E-mail Account.

⑤ Click Next.

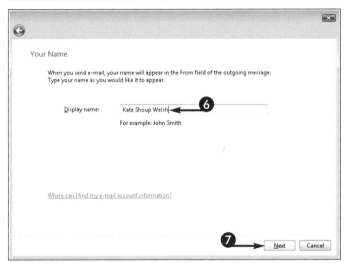

⑥ Type the name you want displayed in the From field of your outgoing messages.

⑦ Click Next.

TIP

More Options!

In addition to creating e-mail accounts, you can also create newsgroup accounts and directory services accounts. (*Directory services* are online address books, and are often provided by universities, businesses, and other institutions.) To set up one of these alternative account types, select the desired account type in Step **4**.

MAIL:
Set Up an Account (Continued)

When you set up Windows Mail, be sure to have handy the e-mail address, username, and password you set up with your ISP, as well as the names of the incoming and outgoing e-mail servers the ISP will use with your account. (Obtain this information from your Internet service provider.)

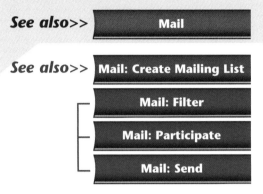

See also>> Mail

See also>> Mail: Create Mailing List

Mail: Filter

Mail: Participate

Mail: Send

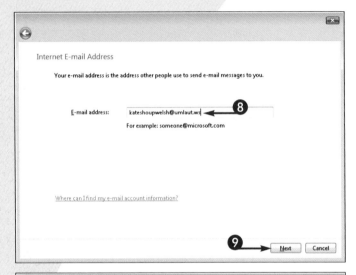

8 Type the e-mail address you set up with your Internet service provider.

9 Click Next.

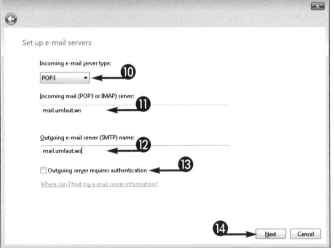

10 If your ISP uses an IMAP or HTTP server rather than a POP server for incoming e-mail (ask your ISP if you are not sure), click the down arrow and choose IMAP or HTTP from the list that appears.

11 Type the address of the incoming e-mail server your ISP will use. (Obtain this information from your ISP.)

12 Type the address of the outgoing e-mail server your ISP will use. (Obtain this information from your ISP.)

13 Select this checkbox if your ISP's outgoing e-mail server requires authentication.

14 Click Next.

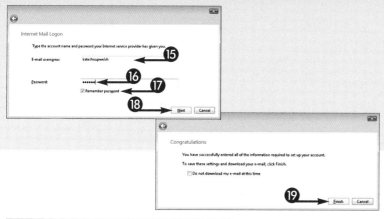

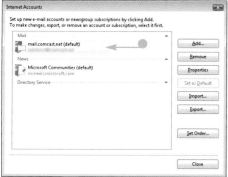

15 Type the e-mail username you set up with your ISP.

16 Type the password you set up with your ISP.

17 If you want Mail to remember your password, select the Remember Password checkbox.

18 Click Next.

19 Click Finish.

● Mail connects to your ISP to authorize the account, and then adds the account to Mail.

TIP

Remove It!

To delete a Windows Mail account, click Tools in the Windows Mail window and choose Accounts. Click the account you want to delete, and click Remove.

MAIL:
Set Up the Newsreader

By default, Windows Mail allows access to Microsoft Communities, which offers hundreds of newsgroups covering various Microsoft-related topics. To access newsgroups outside Microsoft Communities, you must obtain from your ISP the information needed to connect to its news server. News servers run by ISPs typically house thousands of newsgroups, but offer access to countless more by communicating with *other* news servers.

Once you have the necessary connection information from your ISP, you can create a newsgroup account within Windows Mail via the Internet Accounts Wizard. To do so, click the Tools button in Windows Mail and

choose Accounts. The Internet Accounts Wizard starts. (This is the same wizard you used to create your Windows Mail e-mail account.) Click Add, click Newsgroup Account, and follow the onscreen instructions. When you finish the wizard, Windows Mail downloads a list of the newsgroups available to you.

See also>> Mail

See also>> Mail: Participate

Mail: Set Up Account

View Available Newsgroups

① Click Start.

② Click E-mail.

The Windows Mail window opens on the desktop.

③ Click Tools.

④ Click Newsgroups.

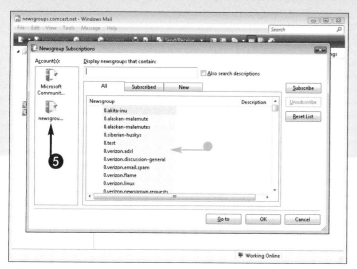

The Newsgroup Subscriptions window opens.

⑤ Click the icon for the newsgroup account you want to view.

Note: *If this is the first time you have opened this newsgroup account in Windows Mail, your PC will download the available newsgroups.*

● The Newsgroup Subscriptions window lists the available newsgroups for that account.

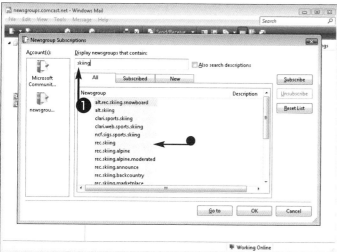

Search for a Newsgroup

① Type a keyword in the Display Newsgroups That Contain box in the Newsgroup Subscriptions window.

● Windows Mail displays those newsgroups whose names contain the word you typed.

Did You Know?

You can also subscribe to a site from within the Newsgroup Subscriptions window. To do so, click the newsgroup and click Subscribe. (To subscribe to multiple newsgroups at once, hold down the Ctrl key and click each newsgroup in the list to which you want to subscribe.)

MAIL:
Set Up the Newsreader (Continued)

Most newsgroups allow you to preview postings without requiring you to sign up, or *subscribe*. If you want to participate in a newsgroup — that is, contribute your own messages, called posts, rather than simply reading posts from others — you must subscribe to it. Subscribing to a newsgroup also saves the newsgroup in your Windows Mail folder list, enabling you to access it with the click of a button.

See also>> **Mail**

See also>> **Mail: Participate**

Mail: Set Up Account

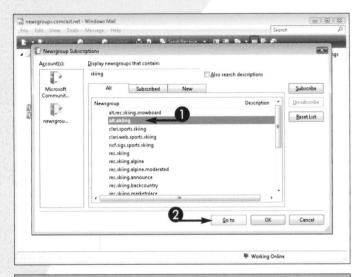

Preview a Newsgroup

① In the Newsgroup Subscriptions window, click a newsgroup you would like to preview.

② Click Go To.

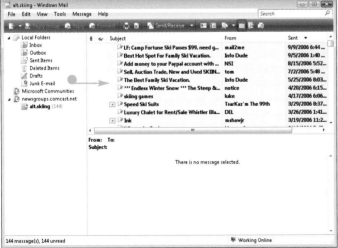

● Postings from the selected newsgroup are displayed in the Windows Mail window.

Subscribe to a Newsgroup

If you have previewed a newsgroup, you can subscribe to it from within the Windows Mail window.

① Right-click the newsgroup in your folder list. (Notice that the icon next to the newsgroup is grayed out.)

② Click Subscribe.

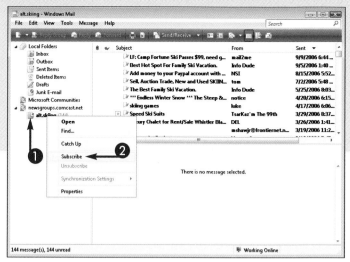

● The newsgroup is added to the list of subscribed newsgroups in Windows Mail. (You can tell that you have successfully subscribed because the icon now appears in color.)

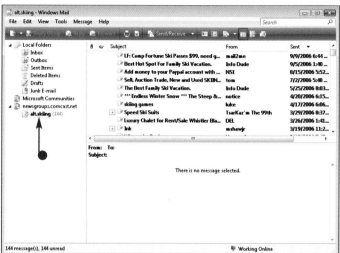

 **Remove It!**

To unsubscribe from a newsgroup, right-click the newsgroup in your folder list and choose Unsubscribe from the menu that appears.

MEDIA PLAYER:
Burn a Music CD

You can use Windows Media Player to burn audio CDs, specifying which songs in your Media Library you want to burn by creating a *playlist*.

You have two options when burning an audio CD: to burn the music files as CDA audio files, meaning that the CD will be playable from any standard CD player, or to burn them as data files (think MP3). If you opt for the latter, only hardware designed to handle data files will be able play back the CD.

In order to burn a CD with Media Player, you need a blank, recordable CD, as well as a CD or DVD drive that is capable of recording audio CDs.

If you are connected to the Internet when you record an audio CD, then Windows Media Player automatically retrieves specific details about each song from the online Compact Disk Database, which is a repository of music data.

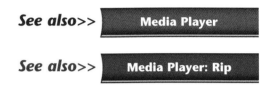

See also>> Media Player

See also>> Media Player: Rip

① In Windows Media Player, click the down arrow on the Library tab.

② Click Create Playlist.

③ Type a name for the playlist.

④ Click the songs in the library that you want to include in the playlist and drag them to the playlist pane.

⑤ Click Save Playlist.

⑥ Click the down arrow on the Burn tab.

⑦ Click Burn *name of CD* to Drive *drive letter*.

⑧ Insert a blank CD in your recordable CD drive.

Windows automatically begins to burn an audio CD (as opposed to a data CD).

⑨ Click the Burn tab to view the progress of the operation.

Caution!
Although Media Player makes it easy for you to copy a prerecorded CD, you are responsible for upholding copyright infringement laws. See your CD package for details of proper use.

More Options!
To burn a data — rather than audio — CD (or DVD), click the down arrow beneath the Burn tab and choose Data CD or DVD.

MEDIA PLAYER:
Find New Content

Windows Media Player provides access to several online stores, where you can buy or subscribe to music, video, and radio services, and other types of content.

Some of the available storefronts are integrated with Windows Media Player and appear in your library. Other stores are less integrated, appearing as separate Web pages within your player. Depending on which stores you use, you may need to install some additional software on your PC.

Much of the content available from these stores is protected by media usage rights, which specify what you can do with the content — play it, download it, buy it, burn it to a CD or DVD, and/or synchronize it to a portable device such as an MP3 player.

See also>>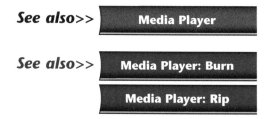

Media Player

See also>> Media Player: Burn

Media Player: Rip

① Click Start.

② Click All Programs.

③ Click Windows Media Player.

The Windows Media Player window opens.

④ Click the arrow under the Online Stores tab.

Note: *If you do not see an Online Stores tab, look for a tab that displays the logo of one of the online stores such as URGE or MSN Music.*

⑤ Choose Browse All Online Stores.

- A list of available stores and content services is displayed.

6 Click a store or service that interests you (here, VCast Music from Verizon Wireless).

7 If prompted whether you want to open the store, click the link.

Windows Media Player displays the store's page.

If you plan to regularly visit this store, add this store to the Online Stores menu. That way, you do not have to browse all the online stores every time you want to visit this one.

8 Click the arrow beneath the store's logo.

9 Choose Add Current Service to Menu.

Did You Know?

One interesting feature of Windows Media Player is its Media Guide — an online resource that is updated daily to provide links to a variety of Internet content, such as movies, music, and video. Access to Internet radio stations is also available here (click the Radio link at the top of the page). To access the Media Guide, click the down arrow under the Online Stores tab and choose Media Guide.

Attention!

The ins and outs of using the online stores differ by store. For information about how to use a specific store, click the Help link on the store's page.

MEDIA PLAYER:
Play a CD or DVD

If you have a vast collection of CDs, you can play them on your PC, assuming your PC has a CD driver. You can also use your computer to play DVDs, again assuming your PC has the appropriate hardware installed. (Note that to play DVDs, you must also have a DVD decoder installed on your machine in order to unlock copy protections applied to the DVD content. Odds are if your PC is new enough to support Windows Vista, it came with a DVD decoder preinstalled. If not, Media Player will alert you to the fact and provide a Help link.)

If your system is configured to use Windows' AutoPlay feature, then a CD or DVD inserted into the proper drive will play automatically. If not, you can launch the CD or DVD from within Windows Media Player.

See also>>   **AutoPlay**

                 Media Player

See also>>   **Media Player: Burn**

                 Media Player: Rip

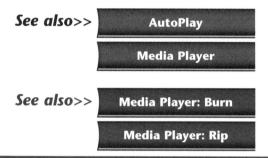

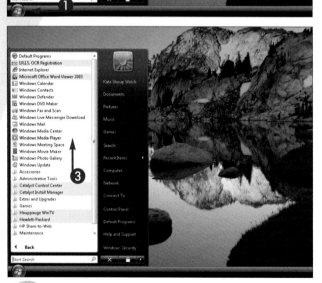

1 Click Start.

2 Click All Programs.

3 Click Windows Media Player.

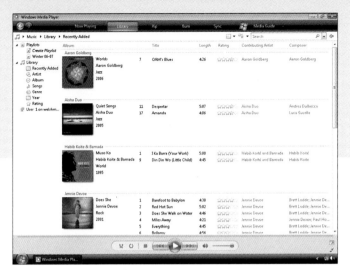

The Windows Media Player window opens.

④ Insert the CD or DVD you want to play in the drive.

⑤ Click the disc's icon in the Navigation pane.

● Windows Media displays the contents of the disc, and the disc begins playing.

TIP

Did You Know?

If there is a song you loathe on a CD you often play, you can configure Windows Media Player to skip it automatically. To do so, insert the disc and click the Now Playing tab. Right-click the track you want to skip and choose Disable Selected Tracks.

MEDIA PLAYER:
Rip Music

Windows Media Player makes it easy to *rip* — that is, copy — music from CDs for storage on your PC. After you rip music, you can listen to the files on your PC, add them to a playlist, burn them to a mix CD, or sync them to a portable music player such as an MP3 player. You can access the files you rip from your Media Player library.

If possible, you should be connected to the Internet when you rip music. That way, Windows Media Player can retrieve information about the tracks you are ripping, such as the track's title, artist, and album — even the album art. Media Player adds this

information to the files during the ripping process to make it easier to find the files when they are stored in your library.

Be aware, however, that unauthorized use and/or duplication of copyrighted material may violate copyright law in the United States or abroad, and can subject you to civil or criminal penalties.

See also>>

Media Library

Media Player

① Click Start.

② Click All Programs.

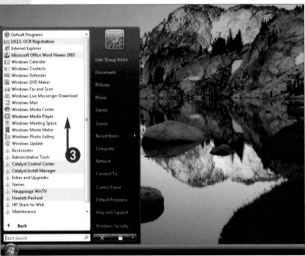

③ Click Windows Media Player.

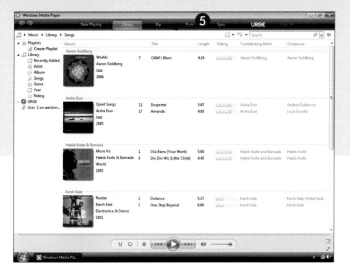

The Windows Media Player window opens.

④ Insert the CD you want to copy in the drive.

⑤ Click the Rip tab.

● If you want to rip only certain songs on the disc, click the checkboxes next to any songs you want to omit to deselect them.

⑥ Click Start Rip.

Media Player rips the selected songs from the CD.

Did You Know?

By default, Windows Media Player saves ripped music files in the Windows Media Audio (WMA) format at a bit rate of 128 Kbps. To change these settings, click the down arrow under the Burn tab, choose Format or Bit Rate, and choose the format or bit rate you want to use. (Note that a higher bit rate means higher quality — but also a larger file size.)

More Options!

To transfer the content in your Media Library to a portable media device such as an MP3 player, connect the device to your computer using the prescribed port (usually USB). Click Windows Media Player's Sync tab, drag the files you want to add your device to the List pane, and click Start Sync.

MICROSOFT MANAGEMENT CONSOLE:

Add Management Tools

The Microsoft Management Console (*MMC* for short) houses more than two dozen administrative tools called *snap-ins*, which are used to manage hardware, software, and network components. Available snap-ins include Device Manager, Event Viewer, Shared Folders, Task Scheduler, and Local Users & Groups. Some of these snap-ins, such as Device Manager, are standalone tools that are accessible

from within Control Panel. Others are accessible only from within the MMC. In order to use a snap-in that is accessible only from within the MMC, or to use a standalone tool from within the MMC, you must first add the tool to the console.

See also>> **Microsoft Management Console**

① Click Start.

② Type **mmc** in the Search box.

The Start menu displays a list of programs that match what you typed.

③ Click the mmc link in the Start menu.

Note: *If prompted, type the administrator password or click Continue.*

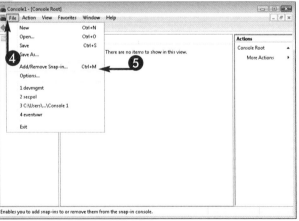

The Microsoft Management Console opens.

④ Click File.

⑤ Click Add/Remove Snap-in.

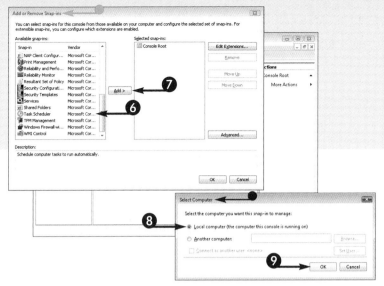

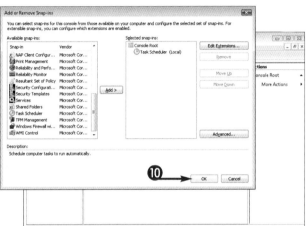

● The Add or Remove Snap-ins window opens.

6 Click the snap-in you want to add to the MMC.

7 Click Add.

● The Select Computer dialog box opens.

8 Specify the computer you want the selected snap-in to manage.

9 Click OK to close the Select Computer dialog box.

10 Click OK to close the Add or Remove Snap-ins window.

The snap-in is added to the MMC.

TIP

Caution!

It is a good practice to close the MMC when you finish working with it. This prevents others from accessing the console while you are away from your machine.

MOVIE MAKER:
Create a Simple Movie

Windows Vista's Movie Maker enables you to create movies from *clips* — that is, digital photos, video footage, and audio files.

Using Movie Maker, you can produce a simple movie in just minutes — although the latest version of Movie Maker offers enough extra tools to produce relatively sophisticated movies as well. For example, the Film Age effect makes your clip look old-fashioned. Transitions, which dictate how your movie moves from one clip to the next, also add polish to a movie, as do text and audio — both a soundtrack and narration. (You access many of these features from Movie Maker's Tools menu.)

To use digital media in Movie Maker, you must import it into Movie Maker. These media files are called *clips*. After you import clips, you add them to a Movie Maker project. You can rearrange them using the Storyboard or Timeline in the Movie Maker window.

See also>>

See also>>

Start a New Project

1 In the Movie Maker window, click File.

2 Click New Project.

Movie Maker opens a blank project on the desktop.

Import Files

1 Click Import Media.

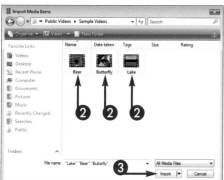

The Import Media Items dialog box opens.

2 Locate and select the file(s) you want to import, be they video footage, digital photos, or audio tracks.

Note: *To select multiple consecutive files, Shift-click them; select non-consecutive files by Ctrl-clicking.*

3 Click Import.

The selected files are imported into Movie Maker.

TIPS

Did You Know?

Movie Maker supports the use of the following types of files as clips: ASF, AVI, M1V, MP2, MP2V, MPE, MPEG, MPG, MPV2, WM, WMV, AIF, AIFC, AIFF ASF, AU, MP2, MP3, MPA, SND, WAV, WMA, BMP, DIB, EMF, GIF, JFIF, JPE, JPEG, PNG, TIFF, and WMF.

Did You Know?

To import footage from an analog video camera, your computer needs an analog capture device and any software associated with that device.

More Options!

To import footage from a digital video camera, connect the camera to your computer using an IEEE 1394 or USB 2.0 connection and set your camera mode to play recorded video. Windows Vista automatically launches the Import Video Wizard to step you through the import process.

MOVIE MAKER:
Create a Simple Movie (Continued)

After you import your clips — that is, the video, photo, and audio files you want to include in your movie — into Movie Maker, you must add them to your project. After that, you can arrange them in the desired order.

When adding clips and rearranging them in your project, start with the Collections pane and Storyboard pane toggled on. Afterward, switch to the Task pane and the Timeline pane. These tools enable you to more easily fine-tune the project by editing your clips, adding transitions, inserting audio, adding titles, and so on.

See also>> **Movie Maker**

See also>> **DVD Maker**

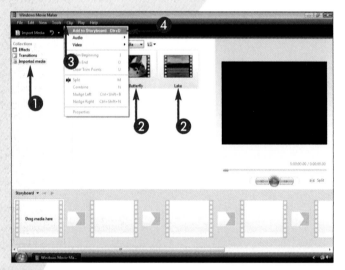

Add Clips to a Project

① In the Collections pane, click the folder containing your clip.

The Contents pane displays the clips in the folder you clicked.

② Click the clip(s) you want to add.

Note: To select multiple consecutive clips, Shift-click them; select non-consecutive files by Ctrl-clicking.

③ Click Clip.

④ Click Add to Storyboard.

● The clip(s) is added to the Storyboard.

Note: You can also add clips to your projects by dragging them from the Contents pane to your Storyboard or Timeline pane.

Rearrange Clips

① In the Storyboard, click the clip you want to move.

② Click Edit.

③ Click Cut.

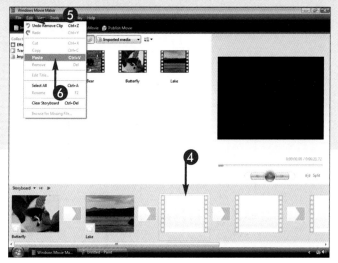

④ Click the next empty cell on the Storyboard.

⑤ Click Edit.

⑥ Click Paste.

● The clip is moved.

Note: You can also move clips in the Timeline pane. To do so, move the playback indicator, which looks like a square with a vertical line beneath it, to the spot where you want to paste the clip in Step 4.

Did You Know?

If you cannot complete your project in one session, save it for later. Click File, click Save Project, type a name for the project, and click Save. To resume, click File, click Open Project, click the project file, and click Open.

Remove It!

To remove a clip — or a transition, a title, or an effect — right-click it in the Storyboard or Timeline and choose Delete.

MOVIE MAKER:
Publish a Movie

When you are satisfied with the arrangement of the clips in your project, you publish it to convert it to a movie file. Movie Maker movie files have either a .wmv file extension or an .avi file extension.

After the project has been published, you can send the movie file as an e-mail attachment, post it on a Web site, or use DVD Maker to burn it to a DVD.

See also>> Movie Maker

See also>> DVD Maker

❶ Click File.

❷ Click Publish Movie.

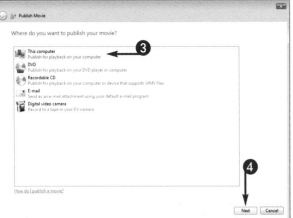

The Publish Movie Wizard opens.

❸ Click This Computer.

❹ Click Next.

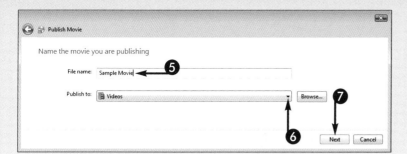

5 Type a name for the movie.

6 Specify where you want the movie file to be saved.

7 Click Next.

8 Choose a quality setting for your movie.

9 Click Publish.

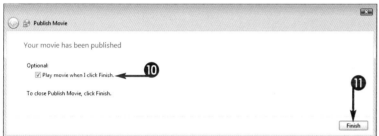

Windows displays a status bar to show the progress of the publish operation.

10 Optionally, in the Your Movie Has Been Published, click the Play Movie When I Click Finish checkbox to select it.

11 Click Finish.

TIP

Did You Know?

You can set the properties of a project, including its title, author, copyright information, rating, and comments. To do so, click File, and click Project Properties. The Project Properties dialog box opens; fill in the fields as desired and click OK.

NETWORK CONNECTIONS WINDOW:
Manage Network Connections

You can manage your network connections in the Network Connections window, which is available through Control Panel or through the Network and Sharing Center.

In the Network Connections window, you can perform all management tasks that are related to various types of network connections. For example, you can check the status of your home or business network or wireless network. You can also troubleshoot the network, remove it, and add connections to it, including those connections that you create for dial-up or broadband Internet service accounts.

Each connection that you set up has an icon in the Network Connections window. You can double-click or right-click a connection icon to display its Properties dialog box.

See also>> **Network and Sharing Center**

① Click Start.

② Click Network.

● The Network folder opens.

③ Click Network and Sharing Center.

● The Network and Sharing Center opens.

④ Click Manage Network Connections.

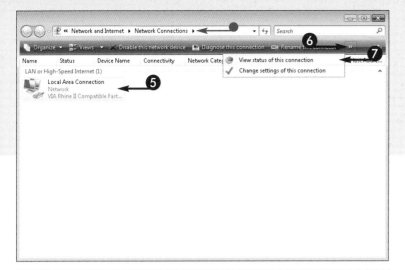

- The Network Connections window opens.

5 Click the connection you want to manage.

6 If necessary, click the right arrow on the right edge of the toolbar to reveal more buttons.

7 Click View Status of This Connection.

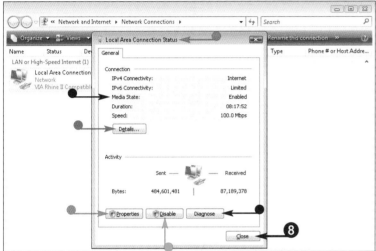

- The connection's Status dialog box opens.

● View general information about the connection here.

● Click Details to view more in-depth information about the connection.

● Click Properties to open the connection's Properties dialog box.

● Click Disable to disable the connection.

● Click Diagnose to troubleshoot the connection.

8 Click Close.

Caution!

Before you change your connection settings, be sure to review the current settings as well as any notes you have on recommended changes. This helps you to avoid making a simple typing error that could disable a connection rather than establish one.

Important!

Different error messages may appear when you try to repair or perform other jobs on your network connections. Follow the instructions in the message window to resolve the problem.

Remove It!

Occasionally, a network connection can become corrupt, which means that some aspect of the connection, such as the settings, no longer allows Windows to establish a connection. If this happens, disable the connection and create a new one.

N

OFFLINE FILES:
Enable Offline Files

You can work on files that are stored on your network even when you are not connected to the network by enabling offline files. This allows you to work on files offline on a laptop computer or Tablet PC, or another computer that is part of the network sharing system.

With offline files enabled, you can copy files from shared folders or drives on your network to your computer hard drive. After moving the files to your hard drive, you can work on them, even if you are not connected to the network. When you reconnect

to the network, Windows Vista synchronizes the files on your hard drive with the files on the network.

Synchronizing is a process by which your computer file system checks the versions of all files on your hard drive against the network files, and then updates the files to make the file contents identical.

See also>>

Offline Files: Make

Offline Files: View

① Click Start.

② Click Control Panel.

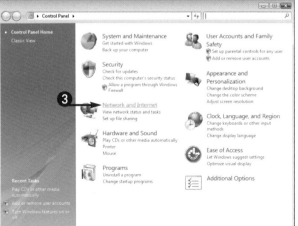

The Control Panel window opens.

③ Click Network and Internet.

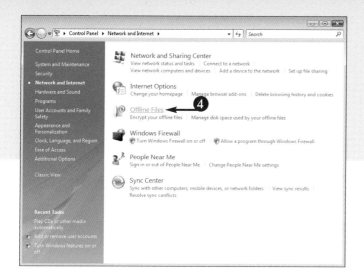

The Network and Internet window opens.

④ Click Offline Files.

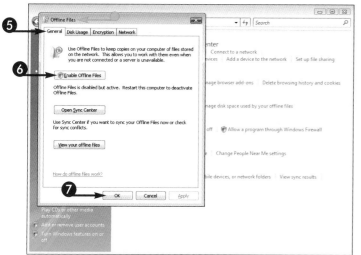

● The Offline Files dialog box opens.

⑤ Click the General tab.

⑥ Click Enable Offline Files.

Note: *If prompted, type the administrator password or click Continue.*

⑦ Click OK.

Windows prompts you to restart your computer in order for the settings to take effect. Click Yes to restart.

Did You Know?

Windows Vista allots a certain amount of disk space for use with offline files. To view how much space is available on your machine — as well as how much is consumed — click the Disk Usage tab in the Offline Files dialog box. To change how much space is available, click Change Limits and use the sliders in the dialog box that opens.

Did You Know?

By default, offline files are not encrypted. To change this, click the Encryption tab in the Offline Files dialog box and click Encrypt.

OFFLINE FILES:
Make Files Available for Offline Use

After you enable offline files, you can work on network files even when you are not connected to the network. This is handy if you plan to use a portable computer away from your network, or if your network connection is painfully slow. Offline files are also invaluable in the event of a network outage.

Before you can work with a network file offline, however, you must make it available for offline use. When you do, Windows Vista automatically creates a copy of the network file on your computer. In the event your network or the network folder housing the file you made available becomes inaccessible, your

computer will automatically access the offline copy of the file, enabling you to continue work without interruption. You can also manually switch to offline mode.

When the network or folder again becomes available, Windows Vista synchronizes the files on your machine with those on the network.

See also>>

Offline Files: Enable

Offline Files: View

Make a File Available

① Click Start.

② Click Network.

The Network folder opens.

③ Navigate to the file you want to make available offline and right-click it.

④ Click Always Available Offline.

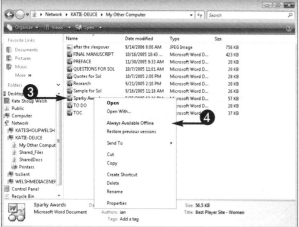

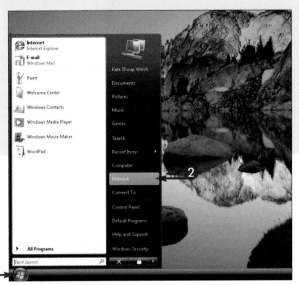

Switch to Offline Mode

1 Click Start.

2 Click Network.

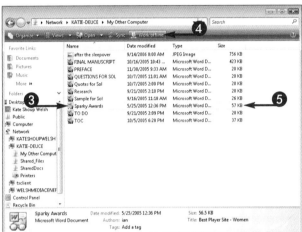

The Network folder opens.

3 Navigate to the file you want to work on and click it to select it.

4 Click Work Offline.

Note: If the Work Offline button is not available, you have not yet made the file available for offline use.

5 Double-click the file to open it and work offline.

TIPS

Try This!

To switch back to online mode and sync your offline document with the version on the network, click Work Online in the Network window.

Did You Know?

If your offline files are scattered across the network, locating each one individually is time-consuming. Instead, to view them all at once, click View Your Offline Files in the General tab of the Offline Files dialog box.

Did You Know?

If you lose access to the shared folder containing the document you are working on, Windows Vista switches to Offline Files mode automatically (assuming you made the file available for offline use). When access to the folder is restored, the offline file will sync automatically with the one on the network.

OFFLINE FILES:
View Synchronization Settings

After you work with shared files offline, those files must be synchronized with the versions that reside on the network. In Windows Vista, this synchronization process occurs automatically, transferring an updated copy of the file back to the original network folder to reflect the changes that you made offline.

If the file on the network changes but the offline version does not, then a copy of the changed network file is transferred to the offline file. If both copies of the file have changed since it was

transferred to your machine, Windows asks you which version you want to keep.

Files can be synchronized only when you are connected to the network. You can view synchronization settings to see the offline file's sync status.

See also>>

Offline Files: Enable

Offline Files: Make

① Click Start.

② Click All Programs.

③ Click Accessories.

④ Click Sync Center.

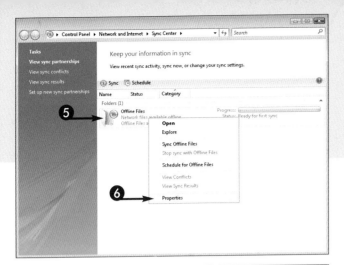

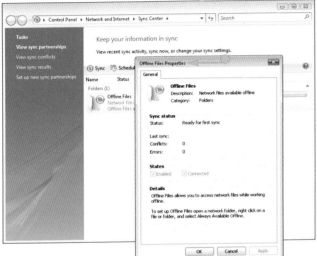

5 Right-click the icon for the Offline Files sync partnership.

Note: A sync partnership specifies how and when files are synchronized. The Offline Files sync partnership was created automatically when you made a network file available.

6 Click Properties.

● The offline file's Properties dialog box opens.

More Options!

Although Windows Vista syncs offline files automatically, you can also instigate a manual sync. For example, you might do so if you are working offline while connected to your network. To manually sync offline files, click the Offline Files sync partnership in the Sync Center and click Sync.

Attention!

To sync the offline files in a specific folder, open the folder containing the files and click Sync. To sync only a single offline file, right-click the file and click Sync.

OPEN WITH COMMAND:
Open a File in a Different Program

When you open a particular file, Windows automatically recognizes and loads the appropriate program for the file. However, you can also open a document or file by using a program other than the default one. For example, you may normally open a Web page — a file that is saved with the .htm or .html file extension — through your Web browser. But if you want to open an HTML file in order to edit its code, you want to open it in a different program, such as WordPad.

There are two reasons why you may want to open a file with an alternate program. First, a different

program may enable you to edit or view the file in a way that the default program does not. Second, when you have trouble opening the file with the default program, you can open the file with a different program and then resave it so that you can open the file with the default program.

See also>>  **Programs and Features**

See also>> **Default Programs Center**

① Click Start.

② Choose the folder containing the file you want to open (here, Pictures).

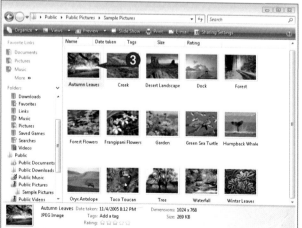

The folder window opens.

③ Navigate to the file you want to open and right-click it.

④ Click Open With.

⑤ Choose the program you want to use to open the file from the list that appears.

The file opens in the program you selected.

Attention!

Match the file type you want to open with an alternate program that can open your file. For example, an image file ending with a .tif, .jpg, or .gif file extension requires a graphics program to open it, such as Microsoft Paint.

Caution!

If you see an error message indicating that the program cannot open the file, or if the file displays strangely, then close the file without saving it and try to open it in another program.

Try This!

If you are worried about making incompatible changes from one program to another in a file, then you can make a copy of the original file, make the changes that you want to the copy, and save your changes with a new filename.

PARENTAL CONTROLS:
Set Windows Media Center Parental Controls

Some of the television available through Windows Media Center is inappropriate for children. Fortunately, Windows Media Center offers parental controls to enable parents to filter inappropriate content.

The first time you access Windows Media Center's parental controls, you must choose an access code. This code is very much like the PIN you use at an ATM. Be sure to select a code that you will be able to remember. (Write this code down and save it someplace safe and private in case you forget it.)

If someone tries to access the types of material that the parental controls are configured to filter out, he or she cannot do so. Moreover, no one can modify or disable the parental-control settings without the access code that you set when you activate the tool.

See also>>

Windows Media Center

See also>> Windows Media Center: Watch Live TV

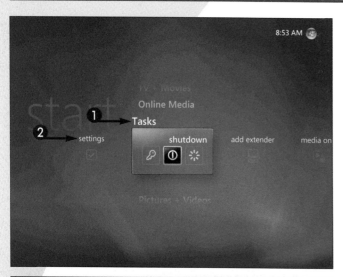

① In Windows Media Center's start screen, scroll to Tasks.

② Click Settings.

③ Click Settings.

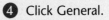

④ Click General.

⑤ Click Parental Controls.

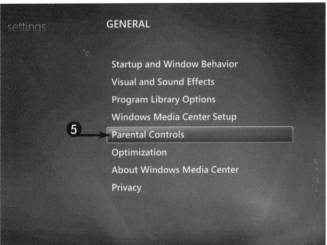

TIPS

Caution!
The ratings cited in the Windows Media Center guide are sometimes inconsistent with the ratings information transmitted with the TV broadcast signal. For this reason, content that you thought would be blocked may on rare occasions be broadcast, and vice versa.

Remove It!
If you find the parental controls too restrictive, you can reset them to their default, nonrestrictive state. To do so, click Reset Parental Controls in the Parental Controls screen.

Did You Know?
To change your access code, click Change Access Code in the Parental Controls screen, enter a new access code, type the code a second time to confirm it, and click OK.

PARENTAL CONTROLS:
Set Windows Media Center Parental Controls (Continued)

You can restrict TV and movie content by rating. The ratings used for movies are those established by the Motion Picture Association of America (MPAA): G, PG, PG-13, R, and NC-17.

TV ratings work a bit differently, and are as follows: TV-Y (appropriate for all children), TV-Y7 (appropriate for children age 7 and older), TV-G (general audience; most parents would find programs with this rating acceptable), TV-PG (parental guidance suggested), TV-14 (parents strongly cautioned), and TV-MA (mature audiences only).

Television shows can also be blocked using the following criteria: fantasy violence, suggestive language, offensive language, sexual content, and violence.

Configuring the Parental Controls involves the same basic process for both TV and movies (except movies do not allow for configuring advanced settings).

See also>>  Windows Media Center

See also>> Windows Media Center: Watch Live TV

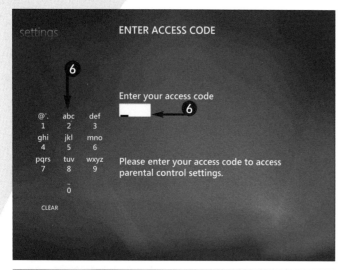

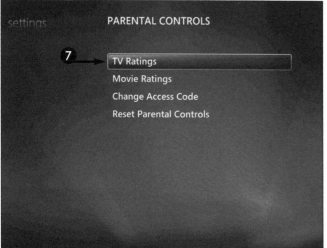

⑥ Enter your access code either by clicking the numbers on the onscreen keypad or typing them.

Note: If this is the first time you have accessed the parental controls, type the access code you want to use, and type it a second time to confirm.

⑦ Click TV Ratings.

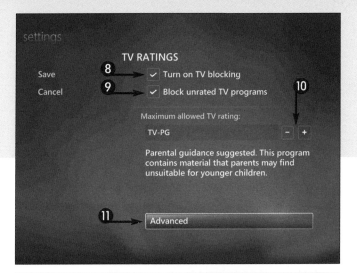

8 Click Turn On TV Blocking.

9 If you want to block programs that are not rated, click Block Unrated TV Programs.

10 Use the plus and minus buttons to adjust the Maximum Allowed TV Rating setting.

11 Click Advanced.

Note: If prompted to save the changes you have made to your settings, click Yes.

12 Click the plus or minus signs next to a content category to allow or disallow shows in that category.

13 Click Save.

14 Click Save again to return to the Parental Controls screen.

TIPS

Did You Know?

Even if you allow suggestive dialogue, offensive language, sexual content, and/or violence, Windows Media Center will still block content by rating. For example, if you chose TV-PG as the maximum allowed TV rating, only the suggestive dialogue, offensive language, sexual content, and/or violence that falls within that rating will be allowed.

Did You Know?

If you like, you can set up Windows Media Center to work with a remote control, which you use just like a television remote control. You can purchase special remote controls designed to work with Windows Media Center at any number of retail outlets. For details on how to use the remote control, see Windows Media Center's help information.

PARENTAL CONTROLS:
Set Windows Vista Parental Controls

You can configure Windows Vista's parental controls to act much like the parental controls in Internet Explorer 7's Content Advisor. For example, Windows Vista can block access to Web sites based on a Web site's content. You can also configure Vista to block (or allow) access to Web sites that you specify, regardless of rating. In addition, Vista can block file downloads.

Before you implement parental controls, be sure each child who uses your computer has his or her own

standard user account. Ensure, too, that you log on using the administrator account; otherwise, you will not be able to set parental controls.

See also>> 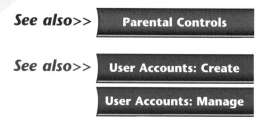 **Parental Controls**

See also>> **User Accounts: Create**

User Accounts: Manage

① In Control Panel, click Set Up Parental Controls for Any User under User Accounts and Family Safety.

Note: *If prompted, type the administrator password or click Continue.*

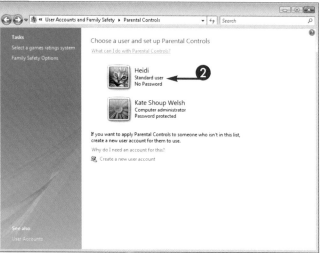

The Parental Controls window opens.

② Click the standard user account to which you want to apply parental controls.

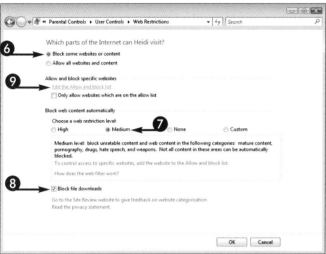

The User Controls window opens.

P

③ Under Parental Controls, click On, Enforce Current Settings.

④ Under Activity Reporting, click On, Collect Information About Computer Usage.

⑤ Click Windows Vista Web Filter.

⑥ Click Block Some Websites or Content if you plan to limit this account's access to Web resources in any way.

⑦ Choose the level of restriction you want to impose.

⑧ Optionally, click Block File Downloads to prevent this user account from downloading files from the Internet.

⑨ Click the Edit the Allow and Block List link.

More Options!

In addition to using any of the built-in restriction levels — High, Medium, and None — you can create a custom level of restrictions. To do so, click Custom; then choose the categories of content you want to block. Categories include Pornography, Hate Speech, Bomb Making, Weapons, Drugs, Gambling, and more.

Did You Know?

When parental controls block access to a Web page, game, or other content, Vista displays a message box indicating that access is restricted. The restriction can be overridden only if you enter the administrator's password.

PARENTAL CONTROLS:
Set Windows Vista Parental Controls (Continued)

Vista offers yet more parental controls — ones that do not relate to the Internet. For example, you can configure Vista to limit a user's access to certain hours of the day on certain days of the week. (If a user tries to log in at a restricted time, Vista blocks access; if the user is logged on, Vista automatically logs him or her off.)

You can also block users from playing games on the computer. Access to games can be restricted completely, by age rating, or by content rating. You can also specify that only certain games be blocked or allowed.

If your computer has programs installed on it that you prefer to keep private — for example, a money-management program that contains information about your finances — you can use Vista's parental controls to prevent unauthorized access.

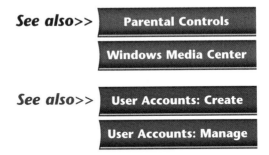

See also>> **Parental Controls**

Windows Media Center

See also>> **User Accounts: Create**

User Accounts: Manage

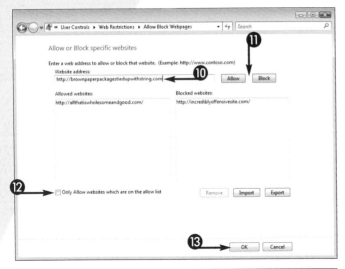

The Allow or Block Specific Websites screen opens.

⑩ Type the URL of a site you want to block or allow.

⑪ Click Allow or Block.

The URL is added to either the Allowed Websites or Blocked Websites list.

⑫ If you want this account to have access only to sites in the Allow list, click Only Allow Websites Which Are on the Allow List.

⑬ Click OK.

⑭ Click OK to close the Web Restrictions page.

⑮ Click Time Limits in the User Controls window.

*Note: Repeat Steps **1** and **2** of this task to open the User Controls window.*

The Time Restrictions window opens.

⑯ Click to indicate the hours you want to block or allow computer use for this account. (To prevent access in large blocks of time, drag the mouse.)

⑰ Click OK.

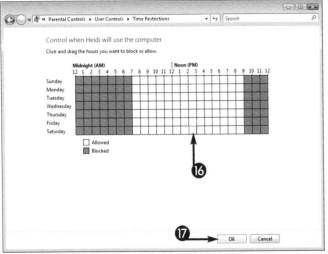

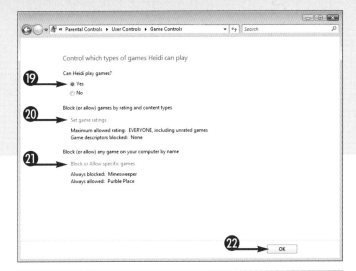

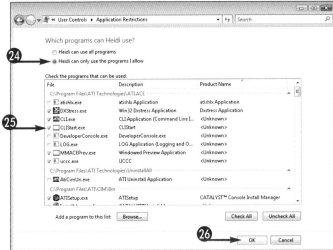

⑱ Click Games in the User Controls window.

Note: Repeat Steps 1 and 2 of this task to open the User Controls window.

The Game Controls window opens.

⑲ Under Can *X* Play Games, click Yes or No.

⑳ If you clicked Yes in Step **19**, click Set Game Ratings to block or allow games by rating and content type.

㉑ If you clicked Yes in Step **19**, click Block or Allow Specific Games.

㉒ Click OK.

㉓ Click Allow and Block Specific Programs in the User Controls window.

Note: Repeat Steps 1 and 2 of this task to open the User Controls window.

The Application Restrictions window opens.

㉔ To limit the programs available to this account, click *X* Can Only Use the Programs I Allow.

Windows displays a list of programs installed on the PC.

㉕ Click the checkbox for each program you want to allow.

㉖ Click OK.

P

More Options!

To view an activity report for an account, click the View Activity Reports link on the account's User Controls window. Activities tracked are broken into the following categories: Web Browsing, System, Applications, Gaming, Email, Instant Messaging, and Media.

Try This!

If you want this account to be able to use most — but not all — programs installed on the PC, click the Check All button in the Application Restrictions window, and then uncheck those programs you want to block.

PARTITION:
Create and Format a Partition

A *partition*, also called a *volume*, is an area of a hard drive that has been formatted and assigned its own drive letter. (To *format* a drive is to configure it with a file system in order to store information on it.) The hard drives on most computers consist of a single volume, typically with the drive letter C. You can, however, divide, or *partition*, the hard drive into multiple volumes if the hard drive contains *unallocated space* — unformatted space that is not part of an existing volume.

Some people partition their hard drive into multiple volumes — one for Windows files, one for program files, one for personal data, and so on. In addition, certain Windows Vista features, such as BitLocker, require multiple partitions to operate.

Hard drives can be divided into as many as four *primary partitions* — partitions that are capable of hosting an operating system and that function like physically separate disks. Additional volumes are called *extended partitions*; these can hold one or more *logical drives*, which function like primary partitions but cannot contain an operating system.

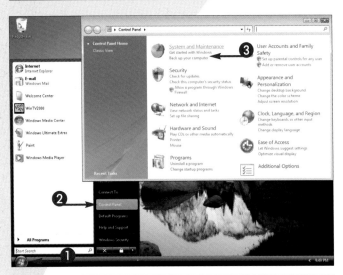

① Click Start.

② Click Control Panel.

The Control Panel window opens.

③ Click System and Maintenance.

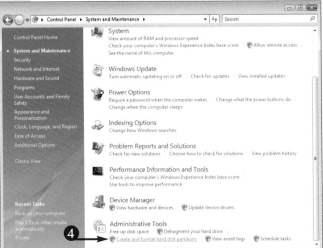

The System and Maintenance window opens.

④ Scroll down to Administrative Tools and click Create and Format Hard Disk Partitions.

Note: If prompted, type the administrator password or click Continue.

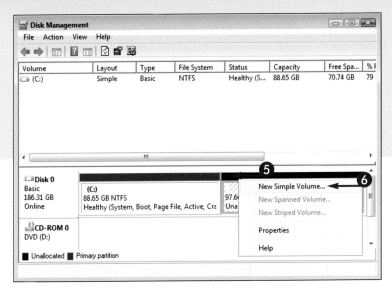

The Disk Management window opens.

5 Right-click an unallocated region on your hard disk, represented by a black bar.

6 Choose New Simple Volume.

The New Simple Volume Wizard starts.

7 Click Next.

Important!

If your hard drive contains no unallocated space (likely the case if your system came with Windows Vista preinstalled) you can create new partitions in the drive by following the steps in this task only if you delete the entire contents of your drive first — which is a Very Bad Idea unless you first back up all your data. Even then, you will have to completely reinstall Windows and any other programs you plan to use. A better approach is to use one of several third-party programs that allow you to repartition your hard disk without erasing data.

PARTITION:
Create and Format a Partition (Continued)

The New Simple Volume Wizard, which starts automatically when you right-click an unallocated region of your hard drive and choose New Simple Volume from the menu that appears, steps you through the process of creating and formatting a

partition. You use the wizard to specify how large the partition should be, assign a drive letter to the partition, apply a file system to the partition, and format it.

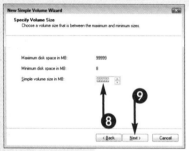

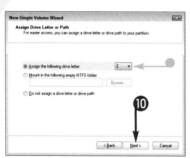

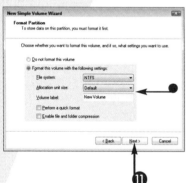

The Specify Volume Size screen opens.

8 Type a size for this new volume in megabytes. (If you ultimately plan to create just one volume, accept the default volume size.)

9 Click Next.

The Assign Drive Letter or Path screen opens.

● Accept the default settings.

10 Click Next.

The Format Partition screen opens.

● Accept the default settings.

11 Click Next.

The Completing the New Simple Volume Wizard screen opens.

12 Review your choices.

13 Click Finish.

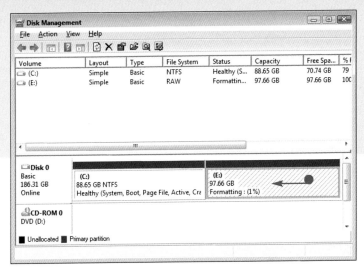

● Windows automatically formats the new partition.

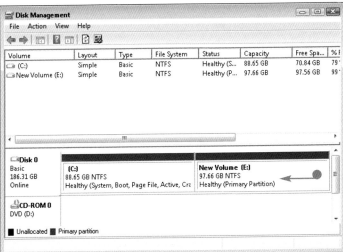

● The partition is now ready for use.

Did You Know?

There are three types of file systems: NTFS, FAT32, and FAT (also known as FAT16), which is rarely used. Of the three, NTFS is the preferred system for Windows Vista. In order to provide better security and improved support for larger hard drives, NTFS can automatically recover from some disk-related errors — something FAT32 and FAT16 cannot do. If, however, you plan to run an earlier version of Windows in a separate partition on your machine, that partition should use a FAT32 file system.

PASSWORDS:
Set a User Password

When you set a password, you prevent anyone who does not know the password from logging on to your PC and accessing your files.

The most frequently used password is the word "password." Pet names and birth dates are also common. These are not good passwords because they can be easily guessed by anyone who knows you. Instead, use a password that is at least eight characters long; does not contain your username, real name, or the name of your company; does not contain a complete word; and contains a combination of uppercase letters, lowercase letters, numbers, and symbols.

For an added layer of protection, you should change your password frequently — ideally every 30 to 90 days. To quickly change your password on-the-fly, log in to the account whose password you want to change, press Ctrl+Alt+Delete, and click Change a Password. Type your old password, type the new password, type the new password a second time to confirm it, and press Enter.

Note that these steps pertain to PCs that are not on a domain. To change a password for a PC on a domain, click the Start button, click Control Panel, click User Accounts once, and click User Accounts again in the screen that appears. Next, click Manage User Accounts. On the Users tab, click the account for which you want to create a password, click Reset Password, type the new password in the New Password field and again in the Confirm New Password field, and click OK.

See also>> **Security Center**

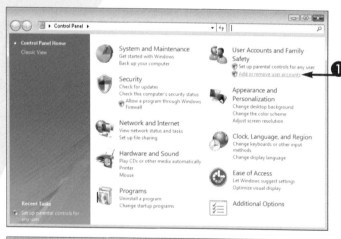

① In the Control Panel window, click Add or Remove User Accounts under User Accounts and Family Safety.

Note: *If prompted, type the administrator password or click Continue.*

The Manage Accounts window opens.

② Click the account for which you want to set a password.

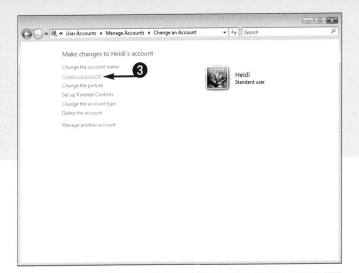

The Change an Account window opens.

3 Click Create a Password.

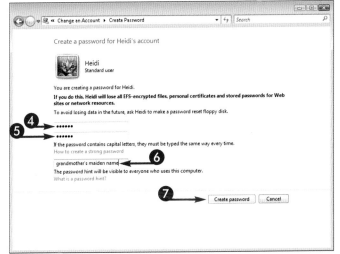

The Create Password window opens.

4 Type the string of characters you want to use as the password.

5 Retype the string of characters.

6 Optionally, type a password hint.

Note: The hint you type will be visible to anyone who attempts to log in to your PC.

7 Click Create Password.

Windows password-protects the user account.

Caution!

You should write your password down — but store it somewhere safe and private. Alternatively, create a password reset disk. (See Vista's Help files for details.) Failure to do so means that if you lose your password, it will need to be reset by the administrator — and as a result, you may lose access to encrypted files or e-mail messages on your PC, as well as stored passwords for Web sites and network resources. Worse, if you forget the password for your PC's administrator account and there are no other user accounts on the computer, your only option is to reinstall Windows — which means you will lose all your files.

Important!

To change passwords for any accounts that are not your own, log in as an administrator.

PERFORMANCE INFORMATION AND TOOLS:
Assess Your Computer's Performance

Windows Vista's Performance Information and Tools window lists your computer's Windows Experience Index base score, which gauges the performance and overall capability of your computer's hardware configuration.

The base score is meant to help users determine what types of software their PC can handle, with higher scores denoting increased performance. For example, a computer whose base score is 2 or lower can handle general tasks such as word processing or Internet searching, but not more complex programs such as some games. In contrast, a computer with

a base score of 4 or 5 can support programs using high-end graphics, 3D gaming, or even HDTV.

To determine the base score, Windows evaluates your PC's RAM, CPU, hard drive, and graphics capabilities, giving each a *sub-score*. Windows then uses the lowest sub-score to establish your system's base score. If your base score is insufficient for the types of programs you want to run, you can upgrade your hardware components; to determine which components need upgrading, view their sub-scores.

See also>>   **Task Manager**

1 In Control Panel, click System and Maintenance.

The System and Maintenance window opens.

2 Click Performance Information and Tools.

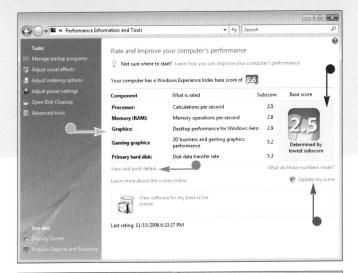

The Performance Information and Tools window opens.

- View the sub-scores for each component here.

- View the base score here.

- If, after installing new hardware, you want to see whether the score has changed, click Update My Score.

- To view more information about your computer's hardware, click View and Print Details.

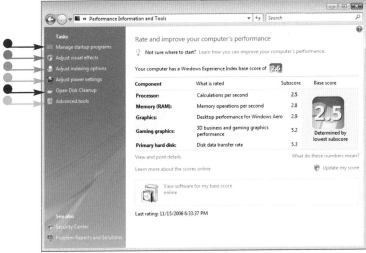

- Click Manage Startup Programs to limit the number of programs that launch at system startup, thereby speeding the startup process.

- Click Adjust Visual Effects to change how menus and windows appear to optimize performance.

- Click here to adjust indexing options in order to improve Windows' search functionality.

- Click Adjust Power Settings to improve your computer's efficiency by adjusting its power settings.

- Click Open Disk Cleanup to delete unnecessary files on your hard disk, thereby increasing storage space.

- Click Advanced Tools to access advanced tools such as Event Viewer and System Information.

Did You Know?

Another way to see information about your computer's performance is via the Performance tab in Task Manager. (To view it, right-click the taskbar, click Task Manager, and click the Performance tab.) At the top of this tab are graphs that illustrate the percentage of the CPU in use (a higher percentage means that more CPU resources are being consumed) as well as how much RAM (that is, physical memory) is being used. Below the graph is a series of tables that provide more information about your PC's consumption of CPU and RAM. For an even more detailed view, click the Resource Monitor.

P

PHISHING FILTER:
Avoid Phishing Scams

Phishing (pronounced *fishing*) is an attempt by a malicious party to obtain private information from an unsuspecting computer user. Typically, phishing involves an e-mail message that appears to be from a legitimate source such as a bank, credit card company, or reputable online storefront. This message informs the user that his or her account information must be updated and instructs the user to click a link in order to access a Web site where he or she can accomplish just that.

When the user clicks the link, however, he or she is not directed to the trusted source's Web site. Instead, the user is directed to a bogus site that is designed to mimic the trusted site in order to steal personal information such as passwords, credit card numbers, social security numbers, and/or bank account numbers.

Internet Explorer's Phishing Filter helps detect these fraudulent Web sites. You can configure Phishing Filter to automatically check all Web sites to determine whether they are fraudulent, or you can run the filter manually on a case-by-case basis.

See also>> Internet Explorer 7

Enable Automatic Site Checking

1. Within Internet Explorer, click Tools.

2. Click Phishing Filter.

3. Click Turn On Automatic Website Checking.

The Microsoft Phishing Filter window opens.

4. Click Turn On Automatic Phishing Filter.

5. Click OK.

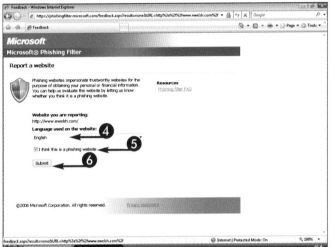

Report a Fraudulent Web Site

① With the site you want to report open in your browser, click Tools.

② Click Phishing Filter.

③ Click Report This Website.

A Microsoft Web page opens.

④ Choose the language used on the suspect Web site.

⑤ Click the I Think This Is a Phishing Website checkbox to select it.

⑥ Click Submit.

Note: *You can also follow these steps to notify Microsoft that a site it has flagged as fraudulent is in fact trustworthy — just leave the checkbox unchecked.*

TIPS

Caution!
Never include personal information in an e-mail or instant message. These types of transmissions are not secure, and may open you up to identity theft.

Caution!
If you receive an e-mail with a suspicious link, do not click it — especially if the e-mail is from a stranger.

Attention!
Regularly review your financial statements. If you discover you have been a victim of fraud, file a report with the local police, change the passwords or PINs on all your online accounts, contact your bank and credit card issuers, and place a fraud alert on your credit reports (your bank or financial advisor can tell you how). Finally, if you are aware of any accounts that were opened fraudulently, close them.

PHISHING FILTER:
Avoid Phishing Scams (Continued)

The Phishing Filter works by determining whether the URL of a Web site you visit appears on a list of known legitimate sites. If not, the filter then analyzes the site to determine whether it features characteristics of phishing sites. If so, the filter deems the site "suspicious."

Optionally, you can configure the Phishing Filter to forward suspicious sites to Microsoft for further assessment. Microsoft then determines whether the site appears on its regularly updated list of known phishing sites.

If the Phishing Filter determines that a site you are attempting to visit is, in fact, fraudulent, it displays a warning page; you can choose to continue or to stop the operation. If the Phishing Filter deems the site suspicious, you will be so notified in your browser's Address bar.

If you opt out of configuring Internet Explorer to use the Phishing Filter automatically, you can use the filter manually to check a site's viability.

See also>> Internet Explorer 7

Disable Automatic Site Checking

① Within Internet Explorer, click Tools.

② Click Phishing Filter.

③ Click Turn Off Automatic Web Site Checking.

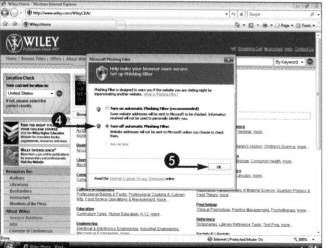

The Microsoft Phishing Filter window opens.

④ Click Turn Off Automatic Phishing Filter.

⑤ Click OK.

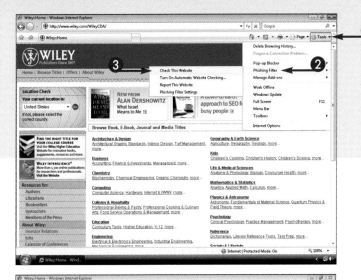

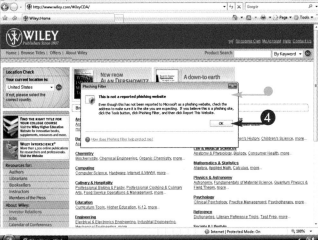

Manually Check a Web Site

① With the phishing Web site open in your browser, click Tools.

② Click Phishing Filter.

③ Click Check This Website.

● Phishing Filter checks the site.

④ Click OK.

Caution!

If you encounter a Web site that tells you to ignore warnings issued about the site by the Phishing Filter, be skeptical. Chances are, the site is indeed fraudulent. If it is not, the owner of the site should contact Microsoft to clear up the problem rather than posting such a message to site visitors.

PHONE AND MODEM OPTIONS:
Set Up a Dialing Location

If you plan to use your PC for telephony or with a dial-up modem, use Phone and Modem Options to set up *dialing locations* so your PC has instant access to the information it needs to place calls or instigate a dial-up connection. If you use your PC in multiple locations — for example, at home and at work — you can establish a dialing location for each.

The first time you launch Phone and Modem Options, you are prompted by the Location Information dialog box to enter the location information for your current dialing location. Fill in the requested information and click OK. Then follow the steps here to add a second location.

See also>> **Phone and Modem Options**

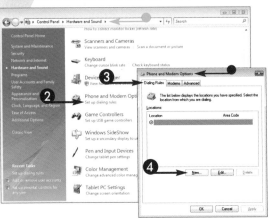

① In Control Panel, click Hardware and Sound.

● The Hardware and Sound window opens.

② Click Set Up Dialing Rules under Phone and Modem Options.

● The Phone and Modem Options dialog box opens.

③ Click the Dialing Rules tab.

④ Click New.

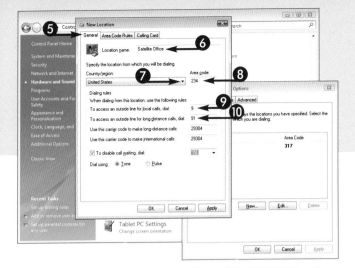

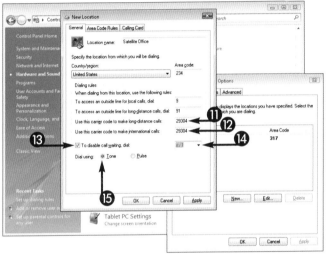

The New Location dialog box opens.

⑤ Click the General tab.

⑥ Type a name for the new dialing location.

⑦ Choose the location's country or region from the list.

⑧ Type the location's area code.

⑨ Type the number required to access an outside line.

⑩ Type the number required to access an outside line for a long-distance call.

⑪ Type the carrier code needed to place a long-distance call.

⑫ Type the carrier code needed to place an international call.

⑬ Click here to disable call waiting when the computer is online.

⑭ Enter the number (obtained from your phone company) the computer should dial to disable call waiting.

⑮ If your phone system uses pulse dialing, click Pulse. Otherwise, click Tone.

Remove It!

If you no longer use one of the locations you have established, you can delete the dialing rules you set for it. To do so, click the location in the Dialing Rules tab of the Phone and Modem Options dialog box and click the Delete button. Alternatively, to change some of the rules for the selected location, click Edit.

More Options!

The Modems tab in the Phone and Modem Options dialog box offers access to modem-related settings, and enables you to install (and uninstall) a modem.

Important!

It is a good idea to disable call waiting if you plan to use a dial-up modem to access the Internet. That way, if someone calls while you are online, your online session will not be disconnected.

P

When you set up a dialing location, you establish *dialing rules*, such as whether your computer must dial a certain number to access an outside line.

In addition to setting up dialing rules, which enable you to dial out, you can also use the Phone and Modem Options to establish area code rules. These rules specify whether or not certain prefixes within an area code are long distance.

You can also configure your system to use a calling card in some circumstances. To do so, click the

Calling Card tab in the New Locations dialog box; then click the New button. Use the tabs in the New Calling Card dialog box that appears to enter the access number you need to dial in order to use the calling card, your account number, your PIN, and any other pertinent information. When you are finished, click OK.

See also>> **Phone and Modem Options**

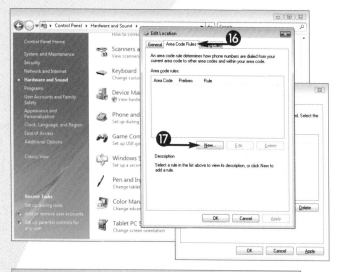

⑯ If some prefixes in your area code are considered local while others are long distance, create a new area code rule. Click the Area Code Rules tab.

⑰ Click New.

● The New Area Code Rule dialog box opens.

⑱ Type the area code.

⑲ Click Include Only the Prefixes in the List Below.

⑳ Click Add.

● The Add Prefix dialog box opens.

㉑ Type the prefix that the rule will affect (this example uses a prefix that is considered long distance).

㉒ Click OK.

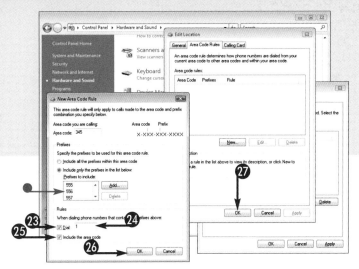

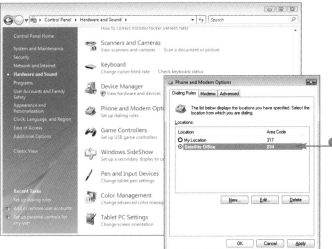

- The prefix is added.

㉓ Click the Dial checkbox to select it.

㉔ Type **1** in the corresponding field.

㉕ Click the Include the Area Code checkbox to select it.

㉖ Click OK to close the New Area Code Rule dialog box.

㉗ Click OK to close the New Location dialog box.

- The new location is added.

More Options!

Click the Advanced tab in Phone and Modem Options to view the telephony providers — that is, the software used to communicate with telephony-related hardware such as modems — installed on your Vista PC. From this tab, you can add, remove, or edit the properties of these providers.

PHOTO GALLERY:
Create and View a Slide Show

Photo Gallery enables you to view and organize pictures and videos on your computer. Photos in your Pictures folder appear in Photo Gallery by default, but you can add pictures from any other folders to Photo Gallery.

In addition to enabling you to edit a digital image — for example, changing its colors, improving its brightness and contrast, straightening it, cropping it, removing red eye, and so on — Photo Gallery makes it possible for you to view your pictures in a full-screen slide show. Not only can you select which images appear in the show, you can specify the speed at which the show plays.

While the slide show runs automatically by default, moving from one picture to the next without any mouse or keyboard input from you, you can take control of the show whenever you like.

See also>>   Photo Gallery

See also>>   Photo Gallery: Edit

Photo Gallery: Manage

1 Click Start.

2 Click All Programs.

3 Click Windows Photo Gallery.

Windows Photo Gallery opens.

④ While pressing the Ctrl key on your keyboard, click the pictures you want to include in your slide show to select them.

⑤ Click the Play Slide Show button.

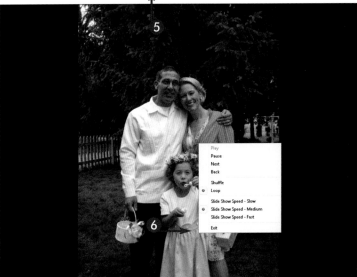

Photo Gallery starts the slide show.

⑥ Right-click the screen to access commands for the slide show.

More Options!

By default, your slide show will play in a loop, stopping only when you exit the show. If you want it to play only once, right-click the screen while the slide show is playing and click Loop to deselect it.

More Options!

To shuffle the order of the photos in the slide show, right-click the screen while the slide show is playing and click Shuffle.

PHOTO GALLERY:
Edit Pictures

Using Photo Gallery's editing tools, you can adjust a photo's brightness, contrast, and color; crop it; and remove the pesky red-eye effect that makes even your angelic grandmother resemble a demon.

To access the editing tools, click the picture you want to edit, and then click Fix. The available tools are arranged in the Fix pane in the order they should be used: Adjust Exposure (that is, brightness and contrast), Adjust Color, Cropping, and Red Eye. Although you are free to edit your photos in any order you choose, editing your photos in this order yields the best results.

Regardless of which editing tools you use, you should always keep a copy of the original image. That way, if you botch the edits, the photo is not permanently damaged. To make a copy of a photo, double-click it, click File, click Make a Copy, and click Save.

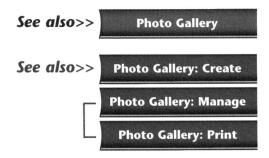

See also>> Photo Gallery

See also>> Photo Gallery: Create

Photo Gallery: Manage

Photo Gallery: Print

Adjust Exposure and Color

① In Photo Gallery, click the photo you want to adjust.

② Click Fix.

③ Click Auto Adjust.

Windows optimizes the brightness, contrast, color temperature, and tint of the image.

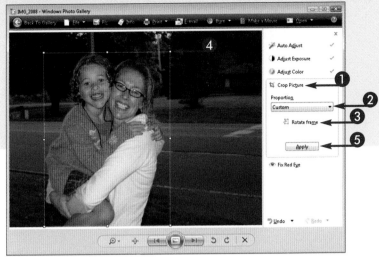

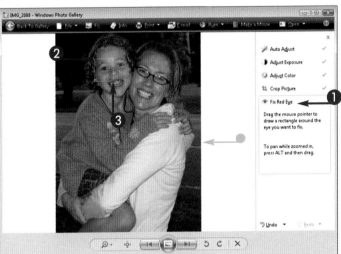

Crop a Picture

1. In Windows Photo Gallery, with the picture you want to edit displayed in the Fix pane, click Crop Picture.

   The Crop Picture settings appear.

2. To change the picture's size, choose a standard print proportion in the Proportion menu or click Custom to set a custom size.

3. To rotate the crop frame vertically or horizontally, click Rotate Frame.

4. Drag the crop frame to the desired spot to crop the picture.

5. Click Apply.

   ● The picture is cropped.

Remove Red Eye

1. In Windows Photo Gallery, with the picture you want to edit displayed in the Fix pane, click Fix Red Eye.

2. Click the upper-left corner of an eye that needs correcting.

3. Drag the cursor to the lower-right corner of the eye to select the eye.

   Windows removes the red eye.

4. Repeat Steps 2 and 3 to remove red eye from any remaining eyes in the photo.

 TIPS

Remove It!
If you do not like the results of an adjustment, click the Undo button. To undo all changes made to the image, click the arrow next to the Undo button and click Revert to Original.

Try This!
You can change a color image into black and white by clicking Adjust Color in the Fix pane and dragging the Saturation slider all the way to the left.

More Options!
If clicking Auto Adjust does not yield the desired results, click Adjust Exposure and drag the Brightness and Contrast sliders to adjust the levels manually. Then adjust the colors manually by clicking Adjust Color and dragging the Color Temperature, Tint, and Saturation sliders.

PHOTO GALLERY:
Manage Pictures

In the days of print photography, people painstakingly organized their favorite photos in albums, haphazardly stashing the rest in shoeboxes. In contrast, digital photos can be stored, located, and viewed on your computer with the click of a button.

Photo Gallery, which displays the photos in your Pictures folder, is Vista's tool for doing just that. For example, you can rename image files in batches, replacing the filenames your camera creates (think DC000591.jpg) with more meaningful names (e.g., MexicoTrip.jpg), on several image files at once.

In addition, you can *tag* your image files — that is, add descriptive keywords to the picture's metadata.

For example, if you enjoy taking photos of insects, you might tag those photos with the word "insect" as you might tag a photo of your mom with the word "mom," or a photo taken during a wedding with the word "wedding" or with the names of the bride and groom.

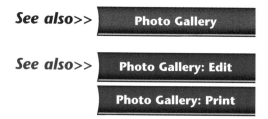

See also>> Photo Gallery

See also>> Photo Gallery: Edit

Photo Gallery: Print

Batch-Name Photo Files

❶ In the Windows Photo Gallery window, click the pictures you want to rename while pressing the Ctrl key on your keyboard.

❷ Right-click a selected picture.

❸ Click Rename.

❹ Type a name for the files and press Enter.

The name is applied to each selected picture, along with a sequential number to differentiate the files.

Tag Photo Files

1 In the Windows Photo Gallery window, click the pictures you want to tag while pressing the Ctrl key on your keyboard.

2 Right-click a selected picture.

3 Click Add Tags.

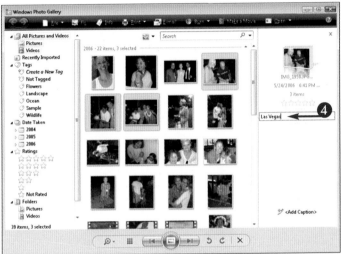

4 Type the tag and press Enter.

Note: You can apply a tag to a photo by dragging the photo to the desired tag in the Navigation pane.

Did You Know?

By default, Photo Gallery displays only the pictures stored in your Pictures folder and all its subfolders. (Note that if Movie Maker is installed on your PC, videos will also be visible in Photo Gallery.) To add other folders to Photo Gallery, click File in the Photo Gallery window, click Add Folder to Gallery, click the folder you want to add, and click OK. Remove a folder you added by right-clicking it and choosing Remove from Gallery.

More Options!

In addition to renaming your files and tagging them, you can apply ratings to your files of no stars to five stars, as well as add captions. You can then organize or search for files based on their rating or caption.

PHOTO GALLERY:
Manage Pictures (Continued)

The easiest way to find pictures that you have recently imported from your camera is to click Recently Imported in Photo Gallery's Navigation pane. If, however, it has been more than a few weeks since you imported the photos, you will need some other way to find them.

You can, of course, click All Pictures and Video in Photo Gallery's Navigation pane and sift through your images, but doing so can be time-consuming — especially if you store many, *many* digital photos on your PC.

Fortunately, Photo Gallery enables you to locate your image files by name, by tag, or by rating. You can

also locate your files by searching by file type or by date taken.

Photo files are displayed as thumbnails by default. To see a larger version, hover your mouse pointer over the thumbnail or double-click it.

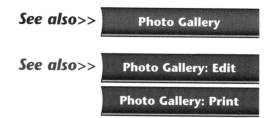

See also>> Photo Gallery

See also>> Photo Gallery: Edit

Photo Gallery: Print

Locate Tagged Files

① In the Navigation pane of the Windows Photo Gallery window, click Tags.

A list of tags you have applied to your photos appears.

② Click a tag to see all pictures that contain that tag.

● Photos containing the selected tag are displayed.

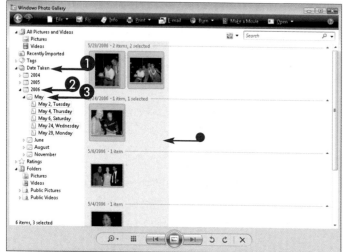

Locate Files by Date

① In the Navigation pane of the Windows Photo Gallery window, click Date Taken.

② Click the year that the photos you are searching for were taken.

③ Click the month the photos were taken.

● Photos taken in the selected month are displayed.

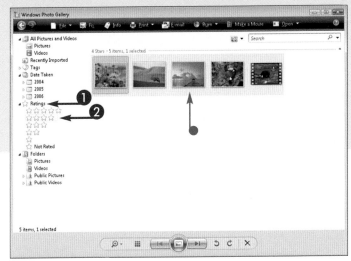

Locate Rated Files

1 In the Navigation pane of the Windows Photo Gallery window, click Ratings.

2 Click a rating.

● Photos with the rating you selected are displayed, as are all photos with a higher rating.

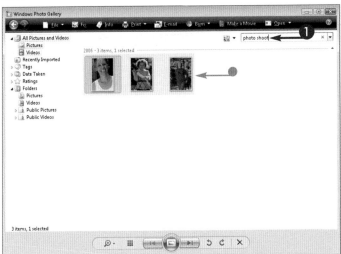

Search for Files

1 In the Windows Photo Gallery window, type the filename, a tag, a caption, or a file extension in the Search field and press Enter.

● Photo Gallery displays photos matching the search criteria you typed.

TIP

Did You Know?

To transfer photos from your digital camera to your PC, connect the devices with a USB cable (or, if the camera and computer support Bluetooth, put them in range), turn on your camera, and follow the instructions in the AutoPlay dialog box that appears. If AutoPlay is disabled, open Photo Gallery's Tools menu, click Import from Camera or Scanner, and follow the instructions. If your camera does not use a USB cable or support Bluetooth, you may need to employ the software that came with your camera to transfer your images from your camera to your computer instead of using Photo Gallery. Alternatively, if your camera stores images on a removable memory card, you can use a card reader to copy the images to your PC.

PHOTO GALLERY:
Print a Picture

Even though you can store and view photos on your computer, sometimes there is just no substitute for a photo print. For example, you might want to store your favorite prints in an album or frame them for display in your home or office.

Assuming you have a printer capable of printing photos, you can make prints of your digital pictures from within Photo Gallery.

How good your print will look depends on several factors, among them the overall quality and resolution

of the digital picture, the type of paper you use, the type of ink you use, and the printer settings you configure.

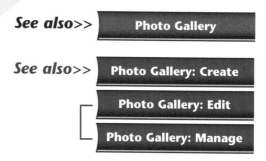

See also>> | Photo Gallery

See also>> | Photo Gallery: Create

Photo Gallery: Edit

Photo Gallery: Manage

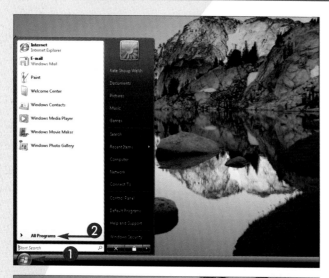

① Click Start.

② Click All Programs.

③ Click Windows Photo Gallery.

Windows Photo Gallery opens.

4 Click the picture you want to print.

5 Click Print.

6 Click Print.

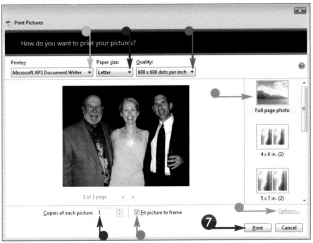

The Print Pictures dialog box opens.

● Select the printer you want to use from this list of available printers.

● Choose the paper size.

● Select the print resolution.

● Choose a print size.

● Specify the number of copies you want to print.

● Click the Fit Picture to Frame checkbox to select it if you want your print to contain no borders.

● For additional print options, click here.

7 Click Print.

Did You Know?
You can also print your photos from within the Pictures folder.

More Options!
Click the Options button for additional print-related options, such as Sharpen for Printing, as well as for access to color-management and printer-properties settings.

Try This!
In addition to enabling you to send a print job to your own printer, you can also use Windows Photo Gallery as a conduit for ordering prints via an online printing company such as Shutterfly. To do so, select the file or files you want to print, click the Print button, and choose Order Prints.

POWER PLAN:
Choose a Power Plan

Windows Vista includes three power plans: Power Saver, designed to save energy by reducing performance and used primarily to prolong battery life on a mobile PC; High Performance, designed to maximize system performance; and the default plan, Balanced, designed for moderate consumption and performance. (Computer manufacturers sometimes provide additional power plans as well.)

If none of these plans suit your needs, you can modify the settings of a plan as needed. Alternatively, create a plan from scratch by clicking Create a Power Plan in the Power Options window and follow the onscreen instructions.

1 In the Control Panel window, click System and Maintenance.

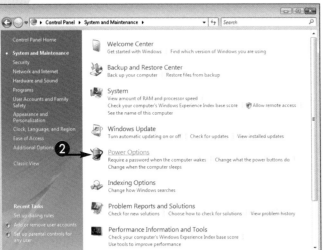

The System and Maintenance window opens.

2 Click Power Options.

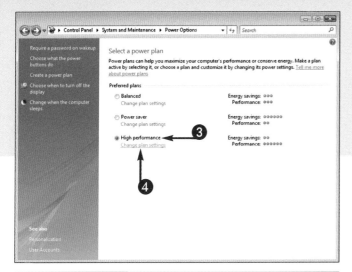

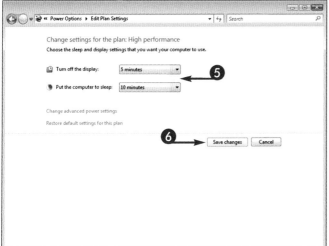

The Power Options screen opens.

③ Click the power plan you want to use.

Note: *If the power plan options are grayed out, click the Change Settings That Are Currently Unavailable link. Then, if prompted, type the administrator password or click Continue.*

④ To modify the selected power plan, click its Change Plan Settings link.

The Change Settings for the Plan window opens.

⑤ Adjust the available settings as desired.

⑥ Click Save Changes.

Caution!
You may want to experiment with power settings to see how your system responds to lower energy modes.

Remove It!
To delete a power plan that you created, open Power Options in Control Panel, click Change Plan Settings under the plan you want to delete, click Delete This Plan, and click OK.

Did You Know?
If you are using a mobile PC, use the battery meter to monitor power consumption. It displays the percentage of battery charge remaining, enables you to choose a different power plan, and indicates whether the battery is, in fact, powering the computer or if the computer is plugged in. To view the battery meter, hover your mouse pointer over its icon in the taskbar.

PREVIOUS VERSIONS:
Revert to a Previous Version of a Document

If you have ever saved changes to a file or folder only to later wish you had not, then Previous Versions is for you. With Previous Versions, you can revert to an earlier version of a file or folder. Being able to revert to an earlier version of a file or folder is also handy in the event a file or folder becomes damaged.

Previous Versions uses two methods to revert to an earlier version of a file or folder. One is to revert to a backup copy of the file — that is, a copy created via

the File and Folder Backup Wizard. Another is to revert to a shadow copy of the file or folder — that is, a copy created by Windows automatically between restore points. (In order to enable the use of shadow copies, System Protection must be turned on.)

See also>>

Backup and Restore

File and Folder Backup

① Click Start.

② Click the folder containing the file or folder you want to roll back (here, Documents).

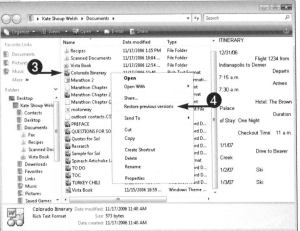

The folder opens.

③ Right-click the file you want to revert to a previous version.

④ Click Restore Previous Versions.

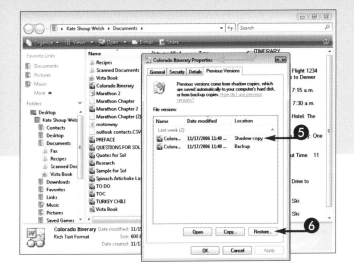

- The file or folder's Properties dialog box opens with the Previous Versions tab displayed.

⑤ Click the backup or shadow file or folder that you want to revert to.

⑥ Click Restore.

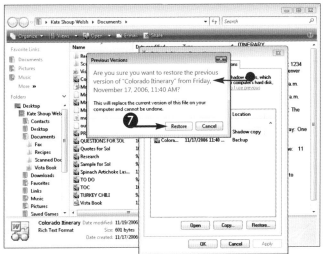

- Windows asks you to confirm that you want to restore the file to its previous version.

⑦ Click Restore.

If the file you selected is a shadow file, the file or folder will be restored.

If the file you selected is a backup file, Windows will launch the Restore Files Wizard; follow the onscreen instructions to restore the file.

Note: If the file you selected is a backup file, you will need to have handy the external media on which the backup file is stored.

Attention!

In certain instances, shadow copies of a previous version of a file or folder may not be available. For example, offline files and folders do not support the use of shadow copies. Alternatively, if your computer is on a network, the network administrator might have disabled the use of shadow copies. Also, some folders, such as those that relate to system operations and settings, do not support shadow copies under any circumstances.

Caution!

Be aware that when you revert to a previous version of a file or folder, the more recent version will be deleted — an operation that cannot be undone.

P

PRINT:
Print a File

If you can view a file on your computer, chances are you can print it — assuming that your PC is connected to and configured to work with a printer and that your printer has adequate paper and ink.

The quickest way to print a file is to right-click it and choose Print. Windows prints the file using your default settings.

If you want to choose print options or change printer settings, you should print the file from within its

associated program rather than from within a folder. For example, if you want to print a WordPad document, open the document in WordPad and choose Print from the File menu.

The quality of your print will depend on your printer and paper quality, as well as the overall quality of the file being printed.

See also>> **Add Printer Wizard**

① Click Start.

② Choose the folder containing the file you want to print (here, Documents).

● The folder opens.

③ Locate the file you want to print and double-click it.

The file opens in its associated program (in this case, WordPad).

● The Windows Print Preview function enables you to see what your print will look like before you send the job to the printer. To use it, click File and click Print Preview.

④ Click File.

⑤ Click Print.

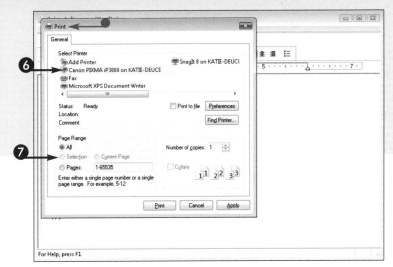

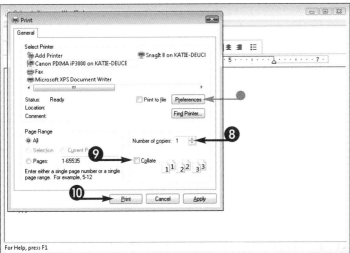

● The Print dialog box opens.

Note: *The available settings in the Print dialog box may differ from what you see here depending on the program and printer you are using.*

6 If your computer is connected to multiple printers, click the one you want to use.

7 Choose the page range. To print the entire document, choose All; alternatively, print the selected portion of the file, the current page, or pages that you specify.

8 Indicate how many copies of the open file you want to print.

9 Click Collate if you want your printer to collate the printed copies.

● You may be able to access more print settings, such as page orientation, paper size, double-sided printing, and so on by clicking a Preferences or Advanced button.

10 Click Print.

The document is printed.

Remove It!
To remove a printer, open the Printers window in Control Panel, right-click the printer, and click Delete.

Did You Know?
You can cancel a print job from the print queue — that is, the window listing print jobs that are currently being printed or waiting to be printed. Access the queue by double-clicking the printer in Control Panel's Printers window; then right-click the job you want to abort and click Cancel in the shortcut menu that appears. (You can also pause or resume a print job from this shortcut menu.) Alternatively, cancel all items in the queue by clicking the Printer menu in the print queue window and choosing Cancel All Documents.

PRINTERS:
Share a Printer

If your home or small office has a network that connects two or more computers, then you can share a printer that is installed on one computer among the other network-connected computers.

To share a printer, you first need to add the printer as a shared resource on your network. Then, from the other computers where you want to share the printer, you can add the printer as an available device. Once you do this, a printer that is directly installed on one computer becomes available for printing to the other computers on the same network.

You can share more than one printer. For example, if you have five computers on a network and one has a standard inkjet printer while another has a laser printer, then you can share both printers, configuring each computer on the network to make both printers available to them. This saves the cost of purchasing a separate printer for each computer.

See also>>  **Add Printer Wizard**

See also>> **Print: Print a File**

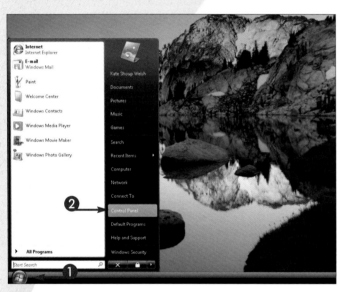

① On the networked computer that is attached directly to the printer you want to share, click Start.

② Click Control Panel.

The Control Panel window opens.

③ Click Network and Internet.

276

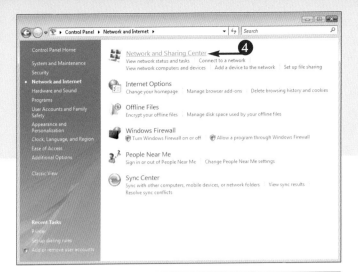

The Network and Internet window opens.

④ Click Network and Sharing Center.

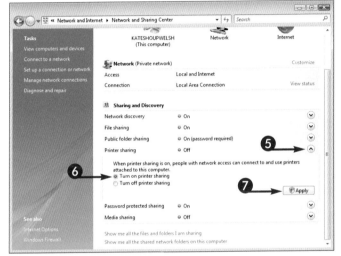

The Network and Sharing Center opens.

⑤ Click the arrow button to the right of Printer Sharing.

⑥ Click Turn On Printer Sharing.

⑦ Click Apply.

Note: *If prompted, type the administrator password or click Continue.*

P

TIPS

Try This!

To use a shared printer, other computers on the network must first connect to it. To connect, click File and click Network on a networked PCs to which the printer is *not* connected; an icon for the printer should appear in the computer's Network folder. Double-click the printer to add it to the computer and install the necessary printer drivers. (These steps assume that other computers on the network are running Vista. If that is not the case, review the computer's Help files for more information.)

Try This!

To send a print job to the shared printer from a computer to which the printer is not connected, simply choose the printer from the list of printer options in the Print dialog box.

PROBLEM REPORTS AND SOLUTIONS:
Review Problem Reports and Find Solutions

If a program on your Windows Vista computer experiences problems, Windows can compile information about the problem, such as the name and version of the program experiencing problems and the date and time at which the problem occurred, into a *problem report*. Windows can then send the problem report to Microsoft via the Internet to determine whether there is a known solution. (Note that if the problem you experience is new, is particularly complex, or will affect a great number

of users, Microsoft may request that you supply additional information about it.)

You can manually send problem reports and check for solutions at the time of your choosing by opening the Problem Reports and Solutions window. This window displays problem reports, as well links to any known solutions to those problems. Alternatively, you can set up your Windows Vista PC to send problem reports and check for solutions automatically when a problem occurs.

① In Control Panel, click System and Maintenance.

● The System and Maintenance window opens.

② Click Problem Reports and Solutions.

The Problem Reports and Solutions window opens.

● If Windows has found a solution to a problem that your computer has reported, click the solution.

● To view information about an unsolved problem, click the problem.

● Click Check for New Solutions to determine whether any of your PC's reported problems are newly solved.

● Click here to view a list of problems your PC has experienced.

③ Click Change Settings.

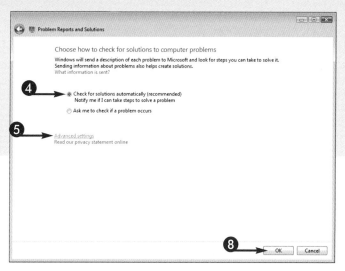

The Choose How to Check for Solutions to Computer Problems window opens.

④ Unless you want to always search for solutions manually, click Check for Solutions Automatically.

⑤ Click Advanced Settings.

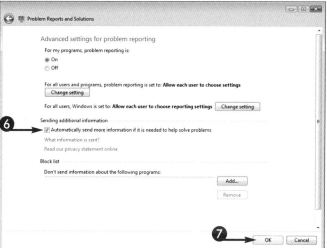

The Advanced Settings for Problem Reporting window opens.

⑥ If you want your PC to automatically send more information about a problem to Microsoft when requested, click here.

⑦ Click OK in the Advanced Settings for Problem Reporting window.

⑧ Click OK in the Choose How to Check for Solutions to Computer Problems window.

Attention!

As mentioned, a typical problem report contains the name and version of the program experiencing problems and the date and time at which the problem occurred. If more information is needed, it will usually be a file or a part of a file that may help identify a problem. Note that Windows does not intentionally collect personal information of any kind. Moreover, before a report that might contain personal information is sent, Windows gives you the opportunity to review the information and cancel the send operation—even if you have configured Windows to send additional information automatically.

PROGRAM COMPATIBILITY WIZARD:
Enable Older Programs to Run

If a program designed to work in an older version of Windows does not run properly in Vista, use the Program Compatibility Wizard to try to enable the older software to operate. The wizard simulates the behavior of earlier versions of Windows in an attempt to "trick" the older software into running. (Note that the Program Compatibility Wizard should not be used with older virus programs, disk utilities, or system programs; doing so may result in lost data or an insecure system.)

When you run the wizard, you can select options that you think will work best with a particular piece of software.

After you run the Program Compatibility Wizard and load the older program, watch carefully for signs of system instability. If Windows misbehaves while the software is open, then you can relaunch the wizard, or consider using a different program.

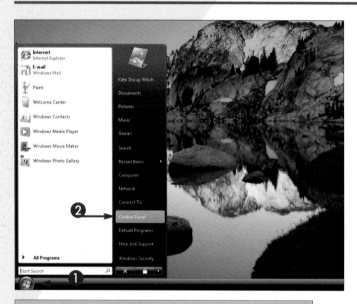

① Click Start.

② Click Control Panel.

The Control Panel window opens.

③ Click Programs.

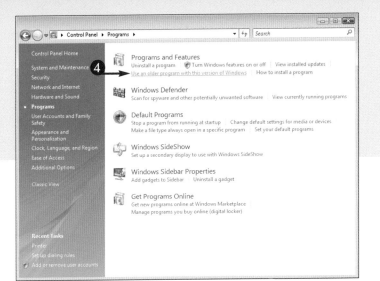

The Programs window opens.

④ Under Programs and Features, click Use an Older Program with This Version of Windows.

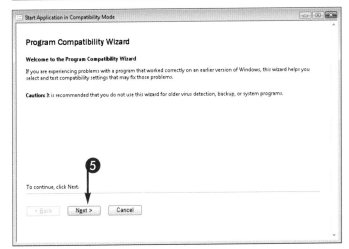

The Program Compatibility Wizard starts.

⑤ Click Next, and follow the remaining steps in the wizard.

Did You Know?
In addition to the Program Compatibility Wizard, Vista includes a feature called Program Compatibility Assistant. It differs from the wizard in that it runs automatically when it detects a compatibility problem, notifying you of the problem and offering to fix it the next time the program is run, or, in serious cases, preventing the program from running.

More Options!
You can run the Program Compatibility Wizard more than once to test different settings. If the wizard does not work, then ensure that the program's drivers are up-to-date, and run Windows Update before you relaunch the wizard or the program.

QUICK LAUNCH:
Add and Remove Programs on the Quick Launch Bar

The Quick Launch bar, located on the Windows taskbar, contains shortcut buttons to some of the more popular programs in Windows such as Internet Explorer. Unlike other shortcuts, such as the ones on the desktop, the Quick Launch buttons are always visible (provided the Quick Launch bar has been enabled).

If you frequently use a certain program, you can add a button for that program to the Quick Launch bar. Then, anytime you want to open the program, you can simply click its button instead of navigating the Start menu.

Of course, adding too many buttons to the Quick Launch bar can make it hard to quickly locate the button you need. For this reason, you should add buttons for only those programs that you truly use on a regular basis. In the event you find your Quick Launch bar has become too crowded, you can remove buttons from it. (Note that removing a program button from the Quick Launch bar does not delete the program from your computer.)

See also>> **Quick Launch**

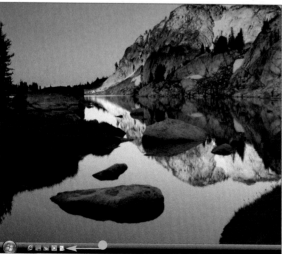

Add a Program

❶ Click Start.

❷ Locate the program you want to add to the Quick Launch bar and click it.

❸ Drag the program's shortcut icon to the Quick Launch bar.

● A button for the program is added.

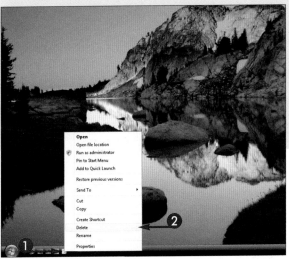

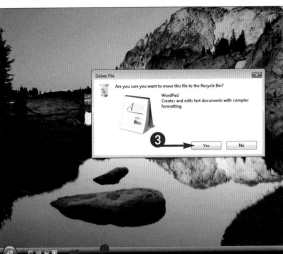

Remove an Icon

1 Right-click the button you want to remove.

2 Click Delete.

3 Windows asks if you really want to remove the button; click Yes.

● The button is removed.

Attention!

If, when you drag a shortcut icon to the toolbar, it fails to "stick," the taskbar might be locked. To determine whether this is the case, right-click the taskbar. If the Lock the Taskbar menu entry has a checkmark, then the taskbar is locked. Unlock the taskbar by clicking Lock the Taskbar to remove the checkbox.

Attention!

If you have buttons for several open programs in the taskbar, the Quick Launch bar may become condensed. Click and drag the toolbar sizing handle on the right side of the Quick Launch bar to the right to expand the bar. (If the handle is not visible, then there is not room on the taskbar to expand the Quick Launch bar.)

QUOTAS:
Set Space Quotas

If you share your PC with others, you might want to set quotas to ensure that no single user monopolizes the space on the PC's hard drive. When you set quotas, you can instruct Vista to warn users as they near their limits, and to deny additional disk space to those users if they attempt to exceed their allotted space.

You can determine how much space your drive has available by opening the Computer folder and locating the drive. (To open the Computer folder, click Start and click Computer.) You can set your quotas based on the information you find here. If, for example, your hard drive boasts 100 gigabytes,

and if four people use the computer, you might allot each user 25 gigabytes. Alternatively, you might allot users different amounts of disk space, based on their needs.

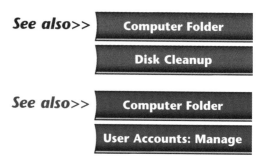

See also>> Computer Folder

Disk Cleanup

See also>> Computer Folder

User Accounts: Manage

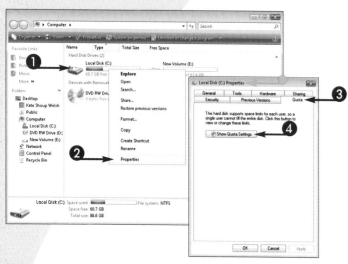

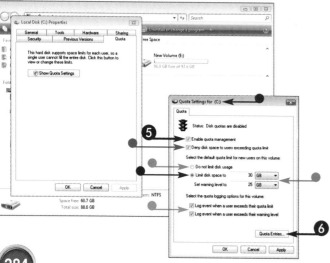

① In the Computer folder, right-click the drive to which you want to apply quotas.

② Click Properties.

● The drive's Properties dialog box opens.

③ Click the Quota tab.

④ Click Show Quota Settings.

   Note: *If prompted, type the administrator password or click Continue.*

● The Quota Settings dialog box opens.

⑤ Click the Enable Quota Management checkbox to select it.

● Click to deny disk space to users who exceed the quota limit.

● Click to provide unlimited disk access to new users by default.

● Click to limit new users' disk usage.

● Set the space limit and the point at which Vista will warn the user that space is low.

● Select these checkboxes to log quota-related events.

⑥ Click Quota Entries.

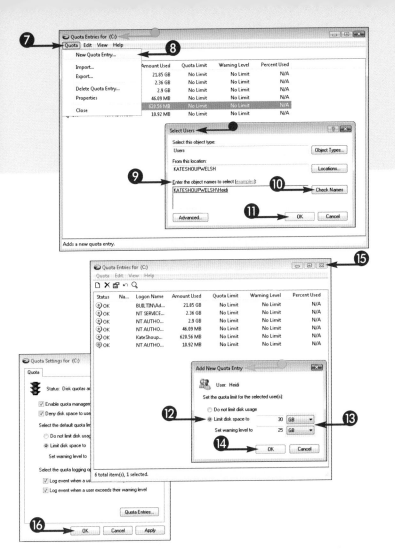

● The Quota Entries window opens.

7 To apply a quota to an existing user, click Quota.

8 Click New Quota Entry.

● The Select Users dialog box opens.

9 Type the user name of the user's account (in this example, **Heidi**).

10 Click Check Names.

Vista ensures that an account with that user name exists on the PC.

11 Click OK.

● The Add New Quota Entry dialog box opens.

12 Click Limit Disk Space To.

13 Set the disk-space limit and warning level.

14 Click OK.

15 Click the Close button.

16 Click OK.

Windows notifies you that enabling the quota system might take a few minutes; click OK.

Attention!

If quotas are enabled, you will likely want to take special care to maintain the hard drive's free space. For example, you should make it a habit to run Disk Cleanup on a regular basis in order to delete the temporary files on your system. Some of these temporary files are the result of Web browsing; others are created by applications to store the contents of open files before they are saved to disk. Over time, you can end up with a gigabyte or more of unneeded files that take up valuable space on your hard drive. Running Disk Cleanup also empties the Recycle Bin.

RATINGS:
Rate Files

In Windows Vista, all files have certain properties, such as Name, Date Modified, Author, File Type, and the like. You can search for files using these properties as criteria.

In addition to providing support for these default properties, Vista also enables you to apply other properties to certain types of files. For example, you can apply a *tag* to some files — that is, a brief description of the file, which is embedded in the file's metadata. In addition, you can rate certain files using a star system — from one to five stars.

After you rate a file, you can locate it by searching by rating.

If a file is rateable, you can rate it using the Details tab of the file's Properties dialog box. Alternatively, set a file's rating using the folder window's Details pane.

See also>>

Search Folder

See also>>

File and Folder Management: View

Tags

Set a Rating in the Details Pane

① Click Start.

② Click the folder containing the file you want to rate (here, Pictures).

The Pictures folder opens.

③ Click the file you want to rate.

④ In the Details pane, click the star that represents the rating you want to apply.

⑤ Click Save.

Set a Rating in the Properties Dialog Box

R

1 Right-click the file you want to rate.

2 Click Properties.

● The Properties dialog box opens.

3 Click the Details tab.

4 Click the star that represents the rating you want to apply.

5 Click OK.

Remove It!

To remove a file's rating — or any other property you have applied to the file, such as a tag or caption — click the Details tab in the file's Properties dialog box and click Remove Properties and Personal Information. The Remove Properties dialog box opens; click Create a Copy with All Possible Properties Removed to make a copy of the file with all its properties stripped but leave the original intact. Alternatively, click Remove the Following Properties from This File and click the checkbox next to each property you want to remove (in this case, Rating). Click OK to close the Remove Properties dialog box, and click OK again to close the file's Properties dialog box.

TIP

RECYCLE BIN:
Empty the Recycle Bin

When you delete files in Windows, they do not completely disappear. Instead, they are transferred into the Recycle Bin, where they stay until you empty it. Only then does the Recycle Bin purge these files from your system. In this way, the Recycle Bin allows you one last chance to restore these files before they are permanently lost. Indeed, the sole purpose of the Recycle Bin is to act as a holding area for deleted files.

The Recycle Bin also provides a Restore feature so that you can recover accidentally erased files. You can choose to recover either a single file or every item in the bin.

You should empty the Recycle Bin on a regular basis to keep your hard disk from becoming cluttered with orphaned and unwanted files. Before you purge, determine whether there are any files you need to restore.

See also>> **Recycle Bin**

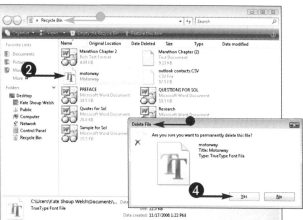

① Double-click the Recycle Bin icon on your desktop.

● The Recycle Bin window opens, displaying files you have deleted.

② To delete a file, click it.

③ Press the Delete key on your keyboard.

● Windows asks if you really want to delete the file.

④ Click Yes.

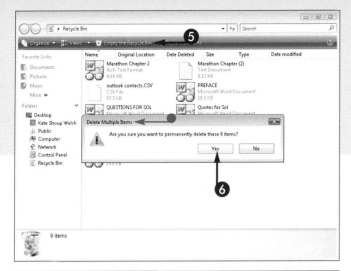

The file is removed from your system.

5 To delete all files in the Recycle Bin, click Empty the Recycle Bin.

● Windows asks if you really want to delete the files.

6 Click Yes.

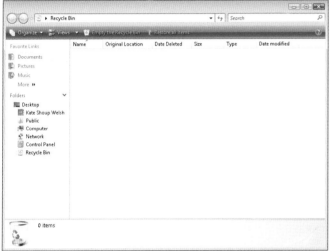

Windows empties the Recycle Bin.

TIPS

Did You Know?
An even easier way to empty the Recycle Bin is to right-click the Recycle Bin icon on your desktop and click Empty Recycle Bin.

Did You Know?
If you accidentally delete a file in a folder other than the Recycle Bin folder, open the Recycle Bin window, right-click the file, and click Restore. (To restore all files in the Recycle Bin, click Restore All Files.) When you restore a file, Windows returns it to the folder from which it was deleted.

More Options!
To immediately remove files from your system when you delete them, bypassing the Recycle Bin, right-click the Recycle Bin icon on your desktop and click Properties. In the General tab of the dialog box that appears, click Do Not Move Files to the Recycle Bin and click OK.

REGIONAL AND LANGUAGE OPTIONS:
Add Language Support

To work with files in a language other than the default language set in Windows, you must add support for that language. When you do, you can specify whether the language should be the input language (i.e., the language you use to enter information into your computer), the display language (i.e., the language used by Windows in wizards, dialog boxes, menus, and so on), or both.

If you plan to use an input language other than English, the standard QWERTY keyboard layout may not suffice. Reconfiguring the keyboard's layout changes which characters appear onscreen when you press certain keys on your keyboard.

When support for an additional input language is enabled, Windows displays the Language bar, which enables you to quickly switch from one supported language to another.

You can also specify that Windows display information such as dates, times, currency, and measurements for a particular region in the world. To do so, click the Formats tab in the Regional and Language Options dialog box and select the desired locale.

See also>> **Regional and Language Options**

Configure an Input Language

1 In Control Panel, click Change Keyboards or Other Input Methods under Clock, Language, and Region.

● The Regional and Language Options dialog box opens, with the Keyboards and Languages tab displayed.

2 Click Change Keyboards.

● The Text Services and Input Languages dialog box opens.

3 Click Add.

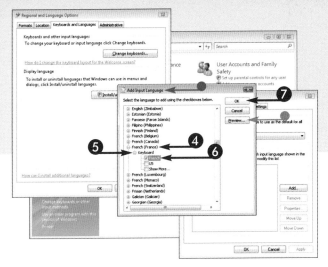

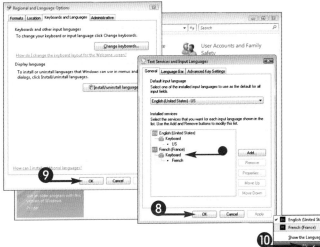

- The Add Input Language dialog box opens.

④ Click the plus sign next to the language you want to enable.

⑤ Click the plus sign next to the Keyboard entry.

⑥ Click the checkbox next to the type of keyboard you want to use.

- To preview the keyboard you selected, click the Preview button in the Add Input Language dialog box.

⑦ Click OK.

- Support for the language you selected is added.

⑧ Click OK.

⑨ Click OK.

⑩ To switch input languages, click the Language bar. (It might be docked on the taskbar. If it is not visible, right-click the taskbar and click Language Bar.)

⑪ Click the language you want to use.

Did You Know?

Vista Ultimate supports several display languages (as opposed to input languages), including French, German, and Japanese. To change Windows Vista's display language, you might have to first download a Language Interface Pack, or LIP for short, from Microsoft's Web site. (Type **www.microsoft.com** in your browser and search for "language interface pack.") You must also be running Vista Ultimate, and must have activated your copy of Windows. Once the LIP has been downloaded, you must install the language you want to use. Then you can select the display language for use on your PC. To do so, run the Install or Uninstall Display Languages Wizard by clicking Install/Uninstall Languages in the Keyboards and Languages tab of the Regional and Language Options dialog box.

REMOTE ASSISTANCE:
Get Help Via Remote Assistance

If you experience a computer problem, you can use Remote Assistance to invite someone to help you — regardless of his or her physical location. In order to use Remote Assistance, you must enable it on your Vista machine.

During a Remote Assistance session, you and your helper can communicate via chat, your helper can view your computer screen, and, with your permission, your helper can use his or her mouse and keyboard to make changes to your system. (To stop your helper from sharing control over your system, click Cancel, click Stop Sharing, or press the Esc key.)

Although all Remote Assistance sessions are encrypted and password-protected, you should engage in a Remote Assistance session only with someone you trust because your helper will have access to your personal files and information during the Remote Assistance session. Also, you should close any sensitive files before initiating the connection.

Note that in addition to obtaining help via Remote Assistance, you can also provide it.

Enable Remote Assistance

1 In Control Panel, click System and Maintenance.

● The System and Maintenance window opens.

2 Under System, click Allow Remote Access.

Note: If prompted, type the administrator password or click Continue.

● The System Properties dialog box opens, with the Remote tab displayed.

3 Click to select the Allow Remote Assistance Connections to this Computer checkbox.

4 Click OK.

Remote Assistance is enabled.

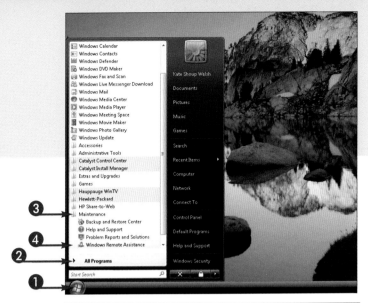

Engage in a Remote Assistance Session

1 Click Start.

2 Click All Programs.

3 Click Maintenance.

4 Click Windows Remote Assistance.

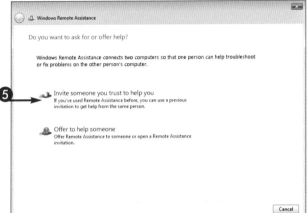

The Windows Remote Assistance Wizard starts.

5 Follow the onscreen instructions to get (or give) help via Remote Assistance.

Did You Know?

Although their names are similar, and although both tools involve connecting to a computer remotely, Remote Assistance differs from Remote Desktop Connection in a few key ways. First, Remote Assistance is used to give assistance to or receive assistance from another user. When connected via Remote Assistance, both you and the other user can view the same screen and control the system. In contrast, Remote Desktop Connection enables you to access a computer remotely and work on it as though it is local. For instance, you might use Remote Desktop to connect to your work computer from home; if so, you have access to all the programs, files, and network resources on your work computer.

REMOTE DESKTOP:
Configure Remote Desktop Connection

With Remote Desktop Connection, you can connect to another Windows PC and work from it without being physically present. For example, you might use Remote Desktop Connection to perform tasks on your work computer from home.

To connect to a remote computer via Remote Desktop Connection, both the remote and the local computers must be powered on, with both connected to a network (or to the Internet). Additionally, the remote computer must have been configured to allow access by the local computer. (Note that if, after you configure the connection, it does not work, your Windows Firewall may be blocking the Remote Desktop port.)

If you intend to use Remote Desktop Connection to connect your home computer to your work PC, and if your work PC is on a corporate domain, you need to establish a virtual private network (VPN) or a Terminal Services Gateway server in order for them to communicate. Contact your system administrator for guidance.

See also>>

Remote Assistance

Windows Firewall:
Manage

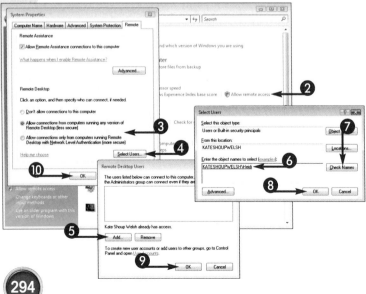

Configure the Remote Computer

1 In Control Panel, click System and Maintenance.

2 Click Allow Remote Access.

Note: If prompted, type the administrator password or click Continue.

3 Under Remote Desktop, click the second or third option button.

4 By default, accounts with administrator privileges can use remote desktop. To add other user accounts, click Select Users.

5 Click Add.

6 Enter the name of the user whose account you want to enable.

7 Click Check Names to verify that the user name you entered is valid.

8 Click OK.

9 Click OK.

10 Click OK.

294

Connect to the Remote Computer

R

1 Click Start.

2 Click All Programs.

3 Click Accessories.

4 Click Remote Desktop Connection.

● The Remote Desktop Connection dialog box opens.

5 Type the full name of the computer to which you want to connect. (You obtain this beforehand by clicking the Computer Name tab in the System Properties dialog box on the remote computer.)

6 Click Connect.

The Remote Desktop Connection engages, with the remote computer's desktop displayed on your screen.

TIPS

Did You Know?

You can copy information from the remote computer to the local one, as well as print via a printer attached to the remote computer. To enable this, open the Remote Desktop Connection dialog box on the local PC, click Options, click the Local Resources tab, select the Clipboard and Printers checkboxes under Local Devices and Resources, and click Connect.

Attention!

While you have the System Properties dialog box open, click the Computer Name tab and jot down the computer's full name. You will need it to establish the Remote Desktop Connection.

RSS FEEDS:
Find and Subscribe to RSS Feeds

RSS, short for *Really Simple Syndication*, is a technology that enables Web site content to be *syndicated* — that is, converted to a Web feed. This Web site content can include blogs, podcasts, news, and so on. (*Podcast* generally refers to an audio-broadcast feed.) Users can check for feeds on a Web site using Internet Explorer 7, and then download this syndicated content to the browser window. Optionally, users can then save their feeds on a portable audio device to enjoy at their leisure.

If you find an RSS feed you particularly like, you can *subscribe* to it, in which case Internet Explorer

automatically checks for and downloads feed updates. (Note that subscribing to a feed is typically free. For example, if you have subscribed to a podcast feed or a blog feed, Internet Explorer automatically downloads new episodes of the podcast or new blog entries.) You can access and view all the RSS feeds to which you have subscribed using a special pane in Internet Explorer 7.

See also>> Internet Explorer 7

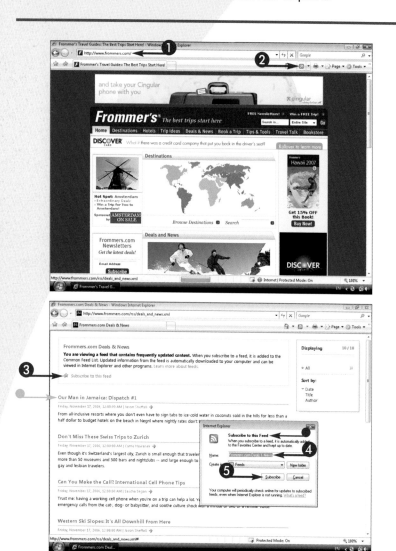

Subscribe to a Feed

① In Internet Explorer, point your browser to a Web site by typing its URL.

 If the Web site you open hosts any RSS feeds, the Feeds button changes from gray to orange.

② Click the Feeds button.

 Internet Explorer displays a list of episodes, blog entries, or feed updates.

● To open an episode, blog entry, or other feed update, click it.

③ To subscribe to the feed, click Subscribe to This Feed.

● The Subscribe to This Feed dialog box opens.

④ If desired, type a name for the feed.

⑤ Click Subscribe.

Launch a Feed

1 In Internet Explorer, click the Favorites button.

The Favorites list is displayed.

2 Click Feeds.

A list of the feeds to which you have subscribed appears.

3 Click the feed you want to view.

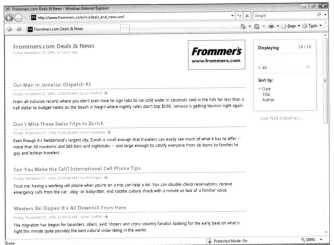

Windows opens the page on which the feed is found.

 TIPS

Remove It!
Delete a feed by right-clicking it in the Favorites list and clicking Delete.

Did You Know?
Internet Explorer 7 includes three feeds by default: Microsoft at Home, Microsoft at Work, and MSNBC News.

Try This!
To view and change a feed's properties, such as how often it is updated, whether a feed is marked as "Read" after it has been opened, and more, right-click the feed in the Favorites pane and click Properties.

SCREEN SAVER:
Choose a Screen Saver

A *screen saver* is a picture that appears on your screen when the mouse and keyboard have been inactive for a prescribed period of time. Using a screen saver can prevent others from seeing your work on your desktop while you are away from your computer. You can also use a screen saver to add fun or personalized images to your desktop.

Windows Vista offers a number of built-in screen savers. If you do not see one you like, you can download and install other screen savers from the Internet. Alternatively, you can use pictures in your

Photo Gallery to create a slide show that acts as a personalized screen saver.

You can configure options such as how long your computer should be inactive before the screen saver appears. In addition, you can configure Windows to require a password in order to return to the desktop. This ensures that unauthorized users cannot simply click your mouse to deactivate the screen saver and work at your keyboard.

See also>>   Photo Gallery

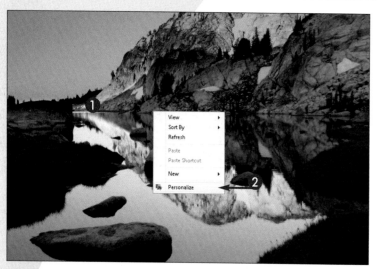

1 Right-click the Windows desktop.

2 Click Personalize.

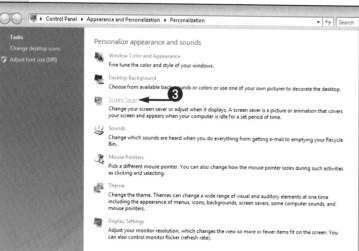

The Personalize Appearance and Sounds window opens.

3 Click Screen Saver.

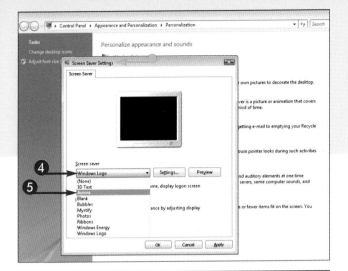

- The Screen Saver Settings dialog box opens.

④ Open the Screen Saver list.

⑤ Click the screen saver you want to use, Aurora in this example.

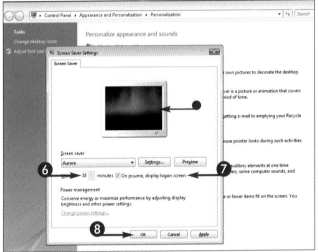

- A preview of the selected screen saver appears.

⑥ Enter the number of minutes of inactivity you want to pass before the screen saver launches.

⑦ To secure your system, click the On Resume, Display Logon Screen checkbox to select it.

⑧ Click OK.

Did You Know?

Some screen savers have settings you can change; they differ by screen saver. To access these settings, make sure the desired screen saver has been selected in the list, and click Settings.

Attention!

If the screen saver is enabled, move your mouse or press a key on your keyboard. The screen saver should disappear and return you to your desktop.

Try This!

To preview the screen saver, click the Preview button.

Try This!

To use a slide show composed of the photos in your Photo Gallery as a screen saver, choose Photos from the Screen Saver list. To access a screen that enables you to select the photos you want to use, click Settings.

SEARCH FOLDER:
Save a Search

Vista offers several search options, with each option serving different needs. For example, if you have a general idea where the file you seek is located — say, somewhere in your Documents folder — you can search for it using that folder's Search box. Another search option, the Search folder, is a good choice when you do not know where a file or folder is located, or when you want to create a more advanced search.

If you find yourself repeatedly searching for the same file, consider saving the search. That way,

instead of manually constructing the search parameters each time you need to find the file, you can simply launch the saved search. Windows will locate the most current files that match the saved criteria. Saved searches are accessible from the Search folder's Navigation pane.

See also>>

Search Box

Search Folder

① Click Start.

② Click Search.

The Search folder opens.

③ Enter your search parameters.

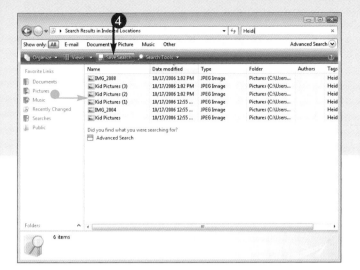

● Windows displays the results of your search.

④ Click Save Search.

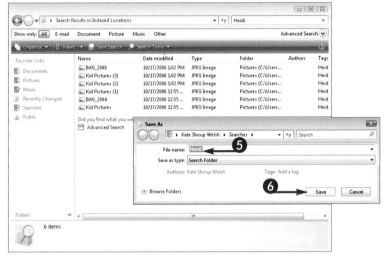

⑤ Type a name for the saved search (or keep the default name, which matches what you typed in the Search box).

⑥ Click Save.

Windows saves your search.

Did You Know?
To access additional search options, click Advanced Search.

Try This!
To launch a saved search, click Searches in the Search folder's Navigation pane. In the list of saved searches that appears, double-click the saved search.

Did You Know?
If you find that the Searches category in the Search folder's Navigation pane has become a bit too crowded, drag the saved search to the Favorites category, or wherever else on the Navigation pane you would like for it to appear.

SECURITY ZONES:
Customize Web Site Security Settings

Not all Web sites are created equal. Some are unquestionably trustworthy, with practices and policies in place to protect visitors. Others are sketchy at best. Attempting to apply the same level of security to all sites on the Internet is a fool's errand.

For this reason, Internet Explorer assigns all Web sites to one of four *security zones*: Internet, Local Intranet, Trusted Sites, and Restricted Sites. The level of security applied to a site depends on the zone to which that site is assigned. For example, the default security level for sites in the Internet

zone is Medium High. The default security level for sites in the Local Intranet, Trusted Sites, and Restricted Sites zones are Medium, Medium, and High, respectively.

If you find that Microsoft has assigned a particular Web site to a zone that you think is too restrictive (or not restrictive enough), you can change zones.

See also>>

Internet Explorer 7

Internet Options

Add a Site to a Security Zone

① Click Start.

② Click Internet.

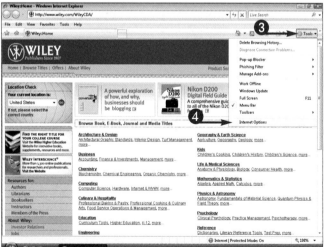

Internet Explorer starts.

③ With a site whose zone you want to change open in Internet Explorer, click the Tools button.

④ Click Internet Options.

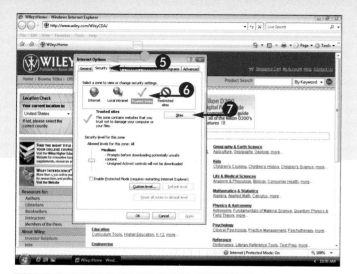

- The Internet Options dialog box opens.

5 Click the Security tab.

6 Click a security zone (here, Trusted Sites).

7 Click the Sites button.

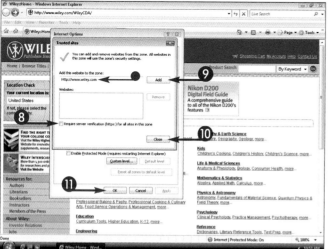

- The open Web site is listed in the Add This Website to the Zone field.

8 If the site is not a secure site, click the Require Server Verification (HTTPS:) for All Sites in This Zone checkbox to clear it.

Note: If the URL for a site starts with http: rather than https:, it is not a secure site.

9 Click Add.

10 Click Close to close the Trusted Sites dialog box.

11 Click OK to close the Internet Options dialog box.

Did You Know?

An *intranet* is a private network with some of the same properties as the Internet, but it is local to your home, small office, or company network.

Attention!

You can tell which zone you are in by checking the bottom-right corner of your Internet Explorer Web browser window in the status bar.

More Options!

Just as you can add a site to a security zone, so, too, can you remove one. To do so, click the security zone of the site you want to remove in the Internet Options dialog box's Security tab, click Sites, click the site you want to remove, and click Remove.

S

SECURITY ZONES:
Customize Web Site Security Settings (Continued)

Each of the four security zones has a recommended level of security applied to it. For example, as mentioned, the Internet zone's security level is Medium High, the Local Intranet and Trusted Sites zones have a security level of Medium, and the Restricted Sites zone's security level is High.

Although the Microsoft Internet Explorer Web browser has security zones preconfigured to the recommended level of security, you can modify the security level for the Internet, Local Intranet, and

Trusted Sites zones to either increase or reduce the level of protection needed. For example, if you experience problems loading a particular page, then you may need to reduce the security level, at least temporarily, to view the page normally. (Note that you cannot change the Restricted Sites zone's security level.)

See also>>

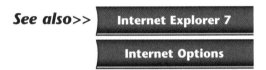

Customize the Security Level of a Security Zone

1 Click Start.

2 Click Internet.

Internet Explorer starts.

3 Click the Tools button.

4 Click Internet Options.

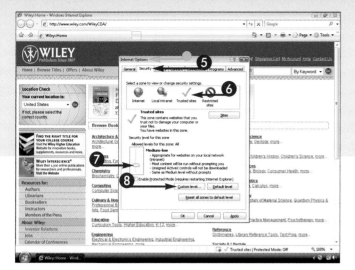

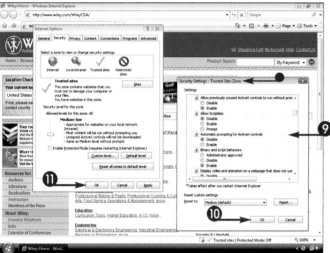

- The Internet Options dialog box opens.

5 Click the Security tab.

6 Click a security zone (here, Trusted Sites).

7 Adjust the slider under Security Level for This Zone to change the security level.

8 To further customize the security settings for the selected zone, click Custom Level.

- The zone's Security Settings dialog box opens.

9 Adjust each of the settings as desired.

10 Click OK to close the Security Settings dialog box

11 Click OK to close the Internet Options dialog box.

Did You Know?

The term "default level" refers to the security level that Microsoft recommends for a particular zone.

More Options!

The Internet Options dialog box enables you to change your security settings as they pertain to *cookies* — the files transmitted from the Web sites you visit to your browser and hard drive. Cookies help sites to identify you. To view the available cookie-related settings, click the Privacy tab in the Internet Options dialog box.

Remove It!

To revert the custom settings to their defaults, open the Internet Options dialog box, click the Security tab, click the zone whose settings you want to change, click the Default Level button, and click OK.

SHORTCUTS:
Create and Manage Shortcuts

A *shortcut* is special icon that you can double-click to launch a program installed on your PC, or to access a drive, folder, or file on your system. Shortcuts can also be used to access network resources such as other computers or a shared printer.

Shortcut icons look different from icons used to represent a regular folder or file in that they feature an arrow graphic in the lower-left corner.

In addition to Windows' pre-fab shortcuts, such as the Recycle Bin shortcut found on the desktop, you can create shortcuts all your own. These shortcuts can be placed on the desktop, on the Start menu, or in a folder.

If the item to which a shortcut links changes or moves, you can edit the shortcut's name or properties to reflect that fact. You can also customize your shortcut by changing the icon's appearance.

Create a Shortcut

① Right-click the item for which you want to create a shortcut. (This item might be in a folder, on the Start menu, or elsewhere.)

② Click Create Shortcut.

Note: *If the item you chose is in the Start menu, right-click it, click Send To, and click Desktop (Create Shortcut).*

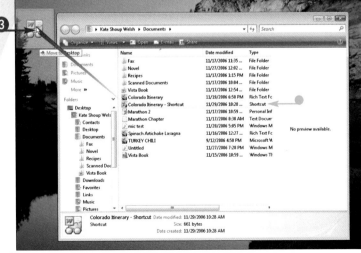

● A shortcut is created.

③ Drag the shortcut to the desired location — the desktop, the Start menu, or a folder.

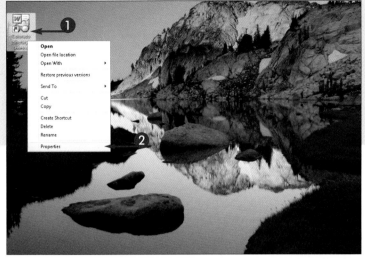

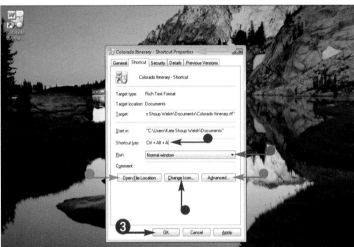

Customize a Shortcut

① Right-click the shortcut you want to customize.

② Choose Properties.

• The Shortcut Properties dialog box opens.

• To associate a shortcut key with the shortcut — for example, Ctrl+Alt+A — type it in the Shortcut Key box. (You can then use this shortcut key to launch the file associated with the shortcut rather than clicking the shortcut icon.)

• Specify whether the file should launch in a window that is normal, minimized, or maximized.

• Click Open File Location to open the folder, menu, or other location where the original file is located.

• Click Change Icon to choose a new icon for the shortcut.

• Access advanced options by clicking Advanced.

③ Click OK.

The shortcut's properties are changed.

Try This!

You can rename a shortcut to make it easier to distinguish from other shortcuts. To rename a shortcut, right-click it, click Rename, type the new name, and press Enter. (If you try to rename a shortcut with the name of an existing shortcut, you will get an error message.) Renaming a shortcut does not change the name of the file or program to which it links.

More Options!

If you prefer, you can cut and paste the shortcut to move it rather than dragging it. To do so, right-click the shortcut icon and click Cut; then right-click in the location where you want to move the shortcut and click Paste. (To copy, rather than move, the shortcut, choose Copy instead of Cut.)

SHORTCUTS:
Create and Manage Shortcuts (Continued)

If, over time, you find that you have added so many shortcuts on your desktop that it is difficult to easily locate the ones you need, you can create a shortcut toolbar on your desktop to store them. This shortcut toolbar tidily houses all your desktop shortcuts in one compact spot.

Alternatively, you can delete those shortcuts that are no longer needed or valid. To delete a shortcut, right-click it and click Delete. (If prompted, type the administrator password or click Continue.) Note that when you delete a shortcut, only the shortcut itself is removed — not the program, folder, file, or other item with which it is associated.

Create a Shortcut Toolbar

1. Right-click a blank area on the desktop.
2. Click New.
3. Click Folder.

A new, blank folder opens on the desktop.

4. Type a name, such as Shortcuts, for the folder and press Enter.
5. Drag the folder to the right, left, top, or bottom edge of the desktop.

A blank toolbar appears.

6 Drag a shortcut to the toolbar.

● The shortcut appears on the toolbar.

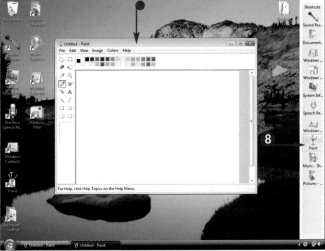

7 Repeat Step **6** to add more shortcuts to the toolbar.

8 Click a shortcut on the toolbar.

● Windows launches the file, folder, or program you associated with the shortcut.

Remove It!

Notice that, after you drag your shortcuts onto the toolbar, they also remain on the desktop in their original position. To delete these shortcuts from the desktop, select them, right-click the selection, and click Delete.

Important!

Programs may sometimes prompt you to install a desktop icon for them. If you click Yes to agree, then a shortcut is created on the desktop.

Did You Know?

If you click a shortcut only to see the Missing Shortcut dialog box, it means that the program, file, folder, or other item with which the shortcut is associated has been deleted or moved. If it has been moved, click Browse to locate it; Windows will update the shortcut accordingly.

S

SOUND SCHEME:
Set Up a Sound Scheme

You can view properties of audio devices and apply a sound scheme to your Windows Vista system in the Sound dialog box.

A *sound scheme* is a collection of sounds used by your computer. By default, Windows uses its own sound scheme, in which certain events trigger specific sounds, such as when you log on or when you receive a new e-mail. You can, however, create your *own* sound scheme in which the events trigger different sounds of your choosing. If you have a microphone, you can even record your own sounds for use in a scheme.

See also>>   **Volume Mixer**

1 Click Start.

2 Click Control Panel.

● The Control Panel window opens.

3 Click Hardware and Sound.

● The Hardware and Sound window opens.

4 Click Sound.

● The Sound dialog box opens.

5 To view the properties of an audio device, click the device in the list.

6 Click the Properties button.

● A dialog box showing the properties of the selected device appears.

7 Click OK.

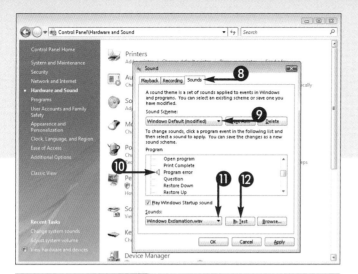

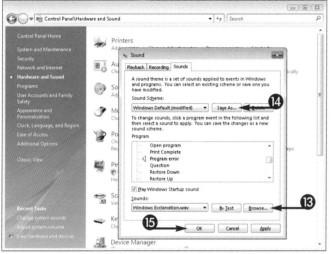

8. Click the Sounds tab in the Sound dialog box.

9. Click the Sound Scheme list to choose a different sound scheme.

10. To change the sound associated with a particular program event, click the program event.

11. Click the Sounds list to choose a different sound for the selected program event.

12. To preview the selected sound, click Test.

13. To select a sound that does not appear in the list (for example, one that you recorded yourself), click Browse and choose the sound from the dialog box that opens.

14. To save an altered sound scheme with a new name, click Save As and type a name for the sound in the dialog box that appears.

15. Click OK.

S

 TIPS

Try This!

To record your own sounds for a scheme, use Sound Recorder. To open it, click Start, choose All Programs, click Accessories, and click Sound Recorder. Record a sound by clicking Start Recording; click Stop Recording to stop. To use Sound Recorder, you need a sound card and a microphone installed on your computer; to set up your microphone, open Control Panel and click Ease of Access. Then click Set Up a Microphone under Speech Recognition and follow the onscreen instructions.

Try This!

To use visual cues instead of sounds, open Control Panel and click Ease of Access. Click Replace Sounds with Visual Clues under Ease of Access Center; then enable Sound Notifications to replace system sounds with visual cues such as flashes, or enable Captions to replace sounds with captions.

SPEECH RECOGNITION:
Set Up Speech Recognition

Setting up Windows Speech Recognition involves two steps. The first step is to set up a microphone. (Note that headset microphones are better suited for Speech Recognition than desktop microphones because they tend to block out extraneous sounds.) To do so, use the Set Up Microphone Wizard.

After the microphone is set up, you are ready for step two of the Windows Speech Recognition setup process: creating a voice profile. A *voice profile* includes information about how you speak, such as whether you have an accent and how you pronounce

certain words, as well as information about your environment, such as whether certain common office sounds are present. As with setting up the microphone, Windows provides a special wizard for creating a voice profile — this one called the Voice Training Wizard.

See also>>

Ease of Access Center

Speech Recognition

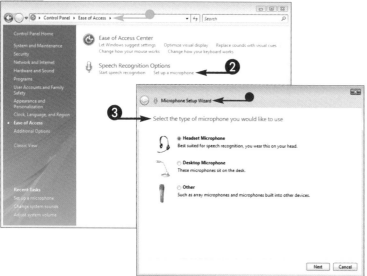

Set Up the Microphone

1 In Control Panel, click Ease of Access.

● The Ease of Access window opens.

2 Under Speech Recognition Options, click Set Up a Microphone.

● Windows launches the Microphone Setup Wizard.

3 Follow the onscreen instructions.

Create a Voice Profile

① In the Ease of Access window, click Speech Recognition Options.

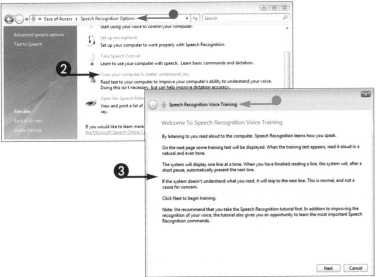

● The Speech Recognition Options window opens.

② Click Train Your Computer to Better Understand You.

● Windows launches the Speech Recognition Voice Training Wizard.

③ Follow the onscreen instructions.

TIPS

Try This!
Configure additional voice profiles by clicking the Advanced Speech Options link in the Speech Recognition Options window and clicking the New button. If multiple voice profiles have been configured, activate the one you want to use by clicking it in the Recognition Profiles list. To delete the selected profile, click Delete.

Did You Know?
To access a handy reference card for use with Speech Recognition, click Open the Speech Reference Card in the Speech Recognition Options window.

SPEECH RECOGNITION:
Set Up Speech Recognition (Continued)

Optionally, you can run the program's Speech Tutorial to learn the various commands required by Speech Recognition to control your computer and to dictate and edit text. (Note that the tutorial takes about 30 minutes to complete.)

Once you have set up Windows Vista's Speech Recognition feature and explored how to use it via the Speech Tutorial, you are ready to use it to dictate and edit text, be it to type a report in a word-processing program such as WordPad or to fill out a form online. As you dictate, you can use special commands to insert punctuation, start a new

paragraph, select text, and so on. For a complete list of commands, see Vista's help information.

In addition to using Speech Recognition to dictate text, you can also use it to control your computer — that is, issue commands to run programs and otherwise interact with Windows — rather than using your mouse and keyboard.

See also>>

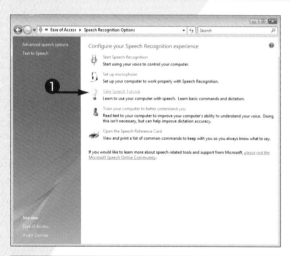

Run the Speech Tutorial

1 In the Speech Recognition Options window, click Take Speech Tutorial.

Windows launches the Speech Recognition Tutorial.

2 Follow the onscreen instructions.

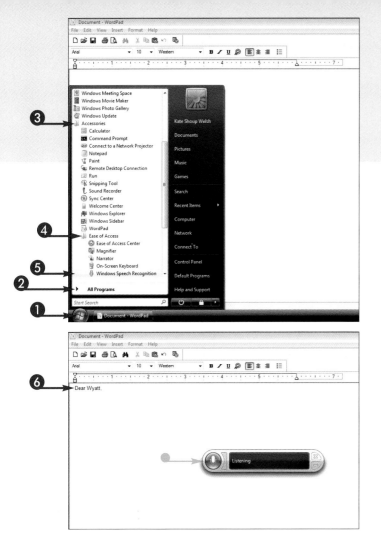

Dictate Text

1. With the program in which you want to dictate text open on the desktop, click Start.

2. Click All Programs.

3. Click Accessories.

4. Click Ease of Access.

5. Click Windows Speech Recognition.

● The Speech Recognition window opens.

6. Speak the words you want to appear in your document.

TIPS

Try This!

If Speech Recognition consistently fails to recognize a word, you can add the word to the Speech Dictionary. To do so, say "Open Speech Dictionary." When the Speech Dictionary dialog box opens, say "Add a new word" and follow the onscreen instructions. Alternatively, if Speech Recognition persistently mishears a word that already appears in the dictionary, correct it by saying "Change existing word" and following the onscreen instructions.

More Options!

You can use Speech Recognition in lieu of your mouse and keyboard to operate Windows and the programs running on it. For example, instead of opening Internet Explorer by clicking the Start button and choosing Internet Explorer, you can say "Open Internet Explorer." For more Speech Recognition commands, see Vista's Help files.

START MENU:
Customize the Start Menu

Windows Vista's Start menu is the starting point to the programs, folders, and files on your PC.

When you launch the Start menu, you will notice that the left pane features a brief list of shortcuts to programs. The bottom part of the left pane includes shortcuts to the programs you have recently used most often, while the top part includes shortcuts to those programs your PC manufacturer deemed critical. (You access the remaining programs on your PC by clicking All Programs.)

If you like, you can change which programs appear on the left pane by default. For example, if the upper portion of the menu's left pane includes a shortcut to a program you rarely use, you can remove the shortcut, replacing it with a shortcut that is more relevant to you on the menu. (When you add a program to the Start menu, it is called *pinning*.)

See also>> **Start Menu**

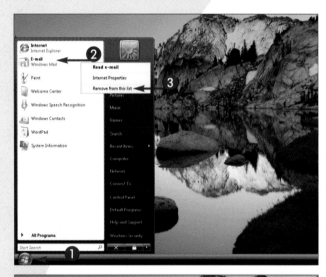

Remove a Program Shortcut

1 Click Start.

2 Right-click the program shortcut you want to remove.

3 Click Remove from This List.

● The shortcut icon is removed.

Pin a Program on the Start Menu

① In the Start menu, right-click the shortcut for the program you want to pin to the left pane of the Start menu.

② Click Pin to Start menu.

● The shortcut is pinned on the left panel of the Start menu.

Note: *To move the pinned shortcut up or down in the program list, click and drag it.*

TIPS

More Options!

If you prefer the classic-style Start menu available in earlier versions of Windows, you can configure Windows Vista to use it. To do so, right-click a blank area of the taskbar, click Properties, click the Start Menu tab, click the Classic Start Menu option button, and click OK. (Note that certain customization options will no longer be available.)

Did You Know?

You can drag the taskbar to any one of the four edges around your screen — and with it, the Start button. (You may have to unlock the taskbar first; to do so, right-click a blank area on the taskbar and click Lock the Taskbar to clear the checkmark.)

START MENU:
Customize the Start Menu (Continued)

In addition to customizing the left side of the Start menu, you can also make certain changes to the right pane, which, by default, includes shortcuts to Windows' common folders such as Documents, Music, Pictures, and so on.

Unlike the left pane, which enables you to add and remove shortcuts by right-clicking, you must make changes to the right pane via the Customize Start

Menu dialog box. In addition to adding, customizing, and removing certain shortcuts using this dialog box, you can also adjust the number of shortcuts to frequently used programs in the left pane, add the Run command to the Start menu, and restore the Start menu's default settings.

See also>>   **Start Menu**

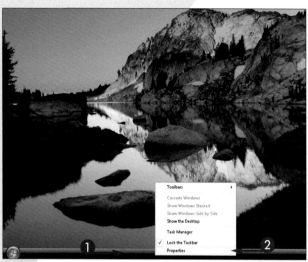

Change Settings in the Customize Start Menu Dialog Box

1 Right-click a blank area of the taskbar.

2 Click Properties.

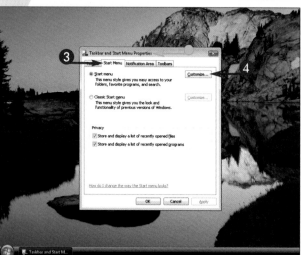

● The Taskbar and Start Menu Properties dialog box opens.

3 Click the Start Menu tab.

4 Click Customize.

- The Customize Start Menu dialog box opens.

- Click the folders and features you want displayed on the Start menu's right pane.

- Enter the number of recently used programs you want to display in the left pane of the Start menu.

- Click Use Default Settings to revert to the default settings.

- To add a link to Internet Explorer or Windows Mail to the left pane, click here.

⑤ Click OK to close the Customize Start Menu dialog box.

⑥ Click OK to close the Taskbar and Start Menu Properties dialog box.

- Your changes are applied to the Start menu.

Try This!

The Start menu's right pane includes a Recent Items list. To clear it, click the Start button, right-click Recent Items, and click Clear Recent Items List.

Remove It!

Restore the Start menu's original default settings by clicking Use Default Settings in the Customize Start Menu dialog box.

Did You Know?

You can choose a different picture to display at the top of the Start menu. To do so, click User Accounts and Family Safety in Control Panel, click User Accounts, click Change Your Picture, click the picture you want to use (or browse to locate a picture in your Photo Gallery), and click Change Picture.

START MENU:
Open a Program, Folder, File, or Feature

Using Windows Vista's Start menu, you can start the programs installed on your PC, as well as launch folders, files, and other features.

To open the Start menu, you click the Start button. When you do, you will notice that the left pane of the menu features a brief list of shortcuts to programs, with additional programs accessible via the All Programs shortcut. The right pane provides access to Windows' main folders (Documents, Pictures, Music, and so on); Windows features, including Control Panel, Help and Support, and games; and buttons that enable you to power off, lock, log off of, shut

down, or restart your computer, and to switch users.

If you want to initiate a search for a program, folder, file, e-mail message, Internet favorite, or recently visited Web site, you can type a keyword or phrase in the Start menu's Search box. Windows displays the results of the search in the left pane; click a result to open it.

See also>>   **Start Menu**

See also>>   **Start Menu: Customize**

1 Click Start.

Windows displays the Start menu.

2 If you see the program you want to launch on the left pane, or the folder, file, or feature you want to launch in the right pane, click it. Otherwise, click All Programs.

More Windows programs are displayed.

③ If you see the program you want to launch, click it. Otherwise, click a category to reveal more programs.

④ Click the program you want to launch.

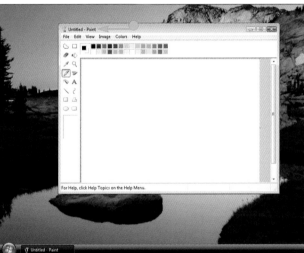

● Windows launches the program you selected.

TIPS

Did You Know?

Windows changes the programs listed in the bottom part of the left pane based on which programs you have recently used the most.

Did You Know?

If you are not sure what a particular program does, place your mouse pointer over its name in the menu to see a description.

More Options!

To quickly find a program, folder, or file, type a keyword in the Start menu's Search box. Items matching your text appear in the left pane of the menu; click an item to open it.

STARTUP FOLDER:
Control Which Programs Launch at Startup

If you find yourself launching a certain program or tool every time you start Windows — for example, Windows Mail or Windows Calendar — you can configure Windows to launch it automatically at system startup. To do so, simply add the program or tool to your Windows Startup folder.

When you add a program or tool to your Windows Startup folder, Windows automatically loads that program or tool each time your system boots or restarts, making it available immediately after your PC starts and Windows loads.

Before you add programs to the Startup folder, keep in mind that every program you add loads and runs each time you launch a session, and this consumes desktop resources. As a result, you want to choose only the programs that you will really need for every session. If you find your system does not boot up as quickly as you would like, consider purging those programs from your Startup folder that are not absolutely necessary.

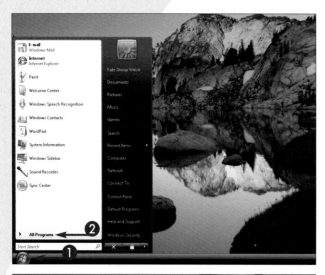

1 Click Start.

2 Click All Programs.

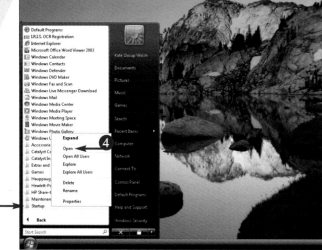

3 Right-click the Startup folder.

4 Click Open.

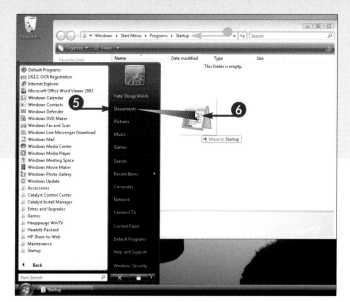

The Startup folder opens on the desktop.

5 Locate the program you want to add in the Start menu.

6 Drag the program's icon from the Start menu to the Startup folder.

Note: If prompted, type the administrator password or click Continue.

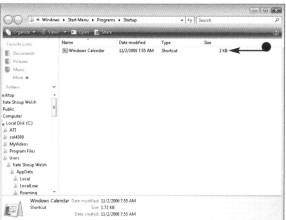

Windows adds the program to the Startup folder; the next time you boot Windows, the program will launch automatically.

More Options!

You are not limited to adding just programs to the Startup folder. If you frequently use the same document when you start Windows, or if you want immediate access to a particular folder, you can add it to the Startup folder. To do so, locate the file or folder, right-click it, and click Create Shortcut. Then drag the shortcut into the Startup folder.

SYNC CENTER:
Sync an Offline Folder or Mobile Device

A *sync partnership* dictates how and when files should be synced between a computer and a network or mobile device. When you connect a new, sync-able device to your computer, Windows will generally detect it and ask whether you want to create a sync partnership with the device. Some devices enable you to establish certain settings during the sync-partnership setup process, such as whether the sync will be one-way or two-way. You will also likely be able to set a schedule for the sync. You can, however, run a manual sync.

If, during the sync operation, Sync Center detects a *sync conflict* — that is, if a file on both your PC *and* on the network or mobile device has changed — you will be prompted to choose which version to keep. To view any active sync conflicts, click the View My Sync Conflicts link in Sync Center's left pane.

See also>>  **Sync Center**

See also>> **Offline Files: View**

1 Click Start.

2 Click All Programs.

3 Click Accessories.

4 Click Sync Center.

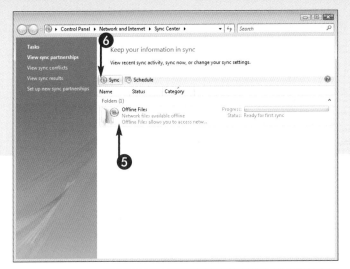

Sync Center opens.

⑤ Click the sync partnership you want to sync.

⑥ Click Sync.

Note: *If you want to sync all your devices and offline folders as opposed to just one, simply open Sync Center and click Sync All.*

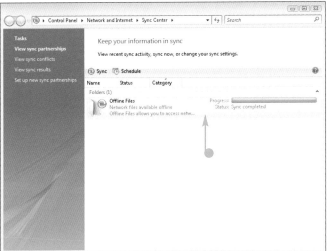

● Windows syncs the selected partnership.

Did You Know?
To change a sync partnership's sync schedule, click the sync partnership in Sync Center, click the Schedule button, and follow the onscreen instructions.

Did You Know?
Some syncs are one-way, with files copied from, say, a PC to an MP3 player, but never from the MP3 player to the PC. Other syncs are two-way; files are transferred to and from each device in the partnership.

Caution!
You system may occasionally experience a sync error, resulting in an aborted sync operation. Sync warnings notify you of problems that may ultimately result in a sync error. (To view any active sync conflicts, click the View Sync Results link in Sync Center's left pane.)

SYSTEM RESTORE:
Create a Restore Point

System Restore, which is enabled by default, is a disaster-recovery utility that you can use to restore your system to the way it worked at a certain time before your computer encountered problems. This enables you to, for example, return the system to the state it was in before you opened a virus-infected file.

System Restore works by taking a virtual snapshot of all the details about your setup and files as they exist at a particular point in time, called a *restore point*. Restore points include information such as your custom user settings, the contents of folders and e-mail messages, and your Web browser history.

Thanks to a feature called System Protection, Windows creates restore points automatically — usually on a daily basis, and before significant system events such as the installation of a new program or hardware device. You can, however, create a restore point manually.

See also>> **System Restore: Roll Back**

❶ Click Start.

❷ Click All Programs.

❸ Click Maintenance.

❹ Click Backup and Restore Center.

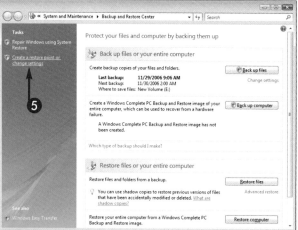

The Backup and Restore Center opens.

❺ Click Create a Restore Point or Change Settings.

Note: *If prompted, type the administrator password or click Continue.*

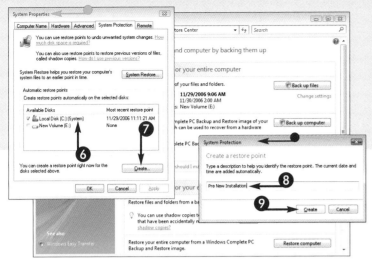

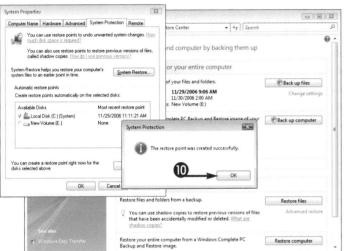

- The System Properties dialog box opens, with the System Protection tab displayed.

6 Click the disk for which you want to create a restore point.

7 Click the Create button.

- The System Protection dialog box opens.

8 Type a description to help you identify the restore point. (Note that the date and time are included automatically.)

9 Click Create.

10 When prompted, click OK.

TIPS

Did You Know?

System Restore uses a feature called System Protection to automatically create restore points on a regular basis. System Protection also creates shadow copies of files that have been modified since the last restore point was made. These shadow copies can then be used in the event you need to use Vista's Previous Versions feature to revert to an earlier version of a file.

Caution!

System Restore is meant only to restore your system to a known good state; it does not affect your personal files. If you delete a personal file, running System Restore cannot restore it for you. That is why you should also run backup utilities such as Windows Backup, CompletePC Backup, and the Back Up Files Wizard.

SYSTEM RESTORE:
Roll Back with a Restore Point

On occasion, a Windows Update or newly installed application or hardware device may wreak havoc on your machine, preventing Windows from loading properly. In these situations, you can attempt to roll back — or *restore* — your computer to a known good state by launching System Restore and choosing a restore point. This returns your system to the state it was in when the restore point was made.

It is usually best to choose the most recent restore point from before the current problems began. If you choose a very old restore point, your restored system

may not reflect more recent changes that you have made.

If System Restore fails to fix the problem, try undoing the restore operation (click Undo System Restore in the first screen of the System Restore Wizard and click Finish); you can then run System Restore again to choose a different restore point.

See also>> **System Restore: Create**

① Click Start.

② Click All Programs.

③ Click Accessories.

④ Click System Tools.

⑤ Click System Restore.

Note: *If prompted, type the administrator password or click Continue.*

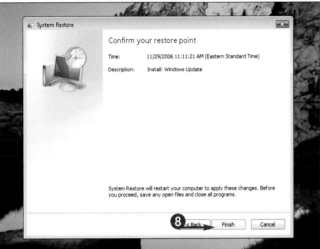

Windows launches the System Restore Wizard.

6 Choose the restore point you want to revert to.

7 Click Next.

8 Click Finish.

Windows restores your system to the earlier state.

TIP

Attention!

If your computer will not start, you cannot run System Restore. Instead, try Startup Repair, which scans for and fixes missing or damaged system files. This tool is preinstalled on many computers; to access it, start your computer and repeatedly press the F8 key. In the Advanced Boot Options screen, select Repair Your Computer and press Enter. Select a keyboard layout, username, and password, and click Startup Repair in the System Recover Options menu. (If your PC does not have Startup Repair installed, insert the Windows installation disc, start your computer, choose your language settings, and click Repair Your Computer. Next, choose the operating system you want to fix and, in the System Recovery Options menu, click Startup Repair.)

SYSTEM WINDOW:
View Your System's Properties

If you want to know which version of Windows you are using or what type of central processor unit, or CPU, you have on your computer, see Control Panel's System window. You can also find out whether a service pack has been installed to the system, and how much memory, or *RAM,* you have installed.

This general information is vital in determining whether you have the necessary system requirements for

adding a particular piece of hardware or software, as well as how powerful and up-to-date your system is.

Another useful piece of information displayed in the System window is your Windows product key. This is helpful if you need to call Microsoft Windows technical support because you will need to provide evidence that your copy of Windows is legitimate and registered with the company.

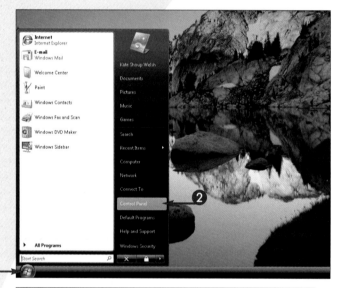

1 Click Start.

2 Click Control Panel.

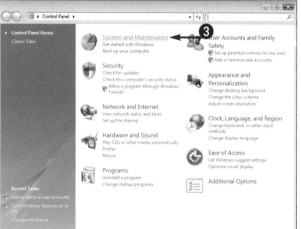

Control Panel opens.

3 Click System and Maintenance.

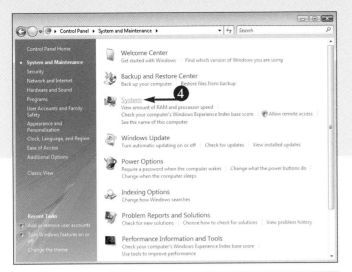

The System and Maintenance window opens.

④ Click System.

The System window opens, displaying information about your system.

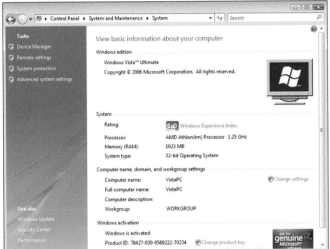

 TIPS

Did You Know?

Although a product key appears in the System window, it does not match the product key you typed in when you first installed the package. Instead, it is a final key that was generated from that initial product key.

Caution!

If your computer appears to have less memory than you thought, the memory may not be correctly installed, or one or more memory modules may be failing.

TAGS:
Tag Files

In Windows Vista, all files are given certain properties, such as Name, Date Modified, Author, File Type, and so on. You can search for files using these properties as criteria.

In addition to providing support for these default properties, Vista also enables you to apply other properties to your files such as tags. A *tag* is a brief description of a file that is embedded in the file's metadata. This description can be anything you choose, such as "Birthday Party," "Expense Account," and so on. Once a tag has been added to a file, you

can then search for the file using its tag as the criterion — which is often easier to remember than other file properties such as Name, Date Modified, and so on.

See also>> Search Folder

See also>> File and Folder Management: View

Ratings

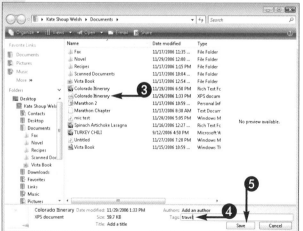

Add Tags in the Details Pane

1 Click Start.

2 Click the folder containing the file you want to tag (here, Documents).

The folder opens.

3 Click the file you want to tag.

4 In the Details pane, type a tag for the file.

Note: *If you want to add more than one tag, simply insert a semicolon between each tag you type.*

5 Click Save.

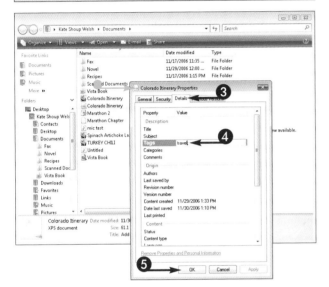

Set a Tag in the Properties Dialog Box

1 Right-click the file you want to tag.

2 Click Properties.

● The Properties dialog box opens.

3 Click the Details tab.

4 Type a tag for the file.

***Note:** If you want to add more than one tag, simply insert a semicolon between each tag you type.*

5 Click OK.

TIPS

Remove It!
Before you share a file with others, you might want to remove its tags — especially if they contain personal information. To remove a file's tags (or any other property you have applied) click the Details tab in the file's Properties dialog box and click Remove Properties and Personal Information. Click Create a Copy with All Possible Properties Removed to make a copy of the file with all its properties stripped but leave the original intact. Alternatively, click Remove the Following Properties from the File and click the checkbox next to each property you want to remove (in this case, Tags).

Did You Know?
In some cases, you can add tags to a file using the Save As dialog box.

TASK MANAGER:
View System Information

You can use Windows Task Manager to see what processes are running on your computer at any given moment, as well as to obtain other useful information. This is helpful when you need to troubleshoot or test your system performance.

Through Task Manager, you can view all of your open applications as well as processes and services that run in the background. By familiarizing yourself with the contents of the Processes tab during normal operation, you can identify any problems that appear when your system is not operating properly. You can

also use Task Manager to view current system performance, as well as network activity.

When an application fails to respond and you need to force it to close, you can do this through Task Manager. This allows you to avoid restarting your computer if you need to shut down only a single misbehaving program. After you shut down the program through Task Manager, you can usually reopen the program again through the Start menu.

See also>> **Task Manager**

View Your System with Task Manager

❶ Right-click the taskbar.

❷ Click Task Manager.

The Windows Task Manager dialog box opens.

❸ Click the Applications tab to view its contents.

❹ Click each of the remaining tabs to view the information they contain.

Force-Quit an Application

1. Right-click the taskbar.
2. Click Task Manager.

The Windows Task Manager window opens.

3. Click the Applications tab.
4. Click the program that you want to close. (This is often a program that is not responding.)
5. Click End Task.

The program closes and disappears from the Windows Task Manager window.

Attention!

Always try to close a non-responding program normally before you resort to using Task Manager. Forcing certain applications or processes to end prematurely can render Windows unstable.

More Options!

If you do not recognize some of the services and processes that are listed in the Processes tab, then you can use the Help and Support Center to search for a process's name to see what it does.

TASKBAR:
Customize the Taskbar

Because you use the Windows taskbar constantly, you can modify it to match the way you work to create a more comfortable desktop experience. For example, you can drag the taskbar to a different position on your desktop. You can also add options such as the Quick Launch bar for fast access to frequently used programs.

You can expand the taskbar to show open applications in two or more tiers. You can also hide the taskbar when you do not need it in order to maximize available desktop space. In contrast, you can

configure the taskbar to always sit on top of other open windows so that it does not disappear when your desktop is very crowded.

By customizing the taskbar, you can make it easier to reopen minimized windows and access the tools that you use most often.

See also>>

> **Quick Launch**

> **Taskbar and Start Menu Properties**

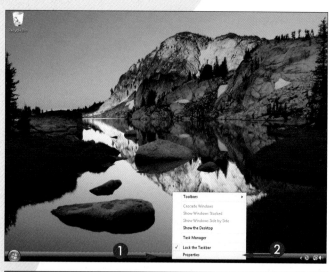

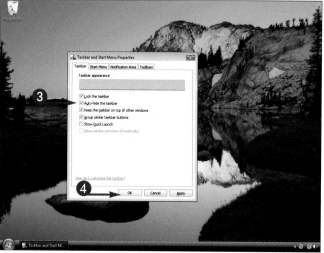

Hide the Taskbar

① Right-click a blank area on the taskbar.

② Click Properties.

The Taskbar and Start Menu Properties dialog box appears.

③ Click to select the Auto-Hide the Taskbar option.

④ Click OK.

Your taskbar disappears whenever it is not in use.

336

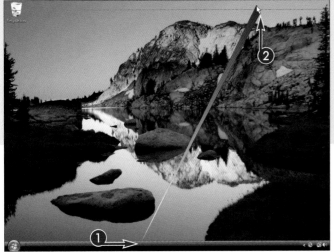

Move the Taskbar

① Click and hold the mouse cursor on the taskbar.

② Drag the taskbar to a different location, such as the top, left, or right side of your desktop, and release the mouse button.

Note: If Vista does not allow you to move the taskbar, it might be that the taskbar is locked. To unlock it, right-click it and choose Lock the Taskbar to toggle the setting off.

● The taskbar drops into place in the new location.

Did You Know?
You can close an open program or program group by right-clicking the program on the taskbar and then clicking Close or Close Group.

Remove It!
If you have moved the taskbar and you want to return it to its original location at the bottom of the screen, then click, drag, and drop it back to the bottom of the window.

More Options!
If you want the taskbar to always appear on top of other windows, then open the Taskbar and Start Menu Properties dialog box and click to select the Keep the Taskbar on Top of Other Windows option. If the Auto-Hide option is selected, then click to deselect it.

TEMP FOLDER:
Locate and Manage the Temporary Files Folder

Windows maintains a Temp folder to store temporary files that are created as you work. If you fail to manage this folder, it can "overflow" such that it limits your available disk space, affects system performance, and costs you time when you perform searches or use an antivirus scanner.

Not everything stored in your Temp folder should be deleted. Occasionally, an important file may end up in there, so you need to review the contents of the folder before you delete files. For example, you may find copies of important files in the Temp folder that

you can move back to their original folder if a crash or other problem causes you to lose the original version. To do so, right-click the file in the Temp folder and click Move; then, in the folder where you want to store the file, right-click and choose Paste. Once you review the contents of the folder, you can use the Disk Cleanup tool to purge the remaining files.

See also>>  **Disk Cleanup**

1 Click Start.

2 Click Computer.

● The Computer window opens.

3 Double-click the drive that contains your Windows installation. (This is usually your C: drive.)

The window displays the folders and files that are located in the main or root folder of the drive.

4 Double-click the Windows folder.

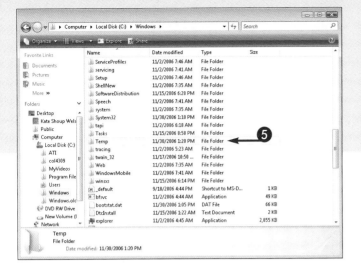

The contents of your Windows folder are displayed.

⑤ Double-click the Temp folder.

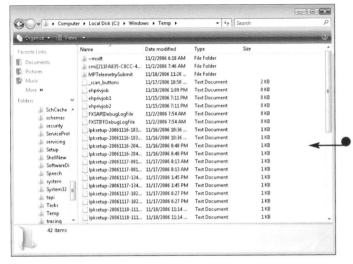

● The contents of the Temp folder appear.

Try This!

If a file that you need to move is located in the Recycle Bin rather than the Temp or other folder, you cannot use the Move command. Instead, right-click the file that you want to move back to its original location and click Restore. The file is automatically moved from the Recycle Bin back to its original location, in its original state.

More Options!

To purge the remaining files in your Temp folder, click Start, click All Programs, click Accessories, click System Tools, and then click Disk Cleanup. Select the drive where your Windows installation is located. From the Disk Cleanup window, click to select the Temporary files option. Click OK to start the cleanup process.

TEMPORARY INTERNET FILES:
Clean the Internet Files Cache

Your system may contain thousands of temporary Internet files that are left behind as the result of browsing the Web. To prevent these files from clogging your system, you need to clean the Internet files cache on a regular basis. Windows stores these files in special folders, which you can easily purge.

If you do not regularly clean the Internet files cache, then you not only lose valuable disk space, but your disk-management tools also take longer to run. You

also increase the risk that your Web browser will experience difficulties when you navigate between different sites on the Web.

Your Internet files may also contain programs or other files that can compromise your privacy, identify your passwords for others to find, or leave behind a computer virus such as an Internet worm.

See also>>   **Disk Cleanup**

① Click Start.

② Click Internet Explorer.

The Internet Explorer window opens.

③ Click Tools.

④ Click Internet Options.

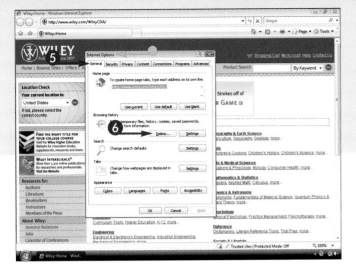

- The Internet Options dialog box appears.

5 Click the General tab.

6 Under Browsing History, click Delete.

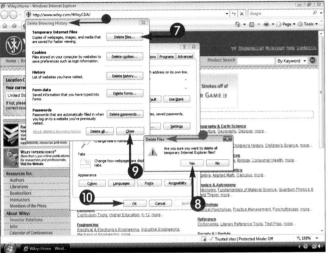

- The Delete Browsing History dialog box appears.

7 Click Delete Files.

- The Delete Files dialog box opens.

8 Click Yes.

9 Click Close.

10 Click OK.

Windows purges the temporary Internet files.

Did You Know?

When you run Disk Cleanup, it purges many of your temporary Internet files.

Important!

To maintain your privacy and to make it more difficult for others who access your computer to track your Web-browsing habits, you should also clear your cookies, browsing history, form data, and passwords. To do so, click Delete All in the Delete Browsing History dialog box.

Try This!

For best results, you may want to purge your temporary Internet files on a regular basis. If you browse the Web daily, then you should clean up the temporary files at least once a week.

THEMES:
Apply a Desktop Theme

When you want to customize your Windows desktop without spending time setting individual options, you can add a desktop theme to change the overall appearance. A *theme* is a package of files that creates a specific look. In addition to appearances, some themes may also include customized sounds to replace the standard ones used by Windows.

By default, Windows is configured with its own theme named Windows Vista. You can use this theme or

select a different one — from the list of themes that come preinstalled with Windows, one that you have downloaded from the Internet, or one that you have created yourself. (To find pre-fab themes online, or instructions for creating your own theme, use a search engine such as Yahoo!.)

See also>>   **Background: Set**

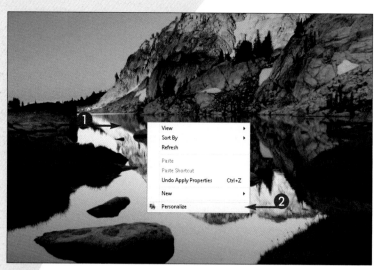

❶ Right-click an empty area on your desktop.

❷ Click Personalize.

The Personalize Appearance and Sounds window opens.

❸ Click Theme.

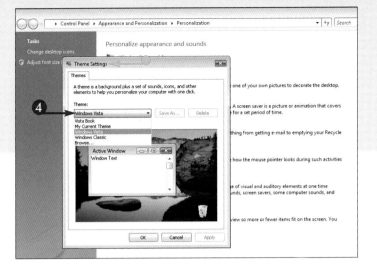

● The Theme Settings dialog box appears.

④ Click to select a theme.

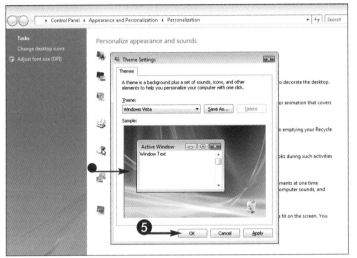

● A preview of the theme appears in the dialog box's Preview window.

⑤ To accept the theme, click OK.

Windows applies your theme to the desktop.

More Options!

If you download additional themes from the Web, you can use the Browse option in the drop-down menu in Step **4** to look for those themes in your system.

USER ACCOUNTS:
Create a New User Account

Each person who uses your computer can have his or her own *user account*, customized to that user's preferences — for example, with the theme, background, and other settings that the user selects. You can create two types of user accounts — Administrator and Standard — each providing its own level of control over the system.

An Administrator account allows the most control over the computer, enabling the user to change security settings, install and remove software and hardware, access all files on the computer, create and make changes to other user accounts, and so on. (Note that there must be at least one Administrator account on a Vista machine.)

Users with Standard accounts can do anything users with an Administrator account can do — but may be prompted to provide the Administrator password before installing hardware or software or changing security settings.

Use an Administrator account only to perform computer-management tasks. For more mundane computing tasks, set up and use a Standard account. (Note that you must use an Administrator account to create a new account.)

See also>>

User Accounts: Enable

User Accounts: Manage

❶ Click Start.

❷ Click Control Panel.

The Control Panel window opens.

❸ Click Add or Remove User Accounts under User Accounts and Family Safety.

Note: *If prompted, type the administrator password or click Continue.*

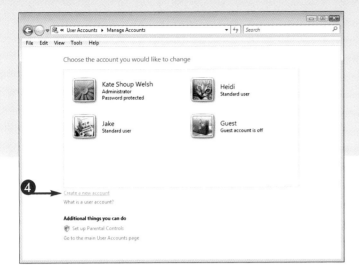

The Manage Accounts window opens.

④ Click Create a New Account.

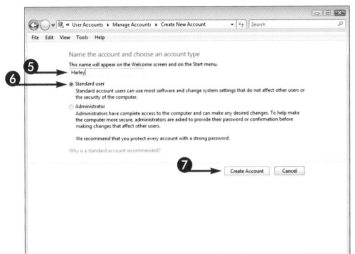

Note: *If prompted, type the administrator password or click Continue.*

The Create New Account window opens.

⑤ Type a name for the new account.

⑥ Choose an account type. (Standard is recommended.)

⑦ Click Create Account.

Windows creates the account.

TIPS

Did You Know?
You can quickly switch user accounts. To do so, click the Start button, click the arrow next to the lock button, click Switch User, and click the account you want. (This feature is called Fast User Switching.) First, however, be sure to save any open files in the account you are switching from.

Attention!
Anyone who can access your Administrator account can change virtually anything on your system. For this reason, creating a secure password and keeping it confidential is especially crucial with Administrator accounts.

USER ACCOUNTS:
Enable Guest Accounts

To give others temporary use of your computer, but without the same amount of access or control that you have, let them use the Guest account in Windows.

The Guest account is a limited account type, which means that it restricts the user's ability to view advanced settings or to modify the Windows configuration or support files. However, a user with Guest access can browse the Internet, play computer games, and use accessories such as Notepad and WordPad.

Be aware that making the Guest account available reduces overall Windows system security because it

allows someone without a user account on the computer to use the system and open files. For this reason, Guest accounts are disabled by default. Nonetheless, there are legitimate reasons for enabling the use of guest accounts — although you should disable guest accounts anytime they are not being used.

See also>>

User Accounts: Create

User Accounts: Manage

❶ Click Start.

❷ Click Control Panel.

The Control Panel window opens.

❸ Click Add or Remove User Accounts under User Accounts and Family Safety.

Note: *If prompted, type the administrator password or click Continue.*

The Manage Accounts window opens.

④ Click the Guest account.

⑤ Click Turn On.

Windows enables the Guest account.

Remove It!
After your guest user has finished with the Guest account, disable the account by clicking the account in the Manage Accounts window and clicking Turn Off the Guest Account in the window that opens.

USER ACCOUNTS:
Manage User Accounts

If several people share your computer, managing their user accounts becomes critical. One key aspect of user-account management is creating and changing a password for each account for users who do not do so on their own — something covered in the task "Passwords: Set a User Password." Another critical aspect of user-account management is implementing parental controls — also covered earlier, in the task "Parental Controls: Set Windows Vista Parental Controls."

Beyond that, user-account management can involve personalizing an account by changing its name, or by

changing the photograph associated with it. The name and photograph will appear on the Welcome screen and on the user's Start menu.

See also>>

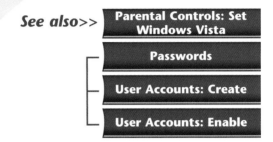

Change the Picture

1 In Control Panel, click Add or Remove User Accounts under User Accounts and Family Safety.

Note: If prompted, type the administrator password or click Continue.

The Manage Accounts window opens.

2 Click the account you want to change.

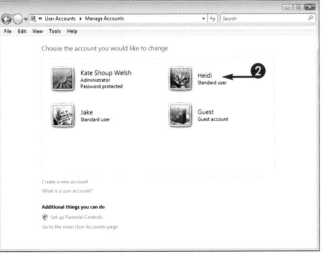

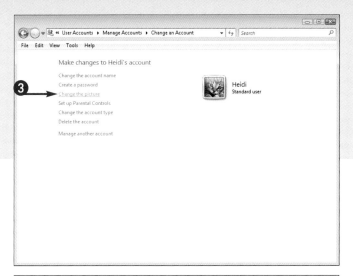

The Change an Account window opens.

3 Click Change the Picture.

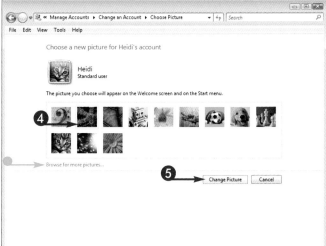

The Choose Picture window opens.

4 Click the picture you want to use.

5 Click Change Picture.

● To use a picture of your own, click the Browse for More Pictures link and locate the image you want to use.

The picture is applied to the account.

Caution!
If a user no longer shares your computer, you should remove his or her account from the system. You cannot delete the account that you are currently using, however. This ensures that an administrator does not delete his or her Administrator account, which would create very serious problems. To delete an account, click the Delete the Account link in the Change an Account window.

Try This!
To change the name of an account, click Change the Account Name in the Change an Account window, type a new name for the account, and click Change Name.

USER ACCOUNTS:
Manage User Accounts (Continued)

Another key aspect of user-account management is ensuring that users have the type of account they need, and changing the account type if necessary. You can change another user's account from Administrator to Standard or vice versa. The main difference between an Administrator account and a Standard account is that an Administrator account can be used to create, modify, and delete any account on the system, as well as specify how users log in, whereas a Standard account can be used only to modify some aspects of an account. The Standard account user cannot perform any changes to other user accounts, nor can they configure the system without first supplying the Administrator account's password.

See also>>

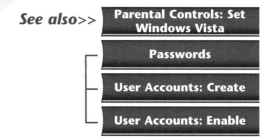

Parental Controls: Set Windows Vista

Passwords

User Accounts: Create

User Accounts: Enable

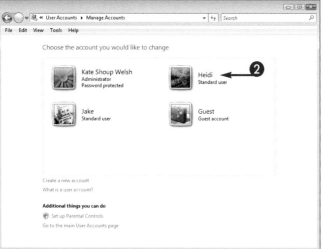

Change the Account Type

1 In the Control Panel window, click Add or Remove User Accounts under User Accounts and Family Safety.

Note: If prompted, type the administrator password or click Continue.

The Manage Accounts window opens.

2 Click the account you want to change.

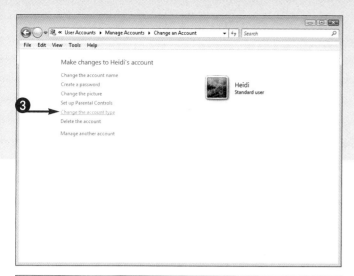

The Change an Account
window opens.

③ Click Change the Account Type.

The Change Account Type
window opens.

④ Click the account type you want
to use for this account.

⑤ Click Change Account Type.

Windows changes the account
type.

More Options!

You can go back at any time to change a
user account from Administrator to
Standard, or vice versa; however, you
must be logged in as an Administrator to
do this.

WINDOWS DEFENDER:
Scan for Spyware

Spyware, which is software that is installed on your computer usually without your knowledge or consent, can overwhelm your system with unwanted pop-up ads, and will almost certainly monitor and record your Web-surfing activities and transmit this data to one or more third parties. Although these third parties are often companies seeking marketing data, they can be more sinister forces: hackers who want your personal information, such as passwords, or who want to sabotage your computer. Even if the spyware on your computer is relatively benign, its presence can dramatically affect the performance of your machine.

Fortunately, you can use Windows Defender to scan your system for spyware. If spyware is detected, Windows Defender can uninstall it automatically. If you like, you can schedule automatic scans to occur on a regular basis. (Windows Defender also offers a real-time protection feature — enabled by default — to alert you if a spyware program attempts to install itself on your machine or if any program attempts to change your Windows settings without your knowledge.)

See also>> | **Windows Update: Check**

① Click Start.

② Click Control Panel.

● The Control Panel window opens.

③ Click Security.

The Security window opens.

④ Click Scan for Spyware and Other Potentially Unwanted Software under Windows Defender.

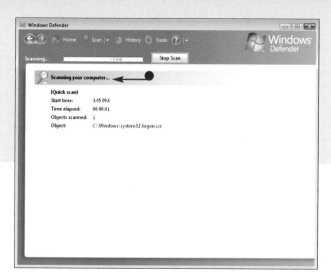

- Windows Defender scans your computer.

  Note: If prompted, type the administrator password or click Allow.

- When the scan is complete, Windows informs you of the results.

Add It Automatically!

To configure Windows to automatically scan your system at an interval you specify, click Tools in the Windows Defender window (accessible via Control Panel), and click Options. Under Automatic Scanning, click the Automatically Scan My Computer checkbox to check it; then set the scan frequency, time of day, and scan type (quick scan or full system scan). Finally, click Save.

Add It Automatically!

To configure Windows to automatically remove spyware it detects during a scan, click Tools in the Windows Defender window, click Options, and, under Automatic Scanning, click the Apply Default Actions to Items Detected During Scan checkbox to check it. Next, under Default Actions, choose Remove from the High Alert Items, Medium Alert Items, and Low Alert Items drop-down lists. Finally, click Save.

WINDOWS FIREWALL:
Configure the Windows Firewall

When you enable and configure the Windows Firewall, you set up a layer of protection to shield your computer or network from intrusion that can put your system at risk. As its name implies, a *firewall* creates a barrier between your system and a network such as the Internet. You should not use more than one firewall on your system at any given time.

System intrusion can take many forms. One example is an *Internet worm*, which is a type of computer virus that can, among other things, leave behind files that create an opening for others who want to access your

computer or steal your passwords. A worm can also send out copies of itself to the people who are listed in your Address Book. Other intruders, such as hackers, may also try to access your files or confidential information.

See also>>  **Windows Firewall**

See also>> **Windows Firewall: Manage**

1. Click Start.
2. Click Control Panel.

The Control Panel window opens.

3. Click Security.

● The Security window opens.

④ Under Windows Firewall, click Turn Windows Firewall On or Off.

Note: If prompted, type the administrator password or click Continue.

● The Windows Firewall Settings dialog box opens to the General tab.

⑤ Click the On option.

⑥ Click the Advanced tab.

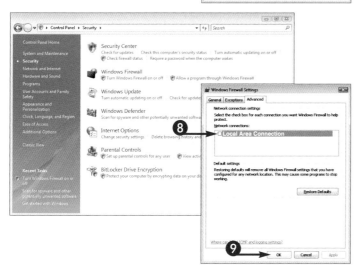

⑦ Review the listing(s) under Network Connections.

By default, all the entries in the Network Connections list are selected.

⑧ Click to deselect any network connection for which you do not want to enable the firewall.

⑨ Click OK.

Your firewall is now configured and enabled.

Important!

Just because you use the Windows Firewall does not mean that you do not need other forms of protection, including common-sense measures that limit your risk of exposure to threats. You should continue to run antivirus software and be careful when opening e-mail attachments or other files from any source, even a trusted one. Also, if you download free software, such as file-sharing programs or screen savers, read the license agreement carefully to ensure that you do not receive pop-up ads from and that the program does not transmit data about your computing habits to the company who developed the software or to any other third parties.

Remove It!

If, after customizing your Windows Firewall configuration, you want it to operate as it originally did, you can restore the default settings by clicking Restore Defaults in the Advanced tab of the Windows Firewall Settings dialog box.

WINDOWS FIREWALL:
Manage Exceptions

When you manage exceptions through Windows Firewall, you can control whether the firewall blocks certain programs or connections from accessing your system or the Internet. An *exception* is a program or connection that you want to allow through the firewall so that it does not limit your ability to work or communicate. It is vital that you manage these exceptions so that your critical network communications are not blocked by the firewall. You can then tell the Windows Firewall how to handle these programs and connections properly.

For example, when you instant-message with someone, you often create a short-term connection between your systems. The firewall may block this connection unless you identify the connection as allowed. You can do this by configuring the firewall ahead of time or when you receive a message from the firewall, asking if you want to block or unblock a connection or program.

See also>> Windows Firewall

See also>> Windows Firewall: Configure

❶ Click Start.

❷ Click Control Panel.

The Control Panel window opens.

❸ Click Security.

The Security window opens.

④ Under Windows Firewall, click **Allow a Program Through Windows Firewall**.

Note: *If prompted, type the administrator password or click Continue.*

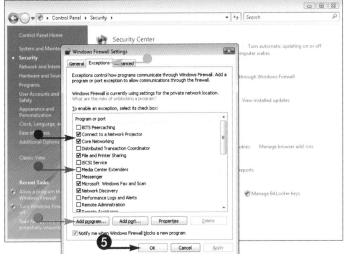

● The Windows Firewall Settings dialog box opens to the Exceptions tab.

In the Program or Port list, a checkmark appears next to any items that are not blocked by the firewall.

● To unblock a program in the list, click to select the checkbox.

● To block a program in the list, click to deselect the checkbox.

● To block or unblock a program that is not in the list, click Add Program and select the program from the list. Then check or uncheck the program's checkbox in the Exceptions tab as needed.

⑤ Click OK.

More Options!

If Windows Firewall prevents you from communicating with a network or running a particular program, one solution is to temporarily disable the firewall. Doing so, however, increases your system's exposure to security threats such as computer viruses. A better approach is to allow the problematic network connection or program as an exception. In the event you do need to disable your firewall, first make sure your computer is running antivirus software. Then click the Off option button in the Windows Firewall dialog box's General tab.

Important!

For maximum security, you can choose to allow *no* exceptions. To do so, click the Block All Incoming Connections checkbox in the Windows Firewall Settings dialog box's General tab.

WINDOWS LIVE MESSENGER:
Create an Account

Although Windows Vista does not include an instant message (IM) program by default, it does provide a link in the Start menu to download Windows Live Messenger, an update of Microsoft's MSN Messenger. After you download and install Windows Live Messenger (click the Start button, click All Programs, click Windows Live Messenger Download, and follow the onscreen prompts), you must create your Windows Live Messenger account.

The account you use with Windows Live Messenger, called your *Windows Live ID*, is the same account you use to take advantage of any other Windows Live

service. (*Windows Live* is a new suite of Internet software designed to make it easier to keep in touch with people and to find information online.) If you already have an MSN Hotmail, MSN Messenger, or Microsoft Passport account, that account automatically becomes your Live ID.

See also>>   **Windows Live Messenger**

See also>>   **Windows Live Messenger: Populate**

Windows Live Messenger: Send

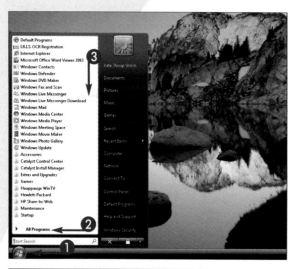

① Click Start.

② Click All Programs.

③ Click Windows Live Messenger.

Windows Live Messenger starts and presents the logon screen.

④ Click Get a New Account.

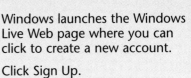

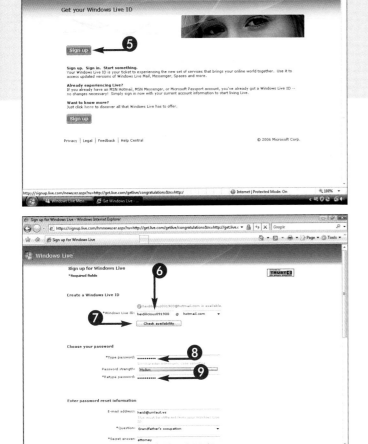

Windows launches the Windows Live Web page where you can click to create a new account.

5 Click Sign Up.

6 Type the username you want to use.

7 Click Check Availability to ensure that the username you typed is available.

Note: If the username you typed is not available, continue typing names and clicking Check Availability until you find one that is.

8 Type the string of characters you want to use as your password.

9 Type the string of characters again to confirm the password.

Did You Know?

If you already have a Windows Live ID — for example, if you created one earlier, or if you previously had an MSN Hotmail, MSN Messenger, or Microsoft Passport account — you can log in to Windows Live Messenger by typing your e-mail address and password in the Live Messenger login screen. If you want to avoid having to sign in for subsequent sessions, click the Sign Me In Automatically checkbox to select it.

WINDOWS LIVE MESSENGER:
Create an Account (Continued)

In addition to standard IM-related tools, such as contact lists and emoticons, Windows Live Messenger includes several new features such as folder sharing, PC-to-PC calling, PC-to-phone service throughout North America and western Europe, and more.

Windows Live also enables you to create a blog through Windows Live Spaces, post or browse ads on Windows Live Expo, use Windows Live Mail as a Web-based e-mail program, protect your computer with Windows Live OneCare, and more. Once you create your Windows Live ID, you can use any or all of these features.

Note that although many of the tools and features offered by Windows Live are free of charge, others, such as the PC-to-phone service and certain Windows Live OneCare tools, involve a fee. Be sure you understand the pay structure (if applicable) of any Windows Live service you use.

See also>> Windows Live Messenger

See also>> Windows Live Messenger: Populate

Windows Live Messenger: Send

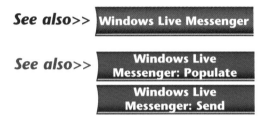

⑩ Type the address for an e-mail account you currently hold.

⑪ Click here to choose a question. (In the event you forget your password, you are prompted to answer the question you select here in order to reset it.)

⑫ Type the answer to the question you selected in Step **11**.

⑬ Scroll down as needed, and fill in your personal information.

⑭ Type the characters shown on the screen.

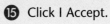

⑮ Click I Accept.

The Live ID is created.

TIPS

More Options!
Using buttons on the Windows Live Messenger screen, you can see which of your contacts are currently online, watch videos on MSN Video, access MSN Shopping, try the Rhapsody music service, find deals on eBay, view personal ads, and more.

Did You Know?
You type the characters shown in Step **14** in order to confirm that a person, rather than, say, an automated program, is attempting to create an account. (This helps prevent misuse of the Windows Live ID system.)

WINDOWS LIVE MESSENGER:
Populate Your Contacts

In order to use Windows Live Messenger to send and receive IMs, you must first add your contacts to the program.

You can enter extensive information about a contact, including his or her home address, home phone, home e-mail address, work address, work phone, work e-mail address, and mobile phone numbers. You can also enter any applicable Web sites, as well as personal information such as the contact's birth date, the name of his or her spouse or partner, and so on. Finally, you can enter notes about the contact.

That said, all that is *required* to enter a contact into your Windows Live Message contacts list is the contact's name and e-mail address or mobile phone number.

See also>> Windows Live Messenger

See also>> Windows Live Messenger: Create

Windows Live Messenger: Send

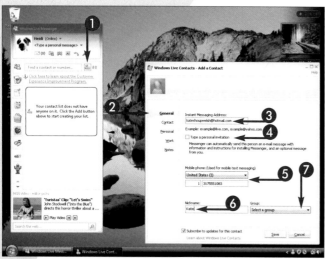

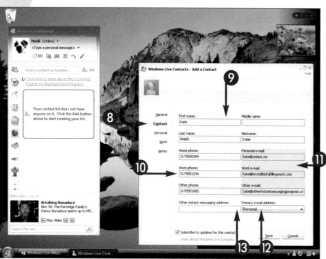

① In the Windows Live Messenger window, click the Add a Contact button.

② In the Add a Contact window, click General.

③ Type the contact's IM address.

④ Optionally, click the Type a Personal Invitation checkbox and invite the contact to install Windows Live Messenger.

⑤ To IM with this contact on his or her mobile, choose the contact's region and type the phone number.

⑥ Type the contact's nickname.

⑦ Click to place the contact in a group.

⑧ Click Contact.

⑨ Type the contact's name.

⑩ Type the contact's phone numbers.

⑪ Type the contact's e-mail addresses.

⑫ Specify the primary e-mail address.

⑬ If the contact uses any other instant-messaging addresses, type one here.

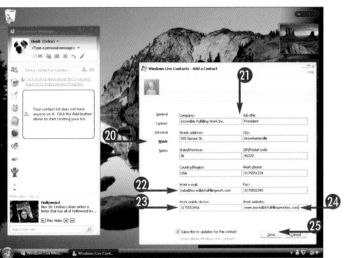

14 Click Personal.

15 Type the contact's home address and home phone numbers.

16 Type the contact's personal e-mail address.

17 If the contact maintains a Web site, type its URL here.

18 Enter the contact's birth date.

19 Type the name of the contact's spouse or partner and enter the contact's anniversary, if applicable.

20 Click Work.

21 Type the contact's company, job title, work address, and work phone numbers.

22 Type the contact's work e-mail address.

23 Type the contact's work mobile device number.

24 Type the URL of the company's Web site.

25 Click Save.

Remove It!

To remove a contact from your list, right-click it and click Delete Contact. In the dialog box that opens, block the contact by clicking the Also Block This Contact checkbox to mark it. (Blocking a contact prevents that contact from seeing whether you are online and from contacting you.) Optionally, click Also Remove from My Hotmail Contacts checkbox. When you are finished, click Delete Contact.

Did You Know?

You can configure Windows Live Messenger to automatically update a contact's information in your contact list if he or she updates it in Windows Live Contacts. To do so, click the Subscribe to Updates for This Contact checkbox to select it.

More Options!

To add notes about the contact, click Notes and type the necessary information.

WINDOWS LIVE MESSENGER:
Send and Receive IMs

Depending on how your and your recipient's e-mail programs are set up, there may be a delay between the time you send an e-mail message and the time it appears in your recipient's inbox. Even if the e-mail message arrives quickly, if your recipient is offline, there is no telling when he or she will actually see your message.

In contrast, instant messages allow for instantaneous communication. Instant-messaging programs such as Windows Live Messenger enable you to determine who among your contacts are currently online and running a compatible IM program. If a compatible contact is online, you can use the program to send

and receive messages with none of the delays that can occur in e-mail communications.

You can also use Windows Live Messenger to send a text message to a mobile phone, place a phone call (provided you have the necessary hardware), and more. (For details, see the program's help information.)

See also>> **Windows Live Messenger**

See also>> **Windows Live Messenger: Create**

Windows Live Messenger: Populate

Receive and Respond To an IM

- When someone sends you an IM, Windows displays it near the taskbar's Notifications Area.

  Note: Messages sent by others will appear here only if Windows Live Messenger is running on your computer.

❶ Click the message.

- A message window opens.

❷ Type your reply.

❸ Press Enter or click Send.

Start a New IM Thread

1 In the Windows Live Messenger window, right-click the contact to whom you want to send an IM.

2 Click Send an Instant Message.

● A message window opens.

3 Type your message.

4 Press Enter or click Send.

More Options!

In addition to typing text in an IM, you can also add emoticons to your messages — that is, special characters meant to convey a facial expression or emotion. Using emoticons can help prevent others from misinterpreting your messages. Also available are *winks*, which are animated greetings you can send to your contacts, and *nudges*, which cause the conversation window to vibrate.

Remove It!

In the event the ads that run along the bottom of the Windows Live Messenger window annoy you, there are some free, third-party programs designed to eliminate them. At the time of this writing, a program called A-Patch leads the pack. For more information, type **"Windows Live Messenger" advertisements** (quotes included) in your favorite search engine.

WINDOWS MEDIA CENTER:
Burn Digital Video to a DVD

If your Windows Vista computer includes a TV tuner, you can use Windows Media Center to record your favorite television shows. You can then burn those recorded shows onto a DVD for use with a traditional DVD player or for use with the DVD drive on your PC.

In addition to burning recorded television programs, you can also use Windows Media Center to burn any other digital video clips on your PC onto a DVD. These might include clips you have downloaded from the Internet, or that you have imported from a digital video camera using the Import Video Wizard. To locate

your video files, scroll to Pictures + Videos in the Windows Media Center Start screen and click Video Library.

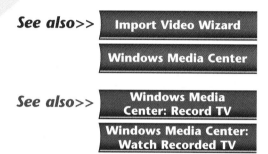

See also>> **Import Video Wizard**

Windows Media Center

See also>> **Windows Media Center: Record TV**

Windows Media Center: Watch Recorded TV

① Click Start.

② Click All Programs.

③ Click Windows Media Center.

④ Insert a blank, recordable DVD into your PC's DVD drive.

⑤ In Windows Media Center, scroll to Tasks.

⑥ Click Burn CD/DVD.

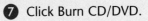
⑦ Click Burn CD/DVD.

The Select Disc Format screen opens.

⑧ Click Video DVD.

⑨ Click Next.

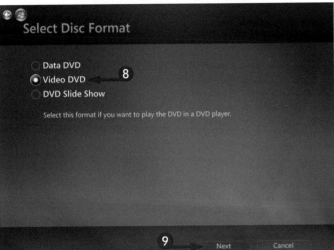

Did You Know?

Note that you can also *play* DVDs using Windows Media Center. To do so, insert the DVD into your PC's DVD drive, scroll to TV+Movies on the Windows Media Center Start screen, and click Play DVD.

WINDOWS MEDIA CENTER:
Burn Digital Video to a DVD (Continued)

When you burn digital video to a DVD, you are required to supply a name for the DVD. Opt for something descriptive so that you can more easily keep track of which DVDs hold which content.

You have the option of choosing to burn recorded television shows or digital video you have imported to your PC. If you like, you can burn video from multiple sources onto a single DVD. For example, you might burn a few recorded shows alongside some video you have uploaded from the Web.

Be aware that burning a DVD can take some time, depending on your system's resources.

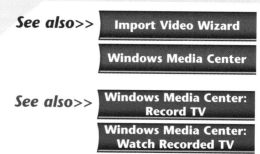

See also>> Import Video Wizard

Windows Media Center

See also>> Windows Media Center: Record TV

Windows Media Center: Watch Recorded TV

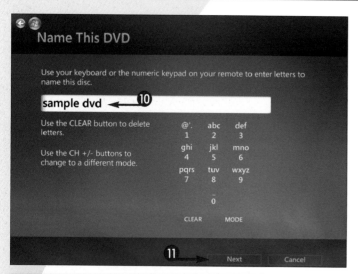

The Name This DVD screen opens.

🔟 Using your keyboard or the keypad on your remote control, enter a name for your DVD.

⓫ Click Next.

The Select Media screen opens.

⓬ Click Recorded TV (or Video Library, depending on the type of video you want to burn).

⓭ Click Next.

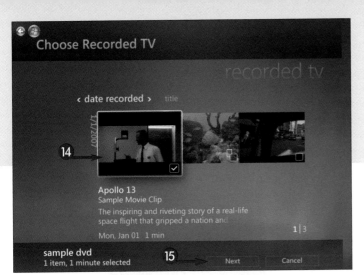

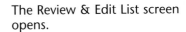

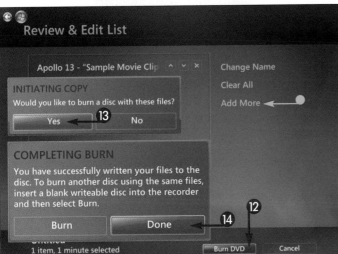

The Choose Recorded TV screen opens.

⑭ Click the TV program (or video) that you want to burn to DVD. A checkmark appears in the bottom-right corner of the selection.

⑮ Click Next.

The Review & Edit List screen opens.

● To burn more content on the same DVD, click Add More in the Review & Edit List screen and select the content you want to add.

⑫ Click Burn DVD.

⑬ In the Initiating Copy dialog box, click Yes.

⑭ Windows Media Center burns the disc. When the Completing Burn dialog box appears, click Done.

Did You Know?

In addition to burning video to DVD, you can also burn a slide show set to music to a recordable DVD for playback in any DVD player. To do so, click DVD Slide Show in the Select Disc Format screen. In the Select Media screen, click Music Library, select the songs you want to include on your DVD, and click Next. In the Review & Edit List screen, click Add More to again see the Select Media screen; click Picture Library, click Next, click each picture you want to include on your DVD, and click Next. Finally, click Burn DVD and follow the onscreen instructions.

WINDOWS MEDIA CENTER:
Listen to Music Files

In addition to using Windows Media Center to watch and record TV, to watch DVDs, and so on, you can also use it to listen to the music files in your PC's Music folder, and to burn music CDs.

Windows Media Center stores your music in the Music Library. If you are not certain what you want to listen to, you might opt to browse the Music Library to see what strikes your fancy. Alternatively, you might opt to search for a specific album, artist, genre, song, playlist, or composer.

Once you locate the song you want to hear, playing it is as simple as clicking a button. You can opt to hear just the song, or the entire album on which the song is found (provided you have the entire album stored on your PC).

See also>> **Windows Media Center**

See also>> **Windows Media Center: Set**

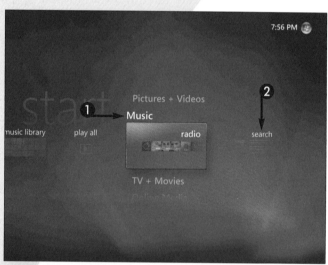

Search for Music

❶ In the Windows Media Center window, scroll to Music.

❷ Click Search.

❸ Click Search.

370

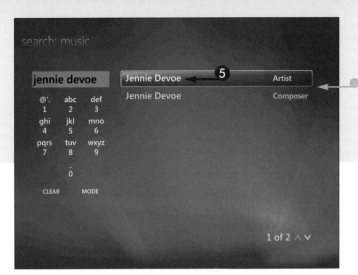

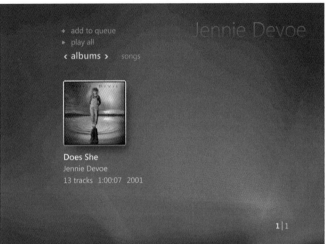

④ Using your keyboard or the buttons on your remote control, type a keyword or phrase. (Note that the keypad on the screen matches the buttons on your remote control.)

● Windows Media Center displays a list of entries that match your search criteria.

⑤ Click the desired entry.

Windows Media Center displays the resulting album or song.

Try This!
Windows Media Center can display *visualizations* — animated colors and shapes that move in time to the music. To view visualizations, click to play the song, album, or playlist you want to hear and click Visualize. For more information, see Windows Media Center's help information.

Remove It!
To delete a music file, click it in your Music Library, click Delete, and click Yes.

WINDOWS MEDIA CENTER:
Listen to Music Files (Continued)

In addition to searching for your music, you can simply browse your Music Library. To open it, scroll to Music on the Start screen and click Music Library. Once you open the Music Library, you can browse your music by album, artist, genre, song, playlist, or composer. After you find the music you are looking for, playing it is a simple matter of clicking a button.

In addition to listening to music files stored on your computer, you can also use Windows Media Center to play CDs. Simply open Windows Media Center and insert an audio CD in your PC's CD drive.

While a queue is still active, it can be edited. That is, songs within the queue can be moved, and songs can be deleted.

See also>>

See also>>

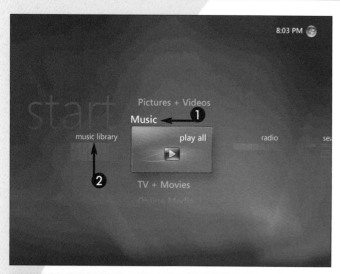

Browse Music

① In the Windows Media Center window, scroll to Music.

② Click Music Library.

③ Click Music Library.

4 Click the category you want to browse (here, Albums).

● Windows Media Center lists the entries in the category you chose.

5 Click the item in the list that you want to hear.

Play a Song

1 After you locate the song or album you want to hear by browsing or searching, click Play Album to listen to it.

More Options!

In addition to using Windows Media Center to listen to the music files stored on your computer, you can also use the program to enjoy FM and Internet radio. You can even create presets to make your favorite stations more easily accessible. For more details, view Windows Media Center's help information.

Caution!

Windows Media Center does make it easy to rip, burn, store, and organize your digital media, but it is up to you to not copy or otherwise use copyrighted material without authorization. Unauthorized use of such materials may subject you to criminal and/or civil penalties.

WINDOWS MEDIA CENTER:
Listen to Music Files (Continued)

If you want to enjoy a longer listening session, you can stack up songs in a *queue*. Windows Media Center then plays the songs in your queue in the order you specify.

If you particularly like a queue you have created, you can save it as a *playlist*. Unlike queues, playlists are not automatically deleted by Windows Media Center when you click a song or album in your Music Library and click Play instead of Add to Queue; access a different type of media such as Internet radio, TV, movies, pictures, or videos; or close Windows Media Center. After you save a queue as a playlist, you can

then open the playlist in a later session to listen to the set of songs it contains. In addition to listening to a playlist, you can also add a playlist to a larger queue or burn a playlist to a CD. In the event you no longer wish to maintain the playlist, you can easily delete it.

See also>>

See also>> Windows Media Center: Set

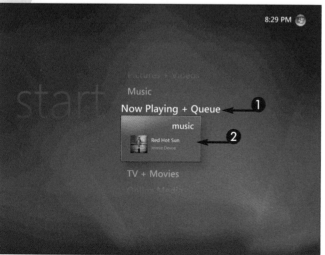

Add Songs to a Queue

❶ After you locate the song or album you want to add to a queue by browsing or searching, click Add to Queue.

Save the Queue as a Playlist

❶ In the Windows Media Center Start screen, click Now Playing+Queue.

❷ Click the queue.

3 Click View Queue.

4 Click Save As Playlist.

5 In the screen that appears, type a name for the playlist and click Save.

 TIPS

Did You Know?

To view a playlist, click Playlists in the Windows Media Center Music Library and click the playlist. Click Play to listen to the playlist; click Add to Queue to add the contents of the selected playlist to your queue; click Burn CD/DVD to burn the songs on the playlist to a CD or DVD; or click Delete to delete the playlist.

Did You Know?

Queues are temporary. Windows Media Center deletes a queue if you click a song or album in your Music Library and click Play instead of Add to Queue; access a different type of media such as Internet radio, TV, movies, pictures, or videos; or close Windows Media Center.

Try This!

You can edit a queue, deleting or changing the order of songs. To do so, click Now Playing + Queue in the Windows Media Center Start screen and click View Queue. Windows Media Center displays the queue; click Edit Queue, click a song you want to move or remove from the queue, and click the up and down buttons or the Delete button respectively. When you finish, click Done.

WINDOWS MEDIA CENTER:
Record TV

If your PC has a TV tuner, you can use Windows Media Center to watch and record TV. Windows Media Center saves recorded programs as digital files, which you can view at your leisure.

To record a program manually as it is playing, click Record on the transport controls. (The transport controls are the ones used to play, pause, fast-forward, rewind, stop, and record media; to change channels; and to adjust the volume.)

Alternatively, to configure Windows Media Center to record an upcoming program, right-click the program in the Media Center guide and click Record. (To record all episodes in a series, right-click an episode in the guide and click Record Series.)

If you like, you can program Windows Media Center to automatically record using criteria you set — for example, all episodes of a particular television series. Or you might record all instances of programs that involve a particular keyword, such as the name of an actor, the title of a program, or a phrase such as "alpine ski."

See also>> **Windows Media Center: Watch Recorded TV**

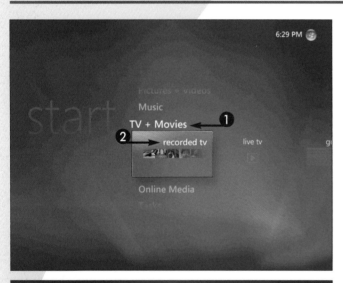

1 On the Windows Media Center Start screen, scroll to TV+Movies.

2 Click Recorded TV.

3 Click Add Recording.

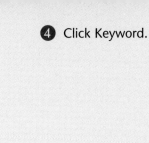

4 Click Keyword.

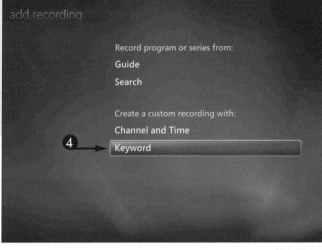

5 Click the type of keyword you want to use — actor name, director name, movie title, program title, or generic keyword.

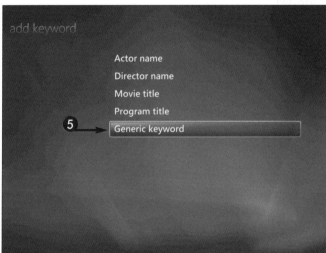

More Options!

To set recording options for a single show or a series, scroll to Tasks on the Windows Media Center Start screen and click Settings. Next, click TV, click Recorder, and click Recording Defaults. In the screen that appears, you can specify how long you want to keep recordings, the recordings' level of quality, and so on.

WINDOWS MEDIA CENTER:
Record TV (Continued)

When you set up Windows Media Center to record a program automatically, you can specify the frequency with which the program should be recorded (every time it plays or once only), the type of show (that is, first run only, first-run shows and reruns, or live shows only), and a daily recording limit (no limit or once per day). You also specify how many episodes of the program you want to keep (a number of your choosing between 1 and 10 or as many as possible), and how long each recording should remain on your hard drive (until you delete it, until you watch it, or until space is needed; alternatively, opt to save the latest recordings only).

See also>> Windows Media Center: Watch Recorded TV

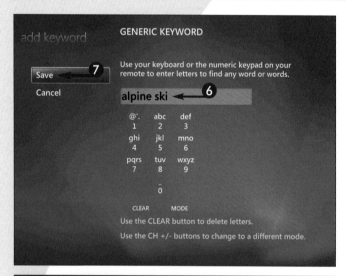

6 Enter the desired keyword or phrase.

7 Click Save.

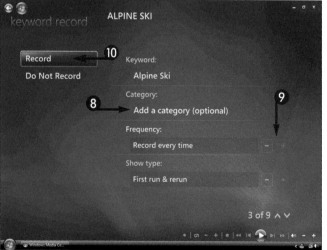

8 Optionally, click Add a Category and choose a category on the screen that appears. (This ensures that Windows Media Center records only those shows in the category you choose.)

9 Click the + or – buttons to specify other criteria, such as frequency, show type, and so on.

10 Click Record.

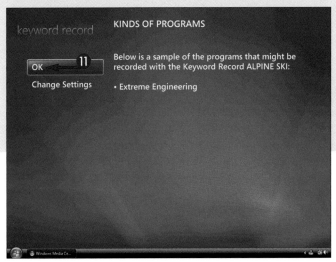

⑪ Click OK.

⑫ To view a list of programs scheduled to be recorded, click View Scheduled.

Windows Media Center displays a list of programs that are scheduled to be recorded.

More Options!

To record a certain channel at a specific time, click Channel and Time in the Recorded TV screen. Enter the channel you want to record, specify how often and when, and indicate how long Windows Media Center should retain recorded files.

WINDOWS MEDIA CENTER:
Set Up Windows Media Center

In order to fully enjoy Windows Media Center's entertainment features, you want to take time to configure its Internet connection, TV signal, and speaker setup.

To facilitate this, Windows Media Center has made all these settings accessible from a single screen: the Windows Media Center Setup screen. To open this screen, scroll to Tasks in the Windows Media Center Start screen and click Settings. The Settings screen opens; click General. In the screen that appears, click Windows Media Center Setup.

Once you are in the Windows Media Center Setup screen, you can simply click Set Up Internet Connection, Set Up TV Signal, or Set Up Your Speakers to launch the appropriate wizard.

(Note that when setting up your Internet connection, your steps may vary slightly depending on whether your Internet connection is always on, as is typically the case with a broadband connection. The steps in this task assume that it is.)

See also>> **Windows Media Center**

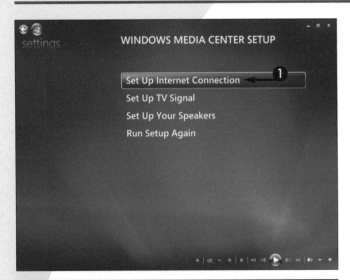

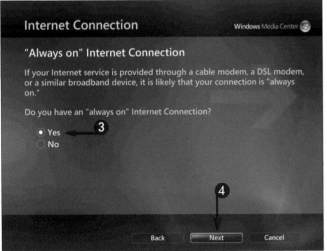

Set Up the Internet Connection

1 In the Windows Media Center Setup screen, click Set Up Internet Connection.

2 In the screen that appears, click Next.

3 When asked if you have an "always on" Internet connection, click Yes or No. (Note that because I have an always on connection, I have clicked Yes.)

4 Click Next.

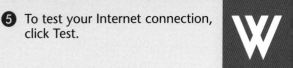

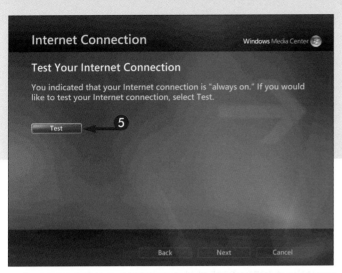

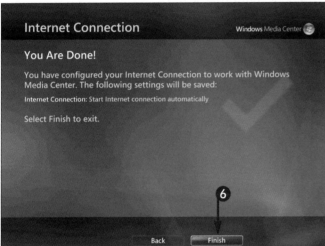

⑤ To test your Internet connection, click Test.

⑥ Click Finish.

Attention!

If you plan to use your Windows Media Center PC to watch television, assuming you have installed the necessary hardware (such as a TV tuner) and set up your system to receive a television signal such as a cable or DSL signal, you will need to configure the TV signal. To do so, click Set Up TV Signal in the Windows Media Center Setup screen and follow the onscreen instructions.

Did You Know?

Windows Media Center is designed to work in conjunction with a remote control, which can greatly enhance the experience of using your Windows Media Center PC to watch television. You can purchase special remote controls designed to work with Windows Media Center at any number of retail outlets. For details on how to use the remote control, see Windows Media Center's help information.

WINDOWS MEDIA CENTER:
Set Up Windows Media Center (Continued)

A key aspect of any home-entertainment center is sound — which is profoundly affected by the system's speaker setup.

The speaker setup you choose will depend on a few factors, including the capabilities of your Windows Media Center computer's audio hardware, the number of speakers you have, and whether or not those speakers are wirelessly connected to your computer (or, if applicable, to your audio receiver).

You access the Speaker Setup settings from the Windows Media Center Setup screen. To open this screen, scroll to Tasks in the Windows Media Center Start screen and click Settings. The Settings screen opens; click General. In the screen that appears, click Windows Media Center Setup.

See also>> **Windows Media Center**

Set Up the Speakers

1 In the Windows Media Center Setup screen, click Set Up Your Speakers.

2 In the screen that appears, click Next.

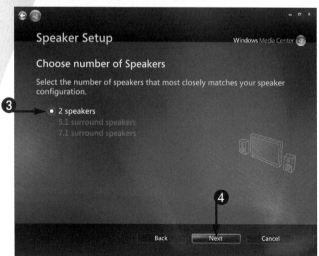

3 Click the speaker configuration that most closely mirrors your own.

4 Click Next.

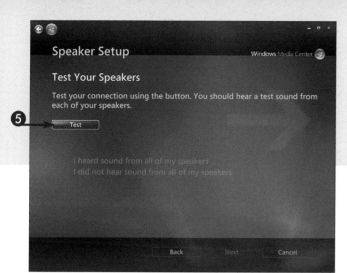

⑤ To test your speaker setup, click Test.

⑥ Click Finish.

Did You Know?

Suppose you used your Windows Media Center computer to record a program, but rather than watching it in the den, where the computer is housed, you want to watch it in your bedroom. The use of a special device called a Windows Media Center Extender enables you to do just that. You can install a Windows Media Center Extender on the TV in your bedroom, and then use that TV to connect to your Windows Media Center PC via your home network.

WINDOWS MEDIA CENTER:
Watch Live TV

You can use Windows Media Center to watch television, provided you have a TV tuner installed on your PC. (Note that you will be able to receive only those channels that the other televisions in your home receive. For example, if your other TVs use a basic cable package, those are the channels that will be available on your Windows Media Center machine.)

To enhance your viewing experience, Windows Media Center enables you to pause a live television program — for example, to answer a telephone call. When you are ready to return to the show, you can resume watching, fast-forwarding through the commercials until you catch back up with the live broadcast. These buttons (along with channel, volume, mute, play, stop, and rewind buttons) are accessible via onscreen controls or from the remote control.

The easiest way to determine what television programs are on is to use the Windows Media Center Guide.

See also>> Windows Media Center

See also>> Windows Media Center: Watch Recorded TV

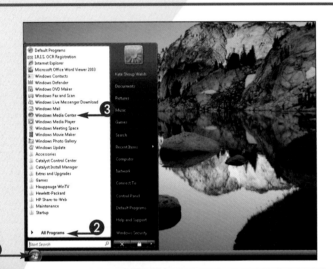

① Click Start.

② Click All Programs.

③ Click Windows Media Center.

④ In the Windows Media Center Start screen, scroll to TV+Movies.

⑤ Click Guide.

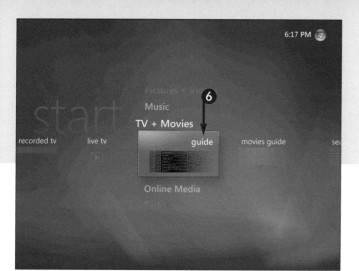

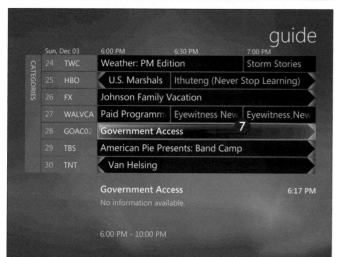

6 Click Guide.

7 Locate the program you want to watch and click it.

Windows Media Center switches to TV mode.

Attention!
Before you use the Guide, which displays programming information in a grid format, listing the date, time, channel number, channel name, and program title, optimize it to match your television service provider's listings. To do so, scroll to Tasks on the Windows Media Center Start screen, click Settings, click TV, click Set Up Guide Listings, and follow the onscreen instructions. (Note that on occasion, TV service providers update their Guide listings; to ensure that your Guide's listings match, download the latest listings by scrolling to Tasks on the Start screen, clicking Settings, clicking TV, clicking Guide, and clicking Get Latest Guide Listings.) To resolve Guide-related issues, see Windows Media Center's help information.

WINDOWS MEDIA CENTER:
Watch Recorded TV

If your PC has a TV tuner, you can use Windows Media Center to record TV programs either manually, as the program is playing, or automatically, using criteria you specify. Windows Media Center saves recorded programs as digital files, which you can view at your leisure.

When watching recorded TV, you can pause, rewind, and fast-forward the program, much as you can when you watch a DVD. This enables you to skip portions of the broadcast that do not interest you, such as advertisements. The buttons that enable

you to do this are accessible via onscreen controls or from the remote control. When you finish watching a recorded show, you can delete it to free up space on your PC for more recordings.

See also>> Windows Media Center

See also>> Windows Media Center: Record TV

Windows Media Center: Watch Live TV

---

① On the Windows Media Center Start screen, scroll to TV+Movies.

② Click Recorded TV.

③ Click Recorded TV.

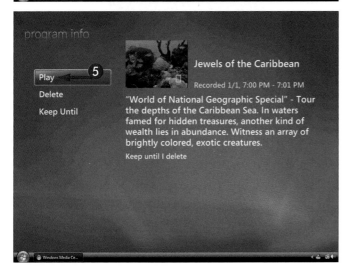

④ Locate the recorded program that you want to watch and click it.

⑤ Click Play.

Windows Media Center plays the recorded program.

Did You Know?

By default, Windows Media Center keeps your recordings until space runs out, at which point it deletes the oldest stored recording. To select a different "Keep" option, scroll to Tasks on the Start screen, click TV, click Recorder, and click Recording Defaults. Then, using the + or − button, select Until Space Needed, For 1 Week, Until I Watch, or Until I Delete. When you finish, click Save.

Did You Know?

The quality of a recording is directly related to how much disk space that recording consumes, with higher-quality recordings consuming more disk space. To change the quality level of your recordings, navigate to the Recording Defaults screen and, under Quality, click the + or − button to select Fair, Good, Better, or Best.

WINDOWS MEETING SPACE:
Share Files, Programs, and Your Desktop

When you are a participant in a Windows Meeting Space session, your workspace includes an icon for each session participant and a Handouts link. The Handouts link enables you to share documents (*handouts*, in Windows Meeting Space parlance) with other session participants, and they with you. These handouts can be edited by any member of the session, and the changes made will appear in each person's copy of the handout (the original file remains intact).

Windows Meeting Space also allows you to *present* programs and even your entire desktop in the Share

a Program or Your Desktop area — that is, to transmit the contents of your screen to the other members of the session, enabling them to take command of those programs or the desktop as needed. You can also use Windows Meeting Space to pass notes. All communication is encrypted to ensure that only authorized session participants can access the shared information.

See also>> **Windows Meeting Space**

See also>> **Windows Meeting Space: Start**

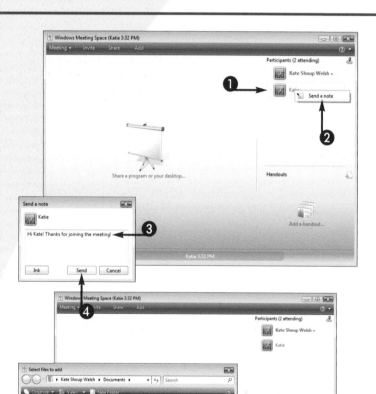

Send a Note to Another Participant

1 To send a note to another participant in your session, right-click the participant's icon in the session window.

2 Choose Send a Note.

3 Type the text for your note.

4 Click Send.

Share a Handout

1 To share a document with the other participants, click Add a Handout.

> **Note:** *If a dialog box appears, read its contents carefully and click OK to proceed.*

2 Click the document you want to share.

3 Click Open.

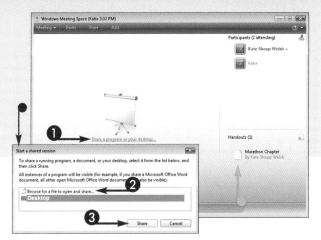

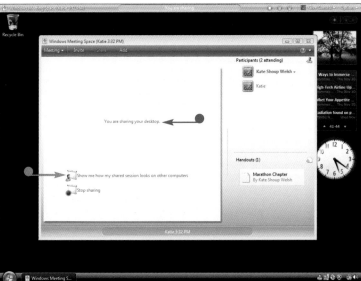

● An icon representing the shared handout appears.

Share a Program

① To share a running application, or even your whole desktop, with the group, click the Share a Program or Your Desktop link.

Note: If a dialog box appears, read its contents and click OK to proceed.

● The Start a Shared Session dialog box opens.

② Click Browse for a File to Open or Share to locate the item you want to share, or click Desktop (shown here).

③ Click Share.

● The session window changes to indicate that you are presenting your desktop or the selected application or file to the group.

● To see how your presentation looks on the other computers in your session, click Show Me How My Shared Session Looks on Other Computers.

Important!

If you have trouble connecting to a session, you may not have the necessary firewall ports open. If your system runs Windows Firewall, fix the problem by checking the Windows Meeting Space checkbox in the Windows Firewall dialog box's Exceptions tab.

Important!

If, when you share an application, other participants see large black areas, minimizing any windows covering that application on your screen should solve the problem.

WINDOWS MEETING SPACE:
Start a Windows Meeting Space Session

Using Windows Meeting Space, you can share notes, documents, programs, and even your desktop with nine other computers on a network (all of which must be running Windows Vista) and vice versa.

Computers in a Windows Meeting Space session connect using *peer-to-peer technology*; each computer in the session communicates with the others over the Internet or a private network, without requiring a server. If no network is present, Windows Meeting Space can set up an *ad hoc network*, in which the computers in the session

connect wirelessly, with wires, or some combination thereof to each other rather than to a network hub or router. All communication is encrypted to ensure that only authorized session participants can access the shared information.

See also>>

Windows Meeting Space

See also>> Windows Meeting Space: Share

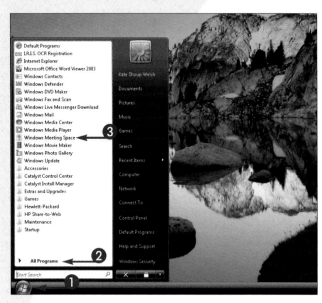

1 Click Start.

2 Click All Programs.

3 Click Windows Meeting Space.

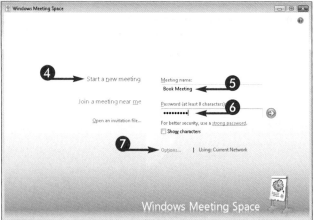

The Windows Meeting Space window opens.

4 Click Start a New Meeting.

5 In the Meeting Name field, type a name for the session.

6 Type a password for the session.

7 To change visibility or network options (for example, to use a different network or to instruct Windows Meeting Space to create an ad hoc network), click Options.

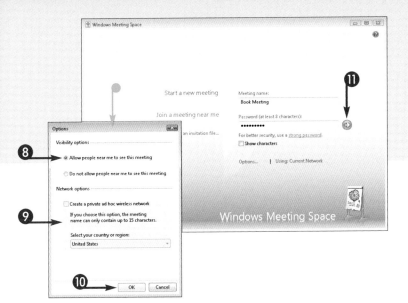

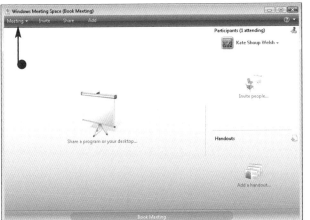

- The Options dialog box opens.
- **8** Change the visibility options as needed.
- **9** Change the network options as needed.
- **10** Click OK.
- **11** Click the green arrow to start the meeting.

The session window opens.

- The meeting will continue until all participants leave the meeting. To leave a meeting, click Meeting in the upper-left corner of the Meeting window and choose Leave Meeting.

Important!
To invite remote users to your session, click Invite People in the session window, choose your invitees from the ensuing list, and click Send Invitations. If an invitee is not listed, click Invite Others; then issue the invitation via e-mail, instant message, or *invitation file*.

Important!
If this is the first time you have launched the Windows Meeting Space program, you will be prompted to enable People Near Me, which is a technology that identifies people using computers near you and allows them to identify you. You may also be asked whether you want Windows Meeting Space to communicate through Windows Firewall; in order to use Windows Meeting Space, you must choose Yes.

Try This!
To join a session, click Join a Session Near Me in the Windows Meeting Space window, type the password (obtained from the host), and click the green arrow. Alternatively, if you receive an invitation via e-mail, double-click the file attached to the invitation, enter the password, and click Join. Finally, to join via an invitation file, click Open an Invitation File in the Windows Meeting Space window, click the invitation file, type the password, and click Join.

WINDOWS UPDATE:
Check for Updates

Windows Vista is a complex operating system that requires *updates* or *patches* — that is, additions to software that can prevent or fix problems or enhance security or performance. Microsoft constantly develops and publishes updates for Windows to make the operating system work to its fullest potential, and to make it more secure and reliable. One way to obtain updates is to manually check for them using Windows Update.

See also>> Windows Update

See also>> Windows Update: Configure

Windows Update: Remove

1 Click Start.

2 Click All Programs.

3 Click Windows Update.

The Windows Update window opens.

4 To manually check for a new update, click Check for Updates.

● Windows Update checks for updates.

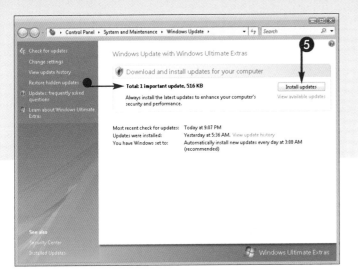

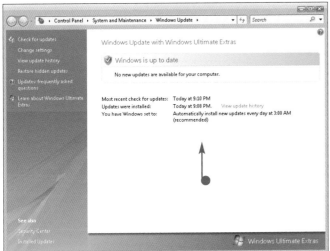

- If Windows Update detects an update, it lists it here.

5 Click Install Updates to install any needed updates.

Note: You may be prompted to restart your computer for the updates to take effect. However, most updates allow you to choose Restart Later if that is more convenient.

- If no required updates are detected, you see this screen.

Caution!

Some updates applied to your Windows Vista setup may cause problems. If you suspect that a recent update does not work well with your system, you can review and, if necessary, remove it.

More Options!

If you use Microsoft Office, you can use a feature similar to Windows Update to apply patches and drivers to your Microsoft Office software. Click Help in your Microsoft Office application and then click the link to Microsoft Office Online to learn more.

More Options!

Just as you need to keep your Vista software up-to-date, you must also keep your Windows Defender *definitions*, which track known spyware and other potentially unwanted software, updated. Windows Defender works with Windows Update to install these definitions.

WINDOWS UPDATE:
Configure Automatic Updates

Although you can manually obtain updates and patches, Windows Update also allows you to automate the update and patch process. For example, you can schedule Windows Update to automatically download and install updates on a regular basis, such as every day at 3:00 a.m.

Updates are downloaded in the background while you are online. Turning on automatic updating ensures that Windows will install the latest important and recommended updates for your computer; failing to update your computer may put it at risk.

If you prefer to have more control over these updates, then you can configure Windows Update to download

the updates but not install them until you direct it to do so. This option offers the advantage of automatic updates and notification, as well as control over when Windows applies these updates.

See also>>

Windows Update

See also>> Windows Update: Check

Windows Update: Remove

① Click Start.

② Click All Programs.

③ Click Windows Update.

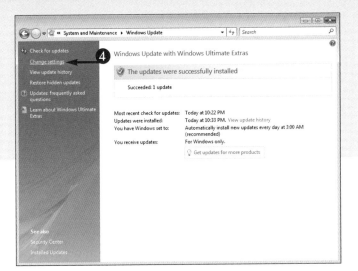

The Windows Update window opens.

④ To change the Automatic Update settings, click Change Settings.

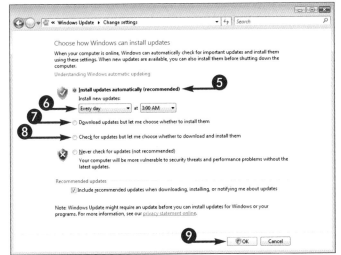

The Change Settings window opens.

⑤ Click the Install Updates Automatically option button to select it.

⑥ Click the lists under Install New Updates to select an update interval, as well as what time the automatic update should occur.

⑦ If you want more control over the update process, click the Download Updates But Let Me Choose Whether to Install Them option button.

⑧ For still more control over the update process, click the Check for Updates But Let Me Choose Whether to Download and Install Them option button.

⑨ Click OK.

Important!

Updates for other programs might not occur automatically. Some programs provide links to check for updates; others can notify you when new updates become available. For updates for other Microsoft programs, visit the Microsoft Update Web site (http://update.microsoft.com).

Attention!

In the event an important update cannot be installed, Windows Update will notify you.

Important!

In order to finish the installation procedure for some updates, you must restart your computer. If you are away from your desk when the update installs, Windows automatically restarts.

Try This!

To see a list of updates, click the View Update History link in the main Windows Update window.

WINDOWS UPDATE:
Remove a Potential Problem Update

If you notice any problems with your system immediately after an update, the update itself may be the culprit. For example, an update to a modem or video driver may leave you unable to connect to the Internet, or it may adversely affect your display. In these cases, you can solve the problem by removing the update.

Some updates, such as updates that relate to the security of Windows Vista, cannot be removed. Likewise, you will be unable to remove the update

if your computer is connected to a network that prohibits this operation.

See also>> **Windows Update**

See also>> **Windows Update: Check**

Windows Update: Configure

1 Click Start.

2 Click All Programs.

3 Click Windows Update.

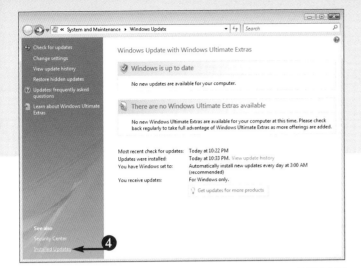

The Windows Update window opens.

④ Click the Installed Updates link.

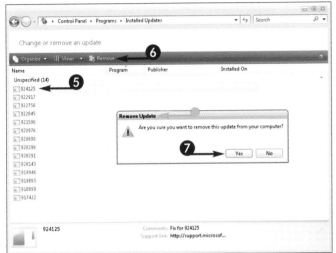

The Installed Updates window opens.

⑤ Click the update you want to remove.

⑥ Click Remove.

Note: *If prompted, type the administrator password or click Allow.*

● A prompt asks you to confirm your change.

⑦ Click Yes.

After you remove the update, it will no longer be visible in the Installed Updates window.

Important!
If the update you removed is automatically reinstalled, or if Windows repeatedly offers you an update you do not want, you must *hide* the update. To do so, click the Check for Updates link (you may need to remove the update first). When Windows detects available updates, click View Available Updates, right-click the update you do not want to install, and click Hide Update.

Attention!
Do not remove an update unless you are positive it is the root of your system's problems. Instead, look for an alternative solution using Windows Vista's Problem Report and Solutions feature. If no known solution is found here, search online; Microsoft Discussions Groups are a good starting point.

WORDPAD:
Save a Document

WordPad is a basic word processor that allows you to format documents with installed fonts and print the files that you create. It also allows you to save those documents to your hard drive, where you can later retrieve them to read and edit.

One advantage to using WordPad is that it is fully compatible with Microsoft Word. In fact, it functions like a light version of a commercial word-processing program. This compatibility makes it easy to open WordPad documents in Microsoft Word and to save these documents in a way that retains all of the formatting when you import them into Word.

By default, WordPad saves your documents to the Documents folder. However, you can change this to save any document that you create to a different folder, or even to save it to a different drive. You can also rename a document that you have already saved in order to store it with a new, more easily identifiable name.

See also>>

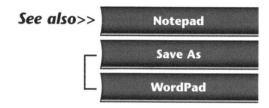

- Notepad
- Save As
- WordPad

1. Click Start.
2. Click All Programs.
3. Click Accessories.
4. Click WordPad.

The WordPad window appears with a blank document open.

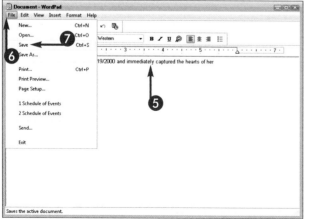

5. Type text in the document.
6. Click File.
7. Click Save.

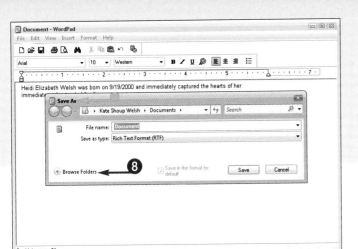

- The Save As dialog box appears.

⑧ Click Browse Folders for more options.

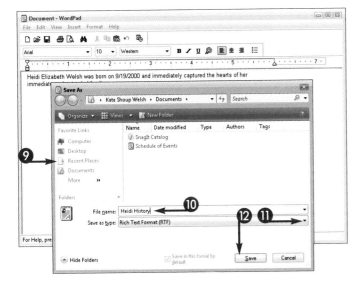

⑨ Click to select the folder in which you want to save the document.

⑩ Type a filename for the document.

⑪ Click the Save As Type list and select a file format.

Note: By default, unless you specify a different format, WordPad files are saved with the .rtf file extension.

⑫ Click Save.

The document is saved in the location that you specify.

More Options!
You can easily print your new document. To do this, you can click the Print icon from the WordPad toolbar, click File, and then click Print. (Alternatively, press Ctrl+P.) The Print window opens, where you can select your print options.

Try This!
To open a document you have saved, open the File menu and choose Open. Navigate to the saved file, click it to select it, and click Open.

Did You Know?
After you save a document in WordPad for the first time, the Save or Save As dialog box does not reappear unless you choose Save As from the File menu. This allows you to save the document with a different filename or format, such as .htm for Web pages.

XPS DOCUMENTS:
View an XPS Document

Microsoft's XML Paper Specification (XPS) enables you to create fixed-format documents that can be easily viewed, shared, printed, and archived — regardless of what program was used to create them — on many different types of computers. Although you do not need the program used to create the original document, you do need a special XPS viewer in order to view and print XPS documents. This viewer is similar to Adobe's Acrobat Reader. Windows Vista includes an XPS viewer by default, which works in conjunction with Internet Explorer.

Windows' XPS viewer can display your document in a few different ways. For example, you can instruct the viewer to display the whole page at its actual size, display it using the page's width as the guide, display the entire page at once, display two pages at a time, or even tile the pages in the document. You can also use the Zoom setting to zoom in or out.

See also>>   XPS Documents: Work

View an XPS Document

① Click Start.

② Click Documents.

The Documents folder opens.

③ Right-click the XPS document you want to open.

④ Click Open With.

⑤ Click XPS Viewer.

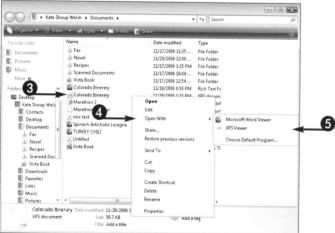

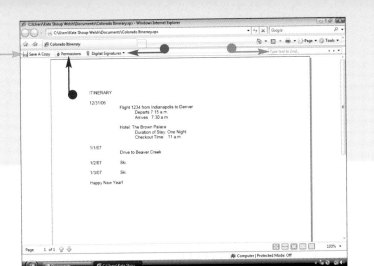

The XPS document opens in the XPS viewer.

- Click Save a Copy to save a copy of the XPS document.

- Click Permissions to specify who can view the document, and for how long.

- Click Digital Signatures to indicate that you have viewed the document.

- To search for a word or phrase in the XPS document, type it here.

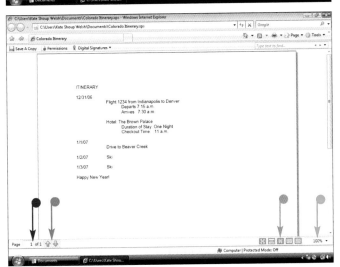

- View the page number here, or type a new page number to jump to that page.

- Click the up and down arrows to move forward and backward through the document.

- Click these buttons to change how the pages are displayed.

- Click here to access Zoom settings.

Attention!

If you have received an XPS document as an e-mail attachment, open it by double-clicking the attachment on the e-mail message. You can then save the XPS document to your own computer by clicking the Save a Copy button in the XPS viewer.

More Options!

If an XPS document contains sensitive information, you can apply permissions to it to limit access to only those users specified.

Did You Know?

Attaching a digital signature to an XPS document enables subsequent viewers to ascertain if, when, and by whom a document has been modified — which is helpful when trying to determine whether a document is legitimate.

XPS DOCUMENTS:
Work with XPS Documents

Like Adobe's Portable Document Format (PDF), Microsoft's XML Paper Specification (XPS) allows for the creation of fixed-format documents. XPS documents can be easily viewed, shared, printed, and archived — regardless of what program was used to create them — on many different types of computers.

You can view or print an XPS document even if your computer does not have the program used to create the document installed. For example, if someone creates a document in Microsoft Word but saves it as

an XPS document, you can view and print that document even if Word is not installed on your PC.

When a document is saved in XPS format, it mirrors the original document — that is, the document created in, say, Word, Excel, or what have you — page for page. Likewise, if an XPS document is printed, the printed document will mirror the onscreen document exactly.

See also>>   **XPS Documents: View**

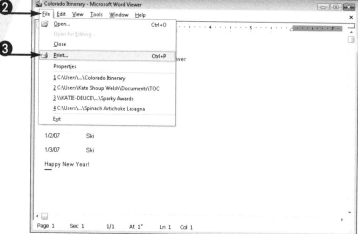

Save a Document in XPS Format

1️⃣ Locate the document you want to convert to XPS format and double-click it to open it.

The document opens.

2️⃣ Click File.

3️⃣ Click Print.

The Print dialog box opens.

④ Choose Microsoft XPS Document Writer from the Name list.

⑤ Click OK.

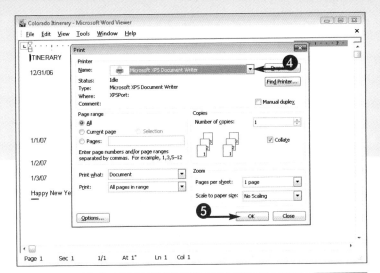

● The Save the File As dialog box opens.

⑥ Type a name for the file.

⑦ Click Save.

Windows saves the document in XPS format.

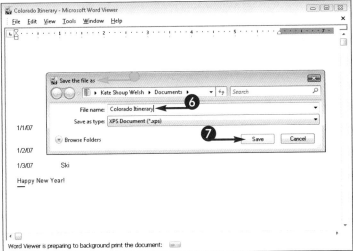

TIP

Attention!

Although PDF offers capabilities — such as editing features — beyond those supported by XPS, XPS is ideal for any user who wants to share a document with a person who does not have access to the program used to create the document.

Index

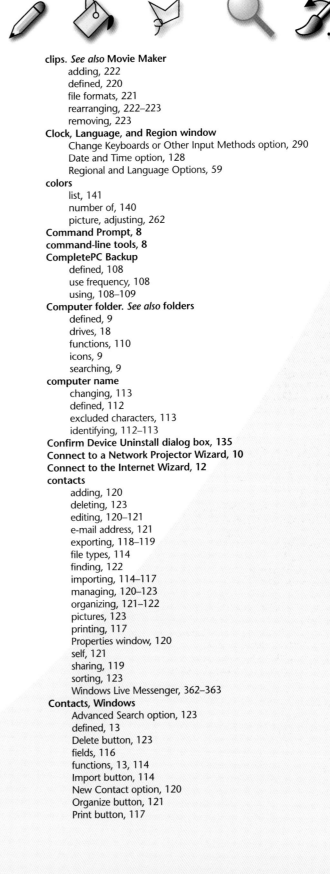

Index

Index

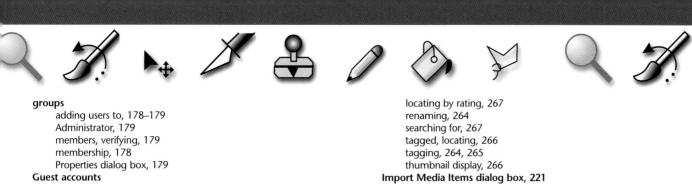

Index

Index

Index

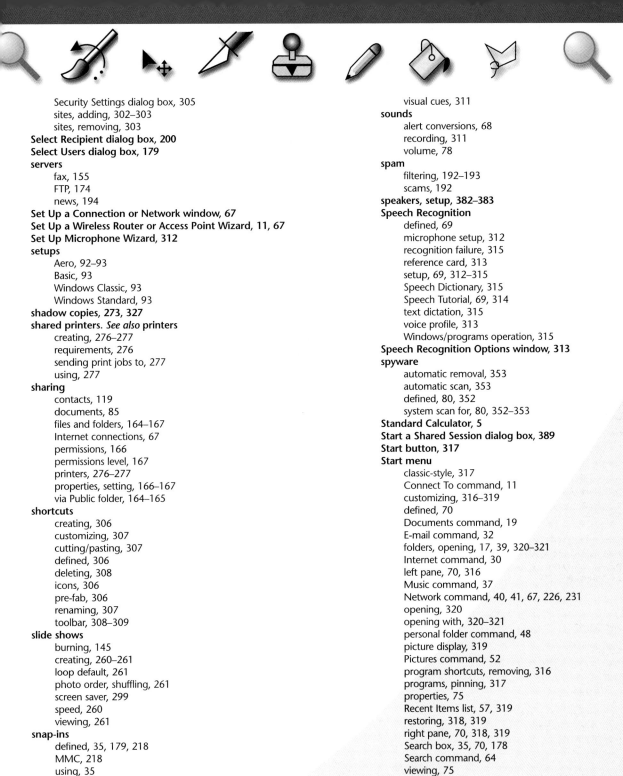

Index

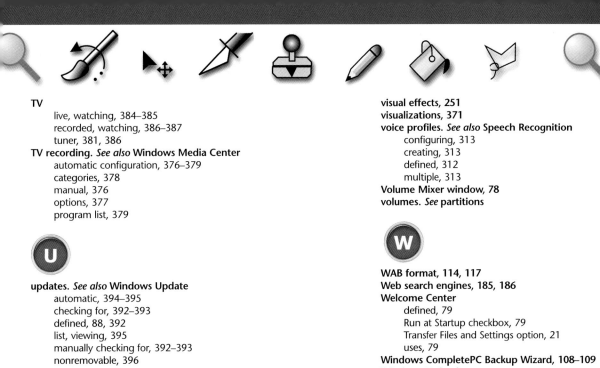

Index